# SHATTERED

*Rhythm*

## RB HILLIARD

Editor: Christian Brose
Proofreader: Joanne Thompson
Cover Model: Andrew England
Cover Designer: Rebel Edit & Design
Formatted by CP Smith

# Dedication

This book is dedicated to my readers. Thank you for taking this ride with me!

I also want to give a special shout out to Oscar, my little Hellion.

# SHATTERED

## Rhythm

# PROLOGUE

## "Living In A Memory"

*Charles*

"Charles! Where are you? Charles!" My mother's yell swept across the yard. I heard it, but I was busy. Super busy. I was making a masterpiece. Mom was going to love it. All it needed was a few finishing touches. "Charles Jones, I better not find you in the mud again!" I glanced up from my mud castle to see my mother bearing down on me. *Uh oh.* She had that look in her eyes, the one she got right before she threatened me with the wooden spoon. She'd only used it once, but one time was enough for me. I didn't care what my friends said. The spoon hurt.

"Charles! Get up! Get up, get up, get uuuuuuuup!" she shrieked. Clearly, she was unhappy, but…why? She always let me make mud castles.

I pointed to my masterpiece and gave her my biggest grin. "Look, Mom. This one has a turret."

"I told you not to get dirty! I told you to stay in the grass!" She glanced at her watch and her face got all scrunchy. Yep, I was definitely getting the spoon. "Come on. We have ten minutes to make you presentable." When she turned on her heel and started back across the yard, I noticed that she was wearing her Sunday dress, the one she saved for church and nice occasions. My heart sank. My fingers drummed nervously against my leg. Tap-tappity-tap-tap. Sigh. It wasn't working. It never worked when Mom was angry. "Now, Charles!" she called over her shoulder. I ran after her as fast as my eight-year-old legs would carry me. "Shoes off," she commanded as we reached the back door.

I quickly toed my shoes off. "Are we going to church?" I quietly asked.

"If you'd stayed in the grass, like I asked, you would know what was happening." She glared down at me and I dropped my eyes to my feet. With a loud sigh, she finally gave in. "I'll explain while I'm getting you cleaned up. Hurry, baby, we don't have much time."

"I'm not a baby," I grumbled as I headed up the stairs after her.

Once we reached the bathroom, Mom got down to business. After a flurry of water, washcloths, and wiping, she stepped back and smiled. "You are my baby, Charles. I love you beyond words. Promise me you'll never forget it. Now, let's get you dressed." I followed her into my bedroom and sat on the foot of my bed while she rummaged around in my closet. I wanted to ask why we were getting dressed up and where we were going, but decided against it. Mom didn't like when I asked too many questions, but still…something was happening, and I was now worried. As I waited for her to explain, I closed my eyes and drummed my fingers on the side of the bed. Tap-tappity-tappity-tap-tap. Slowly, the fear began to recede.

When I opened them back up, she was kneeling in front of me with my least favorite shirt in her hands. Sighing at my unhappy scowl, she ordered, "Hands over your head." Once the shirt was situated, she began to explain. "You know how I've been gone a lot lately?" I nodded my head. "Well, it's because I met someone. His name is Donald and…I really like him." She leaned forward, and whispered, "He really likes me, too, Charley. He's an important man, a police officer. I've told him all about you and he can't wait to meet you." I hated when my mother called me Charley. It made me sound like a baby. The excitement in her voice made my heart race, but her words made my stomach queasy. *What if he doesn't like me?* That question sat like a lead weight on the tip of my tongue. For as long as I could remember it had been Mom and me. My fingers drummed frantically against the side of my leg as I stared down at my knees. "Leg up," she said. I lifted my leg and she helped me into my shorts. All the while, she continued to talk. "Don's going to love you, Charley. He's always wanted kids. Move your hands," she instructed. I shifted my hands to the side of the bed and waited for her to button my shorts. My fingers danced back and forth across the bed while she pulled on my socks. When she was done messing with me, she dropped back onto her heels. "Charles," she whispered. My eyes snapped to hers. "This could be it. You know…what we've been waiting for." I wasn't sure what she was talking about. Seeing my confused expression, she grabbed both of my hands in hers. The urge to rip them from her grasp was overwhelming, but if I did, she would be disappointed.

"Mom, please?" I begged. I didn't like being touched.

"Listen to me, Charley. I want this. Do you hear me?" I nodded my head, yes. "Donald could be your new daddy. Do you understand what I'm saying?" Her face sparkled with excitement. "He'll take care of us, baby. We'll have all the things we've always wanted. All you have to do is smile and show him how amazing you are, okay? No finger twitching or…" she waved her hand in the air, "whatever it is you're always doing with your hands, okay? We don't want to scare him off. Do you understand?" Again, I nodded my head yes. "I need to hear the words."

"I understand," I whispered.

"Great. Donald is going to love you. Just you wait and see..."

# CHAPTER ONE

## "Set Me Free"

*Chaz*

My fingers practically strangled the steering wheel as I stared ominously at the side of the drab looking building. *What the hell am I doing here?* I asked myself for the thousandth time. Chelle's parents might not have posted her bail, but they pulled no punches about hiring a lawyer – a lawyer who apparently was unfamiliar with the word no. He'd contacted me no less than ten times in the past five days. I'd give him this; he was a persistent fucker. Truth be told, I had questions. At first, I didn't want answers. As time passed, however, I realized that I needed them. I needed closure…to move on. Most of all, I needed the truth. Hate, anger, humiliation – you name it, I'd felt it, lived it, wallowed in it. Already twice this month, I'd parked in this exact same spot, stared at this exact same building, and pussed out. Today, I was going in. Grant was up my ass about the band. Evan was downright annoying with his constant texting. Nash was…well, Nash was bitter. Bitter and pissed off. It sucked, but

I understood it. I'd messed up. I now had choices to make, but not until I said my fucking piece. A tap on the window pulled me from my thoughts. I glanced over and scowled at the man standing beside my car door. He motioned for me to roll my window down. As I contemplated whether to stay or to go, I stared at my fingers, willing them to move. Of course, they refused. Fuck them.

"Chaz, is that you?" the man called out. I turned from my traitorous fingers to the douche outside my window. He reminded me of a buttoned-up Gomer Pyle. He'd spent the past month trying to play me with his "pretend I'm stupid when I'm really the smartest one in the room" routine. *I have news for you, buddy. I'm smarter*, I thought as I glared back at him.

One month ago today, I walked away from my sticks, my throne…my life. It was the right thing to do, but I fucking missed it. I missed the guys. Hell, I kind of even missed their women. My thoughts drifted back to Rowan as she lay in the hospital bed fighting for her life, and the look of betrayal on Mallory's face as she realized I was connected to the bitch who'd tried to kill her. I'd spent hours upon hours trying to figure out what the hell happened. Everyone assumed that since I was involved with Chelle, I had to know what she was up to. I didn't know shit. What Chelle and I had was indefinable. Grant dumped her. She moved on to me. We had good sex and she didn't ask questions. Yes, she was selfish and narcissistic, but what did I care? It wasn't like we were married. I didn't keep tabs on her. I should have. I should have listened to my gut. Now, here I sat, staring numbly at the building that housed my biggest mistake, wanting closure…no, needing closure. My life wasn't the only thing I needed back. My internal rhythm: the thing that separated me from all others. The one thing that defined who I was, who I'd become, was gone. Not just that, but my words had stalled. I felt as if I'd been sucked into an emotionless vacuum, that because of my mistakes, I'd been forced to hide away from the world, afraid to push forward, but not daring to move back. Well, my time was officially up. If I wanted to go back, I would have to move forward.

Tap. Tap. Tap. Gomer was getting impatient. Good. After making him stand in the heat of the afternoon for a minute past polite, I finally gave in and rolled down my window.

"Mr. Jones? Is that you?" *Yep, Gomer was definitely irritated.* When he realized I wasn't going to answer, he continued. "I'm Walter Randazzo, Miss Harrigan's attorney. Miss Harrigan will be thrilled that you've finally come for a visit," he drawled in his South Georgia accent. "She's missed you something fierce," he tacked on to the end, and I wanted to smack the smile off his smug face. Fuck him if he thought I was here to save his client. If anything, I was going to bury the lying bitch once and for all. That is, after I got some answers. I swung open my car door and inwardly smiled when it collided with Gomer's nads. He doubled over with a grunt of pain, while I slowly extracted myself from the vehicle.

"Problem?" I asked.

A long moment passed before he waved his hand in the air, indicating that he was okay. "Follow me," he wheezed and, like a good little stooge, I followed along behind him as he limped his way into the county jail. My lips twitched with humor. Sometimes it really was the little things in life…

"Empty your pockets," the guard manning the conveyor belt ordered. I watched Gomer drop his valuables into a small bin and followed his lead. After a rather half-hearted pat down, we grabbed our things, and once again, I followed after Gomer. Dread, resentment, anger…blinding anger, accompanied me on my trek down that hallway. I wasn't a stupid man, but I sure as hell felt like one. I'd been there for Chelle, as much as I could be for anyone, and she'd used me. I'd lied to the only brothers I'd ever known. It didn't matter that it was inadvertently. Lies were lies. Gomer pulled up short in front of a solid steel door.

"I thought we might want some privacy," he announced, and lightly tapped his fingers on the door. A guard stepped out and ushered us into a room, where stark white walls greeted us as well as a dilapidated wooden table, three chairs, and her... Chelle. Her head tilted up and our eyes met. Eyes that I'd once thought were pretty, flared with something that looked a lot like hope. I was instantly engulfed by a million different emotions. It was hard to believe that one person could cause so much damage. I was already damaged, but my friends were not. They didn't deserve any of this. A wave of indecision coursed through me. *Why the fuck am I here?* I could still walk away. Right as I turned to leave, she spoke.

"You came."

Oh, I was here alright. Before I allowed my fucked-up emotions get the best of me, I latched onto the one feeling I could most identify with, and slowly turned to face her.

"You look good."

The voice that had once whispered my name in passion, now grated on my nerves. As I took in the person sitting behind the table, I felt nothing but contempt. It would be so easy to spew the acid that had been corroding my insides for the past month all over her, and walk away. So. Damn. Easy.

"Chaz, please," she rasped.

Memories of her spread out before me, begging for it, swam to the forefront. I shoved them back where they belonged and focused on my task at hand.

"Please talk to me," she urged in her sweet-as-sin voice. The exact same voice that had held me prisoner for the past year. Fuck her. The glasses were off; the curtain had been pulled back. I saw her for what she was. I saw the crazy bitch behind the facade. Something that felt a hell of a lot like shame washed over me. How did I let this happen?

"Let's get seated," Gomer suggested. Once we'd settled onto our respective chairs, the guard stepped out of the room. Chelle stared at me with a pleading expression. I stared back with controlled hatred. She looked like shit. Her dark hair was rooted in gray, her golden skin looked sallow and pale. Wrinkles lined the corners of her eyes. Half-moon circles appeared around her lips as she smiled, and it struck me that in all the time I'd known her, I'd never seen her without makeup on. I could see why. Without her coat of armor, she was exposed, aged...ugly.

She slid her hands across the table and flipped them over in silent invitation. I stared down at them, but made no move to accept her offer. A long moment passed before she got the hint. Slowly, she retracted them. Then she launched in. "I know you're mad, but I wanted the chance to explain. They have it all wrong." And there it was. The reason I was here. "I'm serious, Chaz. You have to believe me. You know me. You can vouch for me."

"Why in the hell would I do that?" Her eyes widened in fake surprise. She opened her mouth to respond, but I beat her to it. "You killed a man and tried to kill two other people. Why in the world would I vouch for you, Chelle?" She glanced nervously at her lawyer.

"Mr. Jones, Miss Harrigan has not been convicted of any wrongdoing. Sh—"

"So, she's rotting in here for shits and grins?" I asked before he could finish his sentence.

"No, she's been accused, but not convicted. In the eyes of the court, she's innocent until proven guilty."

"They found your fingerprints at that guy's apartment. You know, the same guy we saw at Maglioni's restaurant that night. Two days later, you had a diabetic attack, and guess what? Your vial of emergency insulin, you know, the one you kept in your purse for months, was suddenly gone. I saw your insulin vial, Chelle, and funny, the one from your purse looked nothing like the one you used during your attack. You planned it, didn't you? From start to finish, you had it all planned out. Tell me, who was the guy in the apartment? Did you lure him into your deceitful web with your magic snatch and get caught?" She shook her head in silent denial. "For the life of me, I can't figure it out. Please, enlighten me, why did you kill him?"

"Don't answer that," Gomer told her.

At the same time, she blurted, "It wasn't like that."

"Then what was it like? I mean, I know you hated Mallory. Hell, the whole world knew you hated Mallory, but why Rowan? Were you and Conor in on it together? Did you know he had Rowan stashed upstairs? Were you there when he almost beat her to death? Better yet, did you help him?" The more I pushed, the angrier I got. All I could picture was Rowan lying helpless on Conor's floor, while he and Chelle took turns beating the shit out of her.

"Don't answer that," Gomer advised again. I could see the manipulative wheels turning behind her deceptively cagey eyes. Slowly, she swiped her tongue over her lips, a gesture she did when she was nervous, and I wondered for the millionth time what I ever saw in her.

After a long moment, she spoke. "I was aware that Conor knew Rowan, but had no idea that he'd kidnapped her. I had nothing to do with that. You have to believe me, Chaz."

"See, that's where you're wrong. I don't *have* to do shit." Gomer huffed in exasperation. Before he shut me down, I pushed for more. "I get it. You never stopped loving Grant. You used me to get to him. What I don't get is, why kill Conor?"

"Just so you know, Miss Harrigan is pleading not guilty on the grounds of temporary insanity," Gomer stated.

Glancing back and forth between the two of them, I asked,

"Then why in the hell am I here?"

"I can't go to prison, Chaz, please," Chelle quietly begged. "I need you to help me." I leaned forward. She met me halfway. One more inch, and our lips would touch. I hated that I let her manipulate me. I hated that I didn't see her for what she was. I hated that I, of all people, was sitting here trying to get answers so that I could attempt to reclaim a life that I let her steal. I. Hated. Her.

"You spoiled, selfish bitch. You used me. You used Paula. You killed some random guy for who knows what reason, and you almost killed my friends, all because you were obsessed over a guy that gave zero fucks about you. Do you realize how messed up that is?" She reared back as if she'd been struck. She narrowed her eyes in anger.

"Mr. Jones!" Gomer shouted.

"Fine! I killed him! Are you happy?" she screeched.

"Why?" I shouted.

"Don't answer that!" Gomer yelled.

"Because he saw us together! Because I couldn't risk him running his mouth to Rowan and it getting back to Grant!" Finally, we were getting somewhere.

"Why?" I shouted again.

"Because Grant would never want me if he knew I was with you!" It felt as if she'd poured battery acid over the gaping hole where my heart had once been. I might not have loved Chelle, but that didn't mean I didn't care. Fuck this and fuck her.

Gomer pushed back from the table, and angrily announced, "This meeting is over."

"You stupid, stupid bitch," I calmly replied through tightly clenched teeth. "Grant hated you. He didn't give a damn where you were, much less who you were nailing."

An evil sounding cackle shot from her lips. "You act as if you're blameless. Fuck you. It's not as if you're innocent in all of this. You could have told Grant about us, but you didn't. Admit it, you enjoyed sticking it to him, didn't you?"

"I didn't tell him because I knew how much he hated you, Chelle. God, they were right. You really are insane." I topped her cackle with my own burst of laughter. They both stared at me as if I'd lost my mind. Who knows, maybe I'd finally gone over the deep end. Fuck knows I'd had enough to send me there.

"Enough," Gomer growled.

As always, Chelle had to get the last word in. "You think you were the only one? You know nothing, you stupid man."

I was done. I'd gotten all the answers I needed, but the hell if I was giving her the last word. Not this time. Slowly, I pushed back from the table and stood up. "Look around you, Chelle. You're in here," I pointed at the door, "and I'm out there. Tell me, who's the stupid one?" I zeroed in on Gomer, who looked about three seconds away from shitting himself, and warned, "If you contact me again, my team of lawyers will crawl so far up your ass it will take you years to extract them. You and I both know I have the means to do it." I casually walked over to the door and banged my fist on it.

"Wait! Aren't you going to help me?" Chelle shrieked as the guard opened the door. Without so much as a backward glance, I stepped from the room. Halfway down the hall, I smiled.

Finally, I was free.

# CHAPTER TWO

## "Back in the Saddle"

### Olivia

The notice in my hand quivered beneath my shaking fingers as I stared down at it with an overwhelming sense of dread. I'd run the numbers earlier this morning. The numbers didn't lie. I was officially out of money. Disconnecting the cable and reducing my phone minutes hadn't made a dent in the bottom line. The coffers were empty. I couldn't land a job to save my life and now the jig was up. I had two weeks to figure my shit out or I was going to have to move back in with my parents. Something I couldn't do. Something I wouldn't do. As I shoved the notice into the drawer full of bills, my phone trilled from across the room. Pushing the panic aside, I slid the drawer closed and scrambled to see who was calling. Fifty bucks said it was one of my brothers. When I saw the name on the screen, my pulse rocketed. Why was Marcy Kelley calling me? A long time ago, in another lifetime, Marcy and I had been close. We'd spoken once in the past three years. Just before the call went to voicemail, I swiped my finger across the screen and lifted the phone to my ear.

"Hello?"

"Hi, Olivia, It's Marcy…Marcy Kelley."

"Marcy! How are you?" I winced at my stiltedly fake tone.

"I'm doing well. Look, I realize we haven't talked in ages, and apologize for that, but I'm in a bit of a bind. You're the first person who came to mind, and I'm really hoping you can help me out."

Up until about a month ago, Marcy Kelley had been Blane Hamilton's assistant. Blane Hamilton was manager to none other than Meltdown, one of the top rock bands in the industry. According to a source, one of the few I had left, Blane had finally worn out his welcome. He'd been kicked to the curb and Marcy had stepped in to take his place. This meant that Marcy was now running the show. A twinge of excitement, followed by a pulse of trepidation, shot through me.

"Flattery will get you everywhere," I teased. "Now, do tell, what's the situation and how can I help?"

"My father is sick and I need for you to step in and help manage Meltdown while they're on the road this summer. I know you're semi-retired and it's beyond last minute, but I need someone who knows the job, someone I won't have to micromanage. This brings me to you. Please, say you'll consider it?" My heart thrummed a nervous jig inside my chest.

Once upon a time I was road manager for a band. Just like Meltdown, they were full of promise and possibility. I rode fame and fortune all the way to the top, but little did I realize that the higher I climbed the further I had to fall. In the blink of an eye, everything I'd worked for was ripped away. The downward spiral was death-defying. The crash devastating. I'd barely made it out alive. It had taken three years for me to crawl out of that hole, three of the worst years of my life, and now I was being asked to return. I'd be lying if I said I didn't miss it. There was nothing in this world like it: the rush of success, the fast-paced life, the music…God, how I missed the music. Marcy didn't realize what she was asking. How could she? No one did.

I thought about what to say, and opted for a small dose of levity. "Girl, I appreciate it, but I've been out of the business for over three years, now. I'm a rusty old has-been." Marcy laughed.

"Rusty, maybe. Has-been, never. Frank still talks about you, you know. He says you were the best assistant he's ever had. I never understood why you walked away." She paused long enough to realize that I wasn't going to offer an explanation and pushed ahead. "I want you, Olivia. I promise to make it worth your while." Just the mention of my former boss made my eyes sting. I respected the hell out of Marcy. I'd once considered her a friend. That was then. This was now. Now, I had no time for friends. Friendships led to betrayal and betrayal hurt. The right thing to do would be to turn her down. I stared at the drawer full of bills, bills I couldn't pay because I was out of money. Marcy was offering me a lifeline.

Not able to stand it any longer, I asked, "What exactly are you looking for me to do?"

"Well, when I took over management duties, I decided to relocate to Austin. My father fell ill a few weeks ago and I need to be in Utah helping my mother take care of him. I can manage the day-to-day from there, but I can't be there and on the road with the band at the same time. That's where you come in. You've been on the road, so you know what that entails as far as security detail, fans, and media goes." I tried to temper the rush of adrenaline shooting through my veins, but couldn't. Just the thought of going back filled me with excitement. Feelings I hadn't felt since before I'd walked away began to bubble to the surface. "The guys have a month left in the studio to nail down the new album and then they're back on the road."

"How long will they be touring?" I asked.

"Three months." The line fell silent. Where I once would have jumped at the opportunity, I now sat in wary hesitation. Marcy pushed on, "I need you to get to know the guys before the bus takes off. I'll want you in Austin two weeks from today. I'll be there to make introductions before I fly back to Utah. You can stay at my house until the tour starts."

"We're talking three-and-a-half months all in, correct?" If she was asking for six months, I would have said no, but three months on the road was doable.

"Three and a half months, and an upfront bonus for short notice," Marcy clarified. It was tempting, so damn tempting. Could I do this? It had been three years…three long years with surprisingly little residual fallout. What would happen if I just waltzed back in? I would have to get my family on board. I promised them I would never go back, but that was before I ran out of money. Three months on tour with a band like Meltdown could set me up for a few years, if not longer. Still, there was a lot to take into consideration. Like, for example, my sanity.

"Let me think about it. You said I have until the end of the week to decide, correct?"

"I can give you until Friday. I promised Grant a solution by Sunday. Just so you know, he agrees that you're perfect for this job," Marcy answered.

"Shit, Marcy! No pressure or anything. I take it the drummer is back on board?" Meltdown's drummer, Chaz Jones, had walked away from the band after his girlfriend tried to kill Grant's wife. The story had been the talk of the music industry and a prominent part of the 24-hour news cycle for the past month. *Why is it always the drummers?* I thought.

Marcy sighed. "Oh, you heard about that." Her dry tone made me laugh.

"Let me guess, you can't talk without a confidentiality agreement?"

"Which is exactly why you should sign up," she replied. When the laughter died down, she asked the dreaded question. "Have you heard from Sander lately?" My heart squeezed in my chest. Again, I opted for humor over humility.

"Sander is much too busy for little ol' me." In truth, Sander had tried to contact me several times in the past three years. As promised, I'd kept to my end of the bargain.

"According to Frank, the band almost fell apart when you walked away. The only good that came from it was Sander's decision to finally get clean." A punch to the gut would have been less shocking. I grabbed the side of the counter and lowered myself onto the barstool.

"I wasn't aware that he was using," I faintly replied.

"Frank said it got worse after you left. I'm just glad he got help when he did, or he would have been another Dale." Sander James was the lead singer of Indigo Road, and the reason I walked away from a career I loved more than anything in this world. Apparently, he was also an addict, which was something I wasn't previously aware of. I was about to ask for details when Marcy uttered, "Shit, Grant is calling in. I need to get this. Promise me you'll seriously consider taking the job, okay?"

"I will. Thanks for thinking of me, Marcy," I quickly responded.

"Feel free to call if you have any other questions. I look forward to welcoming you back into the fold."

Over the next two days I contemplated Marcy's offer. I had to keep reminding myself that this was Meltdown, not Indigo Road. Meltdown was a different band. This would be a different job with different expectations. Grant Hardy was married. Nash Bostwick was engaged. Evan Walker was married. That left Chaz Jones. *No worries there.* A lot had changed in three years, but especially me. When it came down to it, I was desperate. To slink back to my parents with my tail between my legs would be so easy to do, but it would erase everything I'd accomplished this past year on my own. In order to keep moving forward, there really was only one solution.

I would have to go back.

# CHAPTER THREE

## "Second Chances"

*Chaz*

*"You need to answer your phone, man. Shit is blowing up left and right here. We have a month to finish the album before the tour launches. Marcy's bailing on us because her dad is sick. We've hired a new road manager, and I'm stressed as hell. You're either in or you're out. I'm not kidding this time, Chaz. Either your ass is at my house and ready to record in two days, or you're out... We need you, okay? The band isn't the same without you.*

After playing Grant's message a second time, I thought about my options. Go to Austin or move on. I wanted to go, but was worried things would be different. How could they not be? Thanks to Chelle, my life was a fucking mess. My rhythm was jacked to hell. To an outsider, a messed-up beat didn't compute. It wasn't like losing a set of keys or misplacing a cell phone. A drummer without rhythm was like a writer with no words, an artist with no vision, a singer with no voice. It was essential to life, like breathing, sleeping, or eating. Without it, I felt like a stranger in my own skin, and all because I let that crazy bitch into my life. Even though I wanted to, I couldn't place all of the blame on Chelle. She might have lured me in with her magic pussy, but at the end of the day, it was my decision to stay. I believed the lies. I kept going back for more. Hell, I went back even after I had questions. What did that say about me? Nothing good, that's for sure. I'd always been loyal. In fact, I prided myself on my loyalty to my fellow bandmates. Yet, I'd put that lying bitch ahead of my friends. Lesson fucking learned. I was an idiot who probably deserved to live my life in this rhythmless bubble of silence.

I'd been in this place once before, but that was a time I tried not to think about. A time where things were so dark that I'd lost my desire to play and questioned my reason for being. I'd been helpless back then, lost, suffocating...dying a slow death. I tried to tell myself this was different. I was a kid then. I had no control over what happened. Too bad this didn't feel different. It felt exactly the same. That period in my life nearly broke me. Not this time. This time I would work through it. As much as I'd like to forget, the memories were always there, like harbingers from hell. Always. Fucking. There...

Mom married Don six months from the day we met. For my ninth birthday, they threw me a surprise birthday party and invited my entire class. I thought I'd struck gold. In a way I had, because that's when Don gave me my first drum kit. The drums came with lessons from a guy who knew his shit. Not only did he teach me how to play, but he taught me that part of the reason I had trouble focusing was that I had such a strong internal rhythm. He taught me ways to tame the energy constantly thrumming through my body. For over two years I lived that golden dream, and then Don got demoted. Getting demoted on the police force was a big deal, at least for Don it was. Everything changed after that. My music teacher was let go and my life went to shit. Fucked up became my daily existence. It remained that way until I turned eighteen.

I thought about the difference between now and then. I was a man now. I'd taken my shit life and turned it into something to be proud of. I had more money than I knew what to do with. I had a career that most people would die for. Nash accused me of being closed off. Nash didn't know shit. He was in. They all were. I disliked people in general, but the guys…they were different. I missed the laughter. I missed the bitching. I missed my life. Most of all, I missed the music. I guess I had my answer.

For better or worse, it was time to go back.

*Two days late*

"Enjoy your stay in Austin, Mr. Jones."

"Whatever," I muttered. When the rental car attendant refused to move out of the way so I could close my door, I gave him a scathing look. If the fucker expected me to tip him, he could kiss my ass. "What?" I finally asked.

He nervously shifted his feet. "Ummm, can I have your autograph?"

"Oh, uh, yeah, sure." I held out my hand and waited for him to scrounge up a pen and paper. He stood there with a shit-eating grin on his face while I signed what looked like the back of a candy wrapper. I hated to break it to him, but the second he slid it into his pocket; the ink would smear. I handed it over and stared at him while he gushed all over the fucking place. I shook my head when he slid it into his pocket and waited for him to move out of my way. Finally, he clued in and stepped aside. As I pulled away from the airport and onto the highway, I rolled down my window and breathed in the dry Texas air. I'd forgotten what a pain it was to fly these days. Grant had mentioned getting a security escort. Now I understood why. Shit had gotten real. Even with a baseball cap and sunglasses on, I'd been recognized. Not only that, but I'd been stalked everywhere through the entire damn airport. Before the guy sitting next to me on the plane could engage, I'd put earbuds in, pulled my cap down low, and closed my eyes. When I woke in Austin, I actually felt somewhat rested.

Grant's lawn service was pulling through the front gate when I reached his driveway. Instead of announcing my arrival, I drove in on their coattails and parked next to the back entrance. The kitchen door swung open as I exited the car and Mallory stepped out. A smile spread across her face when she saw me.

Mallory Scott came into our lives in the most fucked-up way possible. It all started with Grant losing his shit on stage one night. We, me included, thought it was drugs. I called mushrooms. Nash thought crank. It turned out that Grant was fucked up, but only because Luke, the dumbshit, had slipped Oxy into Grant's drink before the show. Management freaked, and as part of the damage control, demanded that Grant take a break from the tour and do a stint in rehab. On his return, they hired him his own personal drug counselor. Enter Mallory Scott. Mallory must have been a damned good 'counselor' because she was soon promoted to the position of Mrs. Grant Hardy.

Mallory rounded the car and threw herself into my arms. Shock filtered through me as I rocked back onto my heels. "You came," she whispered in my ear. Her warm welcome felt good but awkward. Not sure what to do, I stiffly patted her on the back.

"Well, it's about fucking time," Grant declared from the doorway. Our eyes met over the hood of the car, mine hesitant, his understanding. Grant's ability to read people made him a damn good leader. After what seemed like years, Mallory released her hold on me, and I quickly stepped back. Just in case she decided to hug me again, I pulled my bags from the trunk and placed them between us. Grant slapped me on the back as I passed by him on my way into the house.

"Same room?" I asked.

"Same room," he replied. I caught his knowing smirk out of the corner of my eye and shook my head. I'd barely stepped into the guest bedroom, when something hit me from behind.

"What the hell?" I growled, and turned right as the culprit whirled past me. All I saw was a blur of fur and teeth while it circled around the bed. As it headed back in my direction, I dropped my bags and lowered to my knees. "Got you," I laughed, and caught it in my arms. Teeth bit, tail wagged, and tongue licked as I attempted to rein it in.

Right as the little fucker bit down on my baseball cap, Rowan yelled, "Hellion, stop!" In a freakishly fast move, the puppy lifted my cap from my head, slipped from my grasp, and took off running for the door. Out it went, along with my hat. Rowan let out an exasperated sounding sigh before dropping her eyes to me. After a long, uncomfortable moment of us both staring at each other, she said, "Welcome back, Chaz." I didn't know what to say, so I went with the first thing I could think of.

"Hellion?" I asked. She smiled.

"She's Grant and Mallory's newest addition. I call her Helly, which annoys them to no end."

"I can see why. Helly is a pussy name."

"I know." When she broke into a fit of laughter, I tried not to smile.

"Hurry up, Chaz!" I tensed as Grant's shout echoed through the house. Mallory and Rowan were clearly taking it easy on me. I had no idea what to expect from everyone else.

Rowan grinned. "Come on. Everyone's waiting for you in the great room."

"Super," I muttered as I followed her out the door.

On the way down the hall, she turned and ruffled my hair. I scowled and she laughed. "Nice hair. What made you change the color?" she asked.

Rowan was an oncology nurse. Nash hired her when his mother was diagnosed with cancer. He had the hots for her for months before he finally made his move. Sad to say, his mother didn't make it, but at least Nash and Rowan were still together. I ran my fingers through my hair and contemplated what to tell her. Truth be told, I'd gotten lazy and didn't feel like bleaching it anymore.

"Just felt like a change," I answered.

"Well, I like it better," she commented as we entered the great room. Grant, Mallory, Evan, Nash, and Marcy all stood there staring at us. Feeling self-conscious about my hair, I made a beeline for Grant. He was holding Hellion, who was happily chomping away on the bill of my cap. As if sensing what was about to happen, the little turd bared its puppy fangs and growled at me. With a pat on the head, I quickly retrieved my hat from her jaws of steel and slipped it on my head. Then I stepped back and assessed the room. Everyone was smiling at me.

"What?" I snapped, and the room erupted in laughter. I didn't see what was so funny.

Evan sidled up and squeezed the back of my neck. "It's damn good to see you." His words made my stomach dip in a funny way.

"Now that we're all here, Marcy has news," Grant announced.

Marcy nodded her head at me and smiled. "First of all, it's good to have you back, Chaz." She scanned over the group, before continuing, "I'm not sure if you've heard, but my father is sick and my mother is too old to take care of him. As you know, I can't be in two places at once."

"Blane seemed to manage," I muttered. Again, the room erupted in laughter, and I wondered what the fuck was wrong with everyone.

"Yes, well, we see where that got him," Marcy sarcastically retorted, before continuing, "You have one month before this album launches. You still need to record the final tracks and finish mastering it. From there it's onto the summer circuit."

"I thought we'd decided to scrap that?" Evan said.

"We talked about it, but Sander called me personally and asked us to headline with Indigo Road," Grant replied. Evan's jaw dropped. Indigo Road had at least three years on us. We were a better band, but they were better known. If we played our cards right, this tour could change that.

"How will that work, exactly?" I asked.

"We'll both get equal time on the stage and will trade off who goes on first each night," Grant answered.

"As I said, I can't be in two places at the same time," Marcy cut in. "Therefore, I called in Olivia Marshall. Olivia will be your road manager, which means she will effectively take the management duties for the tour while I handle the rest from Utah. I expect you to show her the same courtesy you've shown me. Do I make myself clear?" Once she got a nod of acknowledgment from each of us, Marcy continued. "Olivia arrives in two weeks. I will fly in and stay long enough to make introductions and get her settled. Are there any questions?"

"I have one," Nash declared. Slowly, his gaze drifted to me. "Are there anymore hidden girlfriends we should worry about, because I really don't feel like getting blindsided again." *Fuck you*, I thought.

"Yeah, I've got your girlfriend right here," I shot back, as I grabbed my package and pumped my hips. The guys laughed... all but Nash, who stood there glaring at me. Clearly, he was still pissed. The girls both made gagging noises and the dog barked.

Marcy waved her hand in the air. "Okay, children. I'm off to make a few phone calls. If you need me, I'll be in Grant's office."

As I stared at the chaos surrounding me, a sense of peace that I hadn't felt for weeks stole over me. It sure was good to be back.

# CHAPTER FOUR

## "Nobody's Fool"

*Olivia*

My decision to take the job with Meltdown was not an easy one. Three years ago, I'd walked away with the intention of never going back. Promises were made. Documents had been signed. Money was exchanged. I can't say I blamed my family for refusing to support my decision to return to the music industry. Dad was disappointed. Mom was heartbroken. All three of my brothers were angry. I didn't blame them one bit. They'd seen firsthand what the job had done to me. Still, family was family. Eventually they would come around.

The morning I was due to fly out, my baby brother, Banks, stopped by with coffee and donuts. In typical Banks fashion, he pushed his way inside and made himself comfortable on one of my barstools. I was irritated but not angry. It was hard to get angry with someone who really just wanted the best for you. Of my three brothers, Banks was the peacemaker, which was why he was darkening my door hours before he normally got up. It was as clear as day that I was being set up.

"Who sent you?" I asked, and promptly rolled my eyes at his fake, wide-eyed expression. "Was it Mom?" He stared blankly at the coffee cup in his hand. "Dad?" They skittered over my left shoulder to the window behind me. "Both of them?" When they landed back on me, I knew I had my answer. Baby brother couldn't lie worth a damn.

"We're all worried about you, Livvie. This decision is…"

"Mine," I snapped.

"Abrupt," he responded.

"Give it a rest, Banks. I'm fine. You know this is different. Mom and Dad know this is different. When are you all going to let the past go?" Banks eyes flashed with anger.

"You've clearly forgotten how bad it was."

"I will never forget," I snapped, "which is why this is different." We drank our coffee in strained silence, while I tried to think of something to say, something to assure him that I was going to be fine. "Have I mentioned this is only for three months?"

"Why do you have to go at all?" he questioned.

"Because…I need the money. My bills aren't going to pay themselves, you know."

"If this is about money, you know that Mom and Dad are more than willing to help you—" I held up my hand to stop him.

"Yes, and we both know their help comes with conditions. I'm not moving back in with them and I'm not taking any more of their money." A look of defeat skittered across his face. "Look at me." He slowly lifted his gaze to mine. "I was a naïve, stupid little girl back then. I'm no longer that person, okay?" After a long pause, he nodded his head. Just when I thought I had him in my corner, he changed tactics.

"Will Sander be there?" His question caught me by surprise. To buy myself a moment, I opened the fridge and searched for the creamer. The entire time, my mind raced. *Why would Banks ask me about Sander? Did Mom or Dad say something to him? If so, I was going to kill them.*

I held up the creamer. "Want some?" Banks shook his head. As I poured a generous amount into my cup, I contemplated what to say. Finally, I just out-and-out asked, "What does Sander have to do with my working with Meltdown?"

"I dunno," he shrugged. "Mom and Dad were arguing last night and I heard Mom mention his name. I just thought maybe he had something to do with…you know…what happened before." Relief zinged through me when I realized he was simply fishing for answers. *If you only knew*, I thought as I rounded the island and pulled him in for a hug. At nineteen, Banks was the baby of the family. Sometimes I forgot that he was just a kid.

"They're just worried about me. I'm going to be fine. I promise," I whispered against his head.

"I'm going to miss you, Livvie. You're the only one who doesn't treat me like a stupid kid."

I gave him a good, hard squeeze of understanding. "Believe it or not, we're lucky that our parents are demonstrative control freaks." His huff of laughter made me giggle, and soon we were both laughing. That's when it hit me.

"Hey, I have an idea. Why don't you stay here while I'm gone?" His head jerked up in surprise, and I laughed at his slack-jawed expression.

"For real?" he asked.

"Sure. Move your things into the guest room, but no parties and you have to water my plants." His mouth split into a huge smile.

"I can totally do that. Wow!" He pulled me back in for a bone-crushing hug. "You're the best sister ever."

"Yeah, yeah. Tell Mom and Dad that," I muttered under my breath.

I left Banks watching television and eating donuts while I finished getting ready. One of the various things I'd stressed about over the past few days was what to wear on my first day of work. My former boss, Frank, had drilled into my head how important first impressions were, so I decided to forego my usual jeans and t-shirt for a more professional look, which consisted of a sky-blue button-down shirt, black pencil skirt, nude hose, and heels. I contemplated skipping the hose, but felt as if they added an extra level of professionalism. I then swept my hair up into a fancy twist, which I secured with a tortoise shell clip, and finished off the look with my grandmother's pearl earrings. As I stared at my reflection in the bathroom mirror, I began to second-guess my decision. I didn't look at all like myself. I looked… stiff, like I was about to shoot a scene for *Mad Men* rather than meet a famous rock band. *Whatever.* First impressions made lasting impressions, right?

I sent my mother a text message right before I boarded the plane to let her know I'd safely made it to the airport. I also told her that Banks could stay at my place while I was away. She responded with three poop emojis. The fact that she'd responded at all was progress.

During the flight to Austin, I listened to some of Meltdown's earlier music while trolling the Internet for anything I could learn about the band. Had I been given more time, I would have done my due diligence, and thoroughly researched each band member. However, with all of the last-minute back and forth with my family and arrangements to go on the road, I'd been forced to let it slip until the last minute.

As it stood, Meltdown wasn't a complete unknown to me. I'd met Grant and Nash five years ago when Meltdown was opening for Indigo Road. A few short months before I left the industry, Dale overdosed. Sander and Dale had been friends, so Dale's death really hit home for him. Sander wasn't the only one affected. The entire music industry lost a damn fine musician the day Dale Nelson died. Meltdown picked up their new drummer, Chaz Jones, after I'd already left. I never got the chance to meet him, but rumor had it he was extremely difficult to deal with. In layman's terms, he was a giant ass. I stopped at an article written early last year and quickly scanned over it. A feeling of unease stole over me as I read about how Meltdown's keyboardist, Luke Brose, was shot and killed by Grant Hardy's girlfriend, Mallory Scott. The story had been all over the news, but that was a bad time for me, so I didn't remember the sordid details. And the details were definitely sordid. As I dug further into the article, my unease increased. Marcy had conveniently failed to mention any of this. I made a mental note to pump her for information, before clearing the search bar and typing in Chaz Jones's name. Meltdown's most recent scandal had been all over the news for the past month. Several articles described how a love triangle between Grant, Chaz, and a woman named Michelle Harrigan, ended with one person dead and two more seriously injured. I shut down my computer and stared out the window. What was I getting myself into? Obviously, this band had issues. All bands came with their own set of problems. Lord knows Indigo had theirs, but nothing like this. It seemed as if Meltdown was making headlines every other week, and not in a good way.

The day Frank Edwards hired me to be Indigo Road's road manager was one of the best days of my life. My business and communications degrees were finally paying off. Getting hired as road manager was a mere step to the top. However, life on the road came with certain difficulties. In my case it was the band's lead singer, Sander James. Sander hated me at first sight. As it turned out, he was royally pissed that Frank had hired a woman. Forget that I was more than qualified for the job. Also forget that I'd grown up in a testosterone-laden household. I was persona non grata, a woman in a man's world…the enemy. When Frank refused to reassign me to a lesser position, Sander made it his mission in life to torment me.

I was abruptly jerked from my trek down memory lane when the captain came on the loudspeaker and announced our descent into Austin. It was almost showtime. I quickly put my laptop away and brushed a few stray hairs off of my shirt. Regardless of their past issues, I really hoped I received a better reception from Meltdown than I had from Indigo Road.

Marcy was waiting at baggage claim for me. After giving me a welcoming hug, she introduced me to Hank Brown, Meltdown's head of security. Hank was, well…hot. His body screamed muscle junky, but his demeanor was one-hundred-percent military. I almost expected for him to salute me. Instead, he shook my hand and very kindly lugged both of my bags to the car.

On the way to Grant's house, where we were meeting up with the band, Marcy explained the itinerary and my related responsibilities for the next three months. Every so often, Hank would chime in from the front of the car. I got the impression there was something going on between the two of them. Marcy's instructions were clear. Basically, I was never to leave the band's side and was responsible for handling all of the event coordination and logistics. It was the same game as before, only a different team.

"Do you have any questions?" Marcy finally asked. I nervously glanced at the back of Hank's head. Here was my chance to ask about what had happened, but I was hesitant to take it. The old Olivia would have spoken her mind, no matter what the cost, but I wasn't that person anymore. Actions had consequences and words hurt. I'd learned both the hard way. As if reading my mind, Marcy said, "Other than me, Hank will be your closest ally for the next three months. You might as well get used to speaking freely around him. What's on your mind?"

"First of all, let me say how excited I am to be here. Thank you again for thinking of me for the job. That being said, Meltdown has been in the news quite a bit since I left the industry, and not in a positive way. It will be difficult for me to effectively do my job if I don't have all of the facts. Right now, I have none." Marcy sighed. I could tell she was uneasy by the way she kept clasping and unclasping her hands.

"You're right. I apologize for not being straight with you from the beginning. I...ah...just felt that you were so perfect for the job, that if I hammered you with a bunch of negative information you would run for the hills." I gave her a reassuring smile.

"Rest assured that isn't the case, however, I feel as if I'm missing important details. I can't afford to be blindsided, especially when dealing with the press."

Marcy nodded her head in agreement. By the time we pulled up to what I assumed was Grant's driveway; she'd filled me in on the sequence of events from Grant's unwarranted stint in rehab through Chaz's return to the band. It was quite a bit to process. Marcy was right, had I received this information dump from square one, I probably wouldn't have accepted the job.

"We're here," Hank announced, as he rolled down the driver's side window and punched numbers into a keypad. The gates opened and we slowly started up a long driveway flanked by flowering trees. After roughly half a mile, the trees opened to one of the most breathtaking homes I'd ever seen.

Marcy's voice jerked me back to the situation at hand. "Here's what's going to happen. I'm going to introduce you to the guys.

Then Hank is going to drive us to my house, so I can show you where you'll be living for the next few weeks. After that, Hank is going to shuttle me to the airport."

I tore my gaze from the house in order to gawk at her. "You're leaving today?" I thought at least she'd stay for a few days to help me get acclimated. *Don't panic*, I told myself, but I could feel it creeping in. I didn't know these guys. They didn't know me. Marcy reached across the seat to give my hand a squeeze, and I suddenly felt like crying. "Marcy, I-I don't know them," I sputtered.

Hank cut off the engine. Then he turned to us and smiled. "They're easy. Grant prefers a more direct approach, while Nash does better with humor."

"Evan is the peacemaker," Marcy added.

"And Chaz?" I asked.

"Just ignore Chaz." Hank's answer would have been funny had it been delivered with a smile instead of a grimace.

"I agree. Chaz is a troublemaker. Ignoring him is your best line of defense," Marcy stated.

On that overly happy note, Hank slipped from the car and escorted us up several steps to the front door, where an extremely muscular African-American man stood, waiting with a welcoming smile on his face. My pulse fluttered when he held out his hand.

"You must be Olivia. I'm Marcel, Hank's second-in-command, and part of your security detail while you're with us."

"Nice to meet you," I replied as I shook his hand.

Directly inside the front door stood another member of Meltdown's security. This one was shorter in stature, but no less muscular. He had light skin, a military-style haircut, and an intense look on his face. "Olivia, this is Sean. He'll also be watching out for you while you're here with us," Hank introduced. Sean nodded his head and I responded with a smile and a half-wave. I had to give credit where credit was due. Meltdown's security team was top-notch.

As I'd suspected, the interior of the house was every bit as impressive as the exterior. Everywhere I looked was an absolute feast for the eyes. Grant's new wife certainly spared no expense with the interior decorator, that's for sure. Old style wood furnishings with modern touches here and there filled the expansive rooms. I would never have put the two styles together, but in this house, it completely worked. The sound of someone yelling froze me in my tracks. I jerked to locate the source of the commotion and gasped as something small and extremely furry barreled into my legs. On its heels was a very angry looking woman. I tried to step out of the way, but it was too late. The little shit had snagged my hose on both legs and had run them clear through.

"Sorry!" the woman called out as she raced by.

"Oh, no worries," I lied.

"Oh, no!" Marcy cried out. "Look at what that little menace has done!" Everyone stared at the runs in my hose with horrified expressions on their faces. My face flamed with mortification.

Somehow, I managed to keep my cool. "Hey, it's okay. By chance is there a restroom nearby?" Three fingers pointed in the direction of what appeared to be the kitchen.

"Right around that corner," Hank replied.

I strolled across the room as if I didn't have a care in the world. Once I'd rounded the corner and was clearly out of sight, I slumped against the wall. As I stared down in horror at my ruined hose, I failed to see the whirling dervish heading straight for me. Once again, I was nearly barreled over. My left heel slipped on the hardwood floor, and I dropped my purse as I grabbed the counter to steady myself. Clearly, someone needed to get ahold of that animal and beat its ass off. After checking both ways to make sure the coast was clear, I squatted down to retrieve my purse. That's when the little shit tackled me from behind. This time, it latched its razor-sharp puppy teeth onto my hair clip.

"Let go," I whispered between clenched teeth. *Where in the hell is your owner?* I thought. After what seemed like an hour, but was really only seconds, I managed to get Fido to let go of my hair clip. In a one-two motion, I jerked the dog off of me and sprung to a standing position, where I came face-to-face with none other than Chaz Jones. I swallowed down a bubble of hysterical laughter, before letting out a string of mental curse words. *Shit, fuck, hell, shit, shit shit!* This was not my day. As his eyes scanned over me, I wanted to crawl into a hole and hide. The man was good-looking on paper, but in person he was...I had no words. His once white hair was now two-toned. The dark roots made his deep blue eyes stand out. A dark brow shot up in either humor or question, I couldn't tell which.

"I see you've met Hellion," he murmured. Hellion was a very fitting name. I opened my mouth to answer, and remembered that I was warned to ignore him, which was fine by me, because I was too embarrassed to speak anyway. Without so much as a word, I clutched my purse to my chest and strolled back out to where Marcy and friends were waiting.

"You okay?" Marcy asked.

"Never better," I lied.

"Shall we?" Hank asked.

"After you," I replied. With torn hose and messed up hair, I followed the foursome down a steep flight of stairs and into a studio fit for a king, where I was formally introduced to the men I would be spending the next three months of my life with.

So much for first impressions.

# CHAPTER FIVE

## "Territorial Pissings"

*Chaz*

Talk about strange encounters. I grabbed four waters from the fridge and headed back downstairs to practice. I wasn't a hundred-percent sure, but had a sneaky suspicion that the hot mess I'd just run across in Grant's kitchen was none other than our new road manager. As I handed out waters, I told Grant that I was pretty sure his twit of a dog had just jacked up our new road manager.

"What? Where?" he curtly responded, followed by, "Where in the hell is Mallory?"

"Not watching the dog, that's for sure," I muttered. The moment the words left my mouth, we heard someone coming down the stairs. A few seconds later, Marcy, Hank, Sean, and Marcel appeared with the woman from the kitchen. If she was our new manager, she wouldn't be for long. Seriously, the woman looked practically sewn into her clothing. Not only that, but she was wearing pantyhose. I tried to recall the last time I'd seen a pair of pantyhose.

"Boys, I would like to introduce you to Olivia Marshall, your new road manager," Marcy announced. She turned to Olivia, who was doing a relatively good job of feigning normalcy, and said, "You've met Grant and Nash before, but haven't been properly introduced to Chaz and Evan." Olivia, with her ripped hose and wild hair, stepped forward and offered her hand to Grant.

"Good to see you again," she told him.

Grasping her hand, Grant said, "Welcome aboard, Olivia. I'm so sorry about Hellion."

"No harm done. I look forward to working with you." Her calm, cool demeanor was impressive. She turned to Nash and murmured something that I couldn't quite hear, but it must have been funny, because he suddenly let out a loud bark of laughter. After shaking hands with Evan, she gave me a split-second look and a slight nod of acknowledgment, before heading back over to Marcy. *What the fuck?* The bitch just blew me off. Now that I think of it, she'd also blown me off upstairs. *Screw her. She doesn't even know me.* A loud noise on the stairs caught everyone's attention and all eyes in the room jerked in that direction. Mine, however, stayed focused on Hot Mess, who was doing an impressive job of pretending she was unaffected. I knew the truth. I could see it in the way she kept fiddling with her hair and glancing down at her legs. A squeak of surprise slipped from her lips as the little hellhound shot into the room and made a mad dash for Grant. On the dog's heels followed a frazzled looking Mallory. When Mallory saw Olivia, she physically flinched. I inwardly laughed my ass off.

"I'm so sorry!" Mallory gasped. A warm smile spread across Olivia's face.

"Hey, it's really no big deal. It was karma's way of telling me that I shouldn't have worn this outfit to begin with." She lifted a hose torn leg and laughed. "I mean, really, no one wears these things anymore, least of all me." Her levity surprised me. Most chicks would have completely lost their shit by now.

"Olivia, this is Grant's wife, Mallory. Mallory, this is Meltdown's new road manager, Olivia Marshall," Marcy chimed in.

"Nice to meet you," they both replied in unison.

"And this, as you've already learned, is Hellion," Grant said. Hot Mess marched her curvy ass over to Grant and the squirming dog. As she bent over the animal, I had a perfect opportunity to assess her curves. My cock took notice, which surprised the shit out of me, because I was pretty much convinced that Chelle had irreparably damaged my libido. The thought that this…this rude woman was the thing to make him take notice… nope. Not gonna happen. Even if she had a mighty fine ass, Hot Mess was off-limits to me and my johnson.

"What's wrong?" Evan asked. I gave him a questioning look, and he nodded at Olivia. "You're scowling at her, and you're doing that thing with your fingers again." My eyes dropped to my thrumming fingers, and a wave of relief shot through me, followed by a pulse of irritation.

"Haven't we wasted enough time already today?" I asked loud enough for the entire room to hear.

"Don't be a dick," Nash chastised.

"Fuck you," I retorted.

Before he let me have it, Olivia cut in, "You're right, and I apologize. Thank you for taking the time out of your busy schedules to meet me."

Marcy gave me a dirty look, before addressing the room. "Hank is taking us over to my house. Olivia will be staying there until the tour kicks off. I'm leaving this evening for Utah. Olivia will also act as my replacement from now until the end of the tour. Obviously, I will still be available, but on a limited basis."

"Behave," Grant ordered as he lowered Hellion to the floor at his feet.

"Have dinner with us tonight, Hank can pick you up on his way back from the airport," Mallory offered to Olivia. I watched Hellion sniff the floor around where Olivia was standing, and thought, *Someone should probably take her outside.*

"That is very kind of you to offer, but I think I'm going to take it easy tonight, so I can hit the ground running tomorrow. I have a feeling I'm going to have to stay on my toes with this group," Olivia responded with a laugh. Hellion snorfled at her legs. Not missing a beat, she shot out a pantyhose clad leg, and gently shoved her away.

"Are you sure?" Mallory asked. Before she could respond, Hellion was back again. This time with her leg hiked. Hot Mess gasped in horror as piss splashed over her legs and onto her heels.

"Hellion!" Mallory and Grant both shrieked. While Grant dove for the dog, Mallory yanked a towel from the downstairs bathroom and rushed for Olivia. The entire scene was simply too much, and I busted out into hysterical laughter, which earned me shit stares from everyone in the room. I didn't care. I couldn't remember the last time I'd found something to smile about, much less laugh at. I reined the hilarity in long enough to say goodbye, but once the group was out of sight, I let the laughter rip.

"You're such a dick," Nash grumbled, but I could tell by the way his lips kept twitching that he found it funny, too.

Once Marcy and the others had taken off, we laid down tracks for three new songs. It was the most productive we'd been in the entire two-week period. I could have gone all night, but Grant and Nash turned into pansies and insisted they go make nice with their women. Being that I was outvoted, I gave in and called it a night.

After a few hours of not being able to sleep, I decided to make myself a sandwich and watch some television. I was surprised to find Evan parked on the sofa with a beer in hand.

"Want one?" he asked.

"Nope." By the way his voice slurred, I could tell he'd had more than a few. "You're going to feel like shit tomorrow if you don't slow down," I warned.

"Thanks, Mom," he sarcastically replied. He then took a deep draw from his beer, followed it with a loud belch, and asked, "Why don't you drink alcohol?"

I took a bite of my sandwich and thought about what to tell him. Finally, I settled for the truth. "My stepdad was an alcoholic."

"Mean drunk?" he asked.

"Yep."

"Sorry."

"Don't be."

"Was he abusive?" I really liked Evan, but there was no way in hell that I was discussing my past with him any further, or anyone else, for that matter.

In an attempt to redirect, I asked, "You back with the wife?"

He held up his beer in a mock salute, before answering, "The wife wants a divorce." The pain behind his words made me uneasy. Not knowing what to say, I muttered an apology of sorts. After a long, extremely uncomfortable pause, I inhaled the rest of my sandwich and was about to say goodnight, when he said, "Can I ask you something?"

"If it has to do with my family, no." I didn't mean to sound like a dick, but wanted to make it very clear. My family was off-limits.

"Did you really not know what Chelle was up to?" I'd been waiting for this question, or one like it. So far, the guys had been cool about giving me space. I was glad it was Evan doing

41

the asking and not Nash. As I rested my hand on the back of the sofa, I thought about what to tell him. The leather felt cold against my restless fingers as they drummed across the smooth surface.

I opened and closed my mouth a few times, before finally getting the question out. "Have you ever sensed that something bad was happening, but rather than face the possibility that you were right, you buried your head in the sand and ignored all of the red flags?"

He let out a dry laugh. "Yeah, like the failure of my entire marriage."

"Exactly. You know that something bad is happening, but you just don't want to see what's right in front of your eyes…"

"Until you have to, and by then it's too late, or in your case, almost too late," Evan finished for me. He let out a tired sounding sigh. "Some days I wish I'd never met her." Funny, I wished that every day. "What's up with you and Olivia?" he asked.

Talk about a one-eighty. I shot him a questioning look, and asked, "Who?" Knowing full well who he was referring to.

"Uh, Olivia, the new road manager."

"Nothing's up. I don't even know her. Why do you ask?" If Evan saw my fingers tapping frantically against the back of the sofa, he would know that I was lying. The fact that my fingers were moving at all, and had been ever since Olivia had shown up, was disturbing enough. The last thing I wanted was for someone else to notice.

"Yeah, well did you know that she managed Indigo Road?" My fingers stilled. Indigo Road was the band we strived to be. They were the best of the best, and had been for years. They were our number one competition, which brought one question to mind…

"Why'd she quit?"

"No clue," he shrugged. "Apparently, she hasn't been in the

game for at least three years."

"How do you know all of this?" I asked.

He smiled. "It's easy, I listen." I flipped him the bird, and he laughed.

As we settled in to watch an episode of *Storage Wars*, I thought about the woman I'd met today managing a band like Indigo Road. Talk about a strange fit. My curiosity was piqued. Several questions came to mind, the main one being, was she fired or did she quit? Hmmm, apparently little Miss Hot Mess had an intriguing past. It had been awhile since I'd talked to Sander. Maybe I would give him a call tomorrow, just to see how he was doing. Better yet, I'd call Gio. We'd hit skins together a time or two. I bet Gio would have the lowdown on Miss Olivia Marshall.

For the first time in what seemed like a very long time, I fell asleep looking forward to something.

# CHAPTER SIX

## "The World Turned Upside Down"

*Olivia*

When we finally made it back upstairs at Grant's house, I excused myself to the bathroom, where I stripped out of the pee covered hose and attempted to rinse off my shoes. The entire time, Chaz's laughter echoed through my head. Chaz Jones was an insufferable ass. Thankfully he wasn't standing in the kitchen when I exited the bathroom, or I would have throat punched him.

Mallory caught up with me at the front door with another apology. I played it off to the best of my ability, but the damage was done. I'd been utterly and completely humiliated, and by a pint-sized furball, no less. Marcy and Hank discussed the day-to-day aspects of the job again on the drive to Marcy's house, while I contemplated how to get out of my contract without getting sued.

Upon arrival, Marcy showed me straight to my room. As if sensing my need to be alone, she gave some excuse about needing to make phone calls, and promptly closed the door on her way out. I refused to break down in front of an audience, but damn if I didn't want to.

This was bad, as in epic fail bad. During a scalding hot shower, I contemplated all of the things I could have done differently. When I thought about the tiny terror peeing on my shoes, I started laughing. It really was quite funny. Pretty soon, however, the laughter dissolved into tears. Why me? Why now, just when I was trying to get back on my feet? After a good hard cry, I dried myself off. Today was right up there with the time in ninth grade when my oldest brother picked me up from school. I was so busy socializing I didn't see him waiting for me. To get my attention, he rolled down the window and shot a rubber band at me. I thought a large bug had landed in my hair. In my haste to get it off of me, I literally peed my pants. In front of all of my friends. In front of the guy I was trying to impress. I peed myself. I thought nothing could possibly top the roach-pee incident, but today didn't only top it. It surpassed it. Once again, I contemplated quitting. Then I thought about all of the things I would be able to do with the money. *Screw it.* For better or worse, I was stuck. I quickly got dressed and made my way out to Marcy's deck. As I overlooked the city of Austin, I focused on my breathing. Today was a definite hit. Tomorrow would have to be better. I heard the sliding door open.

"You okay?" Marcy asked. No, I wasn't okay. Of course, I didn't tell her this. Instead, I deflected.

"The house is amazing, Marcy."

"Thanks. There's wine in the fridge, if you'd like some."

"I'm good, but thanks." I didn't bother to tell her that I'd quit drinking.

"Look, what happened today could have happened to anyone—" she started to say.

"I'm fine, Marcy, really." We both knew that was a boldfaced lie. I felt embarrassed and humiliated, but she needed to be with her father and I needed to do this. I addressed her look of concern with a smile. "Seriously, shit happens, especially in this business, right?"

"You sure? Those guys can be a tough audience."

"Trust me, I've had much worse." I bumped her with my shoulder and she smiled. An unspoken feeling of solidarity passed between us. We were women trying to prove ourselves in a very masculine world. Nothing about this was easy.

"Are you ever going to tell me why you left the business?" Her question took me by surprise.

I contemplated what to tell her as I stared out at the skyline before me. There really wasn't much I could say. "I got too involved. The job...it changed who I was. It was like I woke up one day, looked in the mirror, and didn't recognize the person staring back at me." This wasn't necessarily a lie, but it wasn't exactly the truth, either.

"So, you just up and quit?" she asked in a surprised tone of voice. I swallowed thickly and nodded my head, yes. I could tell that she wanted to ask for more details, and was relieved when she didn't, because I really didn't want to lie to her again. "Damn. I'm sorry, hon. I know how tough it can be. I wish you'd reached out to me."

"Don't feel bad. No one knew. Look, what's done is done, and now I'm here with you, sooooo," I nudged her arm, "why don't you give me a tour of this gorgeous house of yours?"

Shortly after she showed me the house, Marcy gave instructions on how to manage fan interactions and such, before she and Hank took off for the airport. Hank offered to swing back by the house to give me a ride to Grant's for dinner, but I kindly turned him down. I needed some quiet time to shore up my defenses before returning the next morning for round two. That night I barely slept a wink. I was going to have to make epic strides to prove myself. I racked my brain for a solution, but other than killing the dog and kicking Chaz Jones where it counted, I came up with nothing useful.

The next morning, I woke in a better frame of mind. Screw first impressions. Screw pantyhose and business wear. From this point forward, like it or not, Meltdown was getting the real Olivia Marshall. After a shower and half a pot of coffee, I sent a quick text message to my parents and brothers, letting them know that I'd made it safely to Austin and was doing well. Two of my brothers shot back minimal responses and Mom sent another poop emoji. Definite progress. The new improved Olivia threw on a pair of jeans and a vintage Aerosmith t-shirt. I decided to leave my hair down, but slid a few ponytail holders on my wrist, just in case. After applying a minimal amount of makeup, I slipped my feet into my favorite pair of Converse and grabbed my bag containing everything I needed for the day. On my way out the door, I snatched up a satchel of fan mail and headed to the garage where Marcy kept her car. When I spotted a vomit green colored Beetle sitting there, I stopped dead in my tracks.

"I can't drive this," I announced to the empty garage. It was...heinous, not to mention ancient. I was pretty sure it was also a liability.

By the time I grabbed an Uber, stopped at the grocery store, and made it to Grant's house, I would be late. Yesterday was an epic fail. I wasn't about to give a repeat performance. With a frustrated sigh, I wrenched open the driver's side door and sank into the seat. I adjusted the mirrors and shook my head in disgust. And here I thought it couldn't get much worse. The car started with a loud belch. I warily backed out of Marcy's garage. The moment I shifted to drive, it backfired. I let out a shriek of surprise and then burst into gales of hysterical laughter. This was not how I'd planned on starting my day. Just when I thought it couldn't get any worse, the damn thing began sputtering as if the engine might cut out entirely at any moment. At the rate I was going, I would be lucky if I ever made it to Grant's house. One thing was for sure; Marcy's good taste did not extend to her vehicle.

Thirty minutes later, I pulled out of the grocery store parking lot. As I hit the gas to accelerate onto the highway, the car backfired again. From where I was sitting, it sounded like a mini cannon had exploded. I let out another shriek of surprise, followed by a burst of laughter. Between sputters and backfires, I thought about my plan of action. Hellion might have gotten the best of me yesterday, but not today. Today I was locked and loaded. I just prayed I made it to my destination in one piece.

It was a good thing that the gate was open when I pulled into the driveway, because I wasn't a hundred-percent sure that the car wasn't on the verge of stalling out on me. Slowly, I puttered up the drive to the house and found a nice spot off the beaten path to park. My nerves were completely shot. I took a few moments to get it together, before exiting the car. Marcy and I were going to have to have a little talk about the dangers of improper car maintenance.

To my surprise, an elderly woman answered the door. She'd barely gotten the chance to introduce herself as Ava, the housekeeper, before the tiny terror shot out of nowhere and made a beeline straight for me.

"Hellion!" Ava shouted, but before he could eat my shoes, or better yet, urinate on me, I dropped my bags at my feet, and scooped her into my arms. She wiggled like mad until I whipped a package of dog treats from one of the grocery store bags, and loudly shook the contents back-and-forth in front of her face. Not quite sure what to do, she froze, her eyes riveted on the treats in my hands.

"Hello, Hellion. Remember me?" I quietly asked. I noticed Mallory standing off to the side, and held up the package. "May

I? A reward system will help with teaching beastie here some manners."

"You're a dog trainer, too?" The sound of awe in her whispered question made me laugh.

"For like thirty seconds in college," I glibly responded as I placed Hellion on the floor at my feet. The truth was I'd actually spent two summers working at an animal clinic. The vet I worked under was amazing with animals. He was also amazing with other things. Too bad I was a minor and he was married. Hellion watched me open the treats without so much as a peep. The dog was far from dumb. Clearly, she knew that something good was inside. "You're such a good girl. Do you want to learn a trick?" She practically preened at the sound of my praise. I was about to teach her to sit when I noticed movement from across the room. Grant, Evan, and Chaz stood in the kitchen doorway watching me. Suddenly, I began to doubt my decision to tame the beast. As if sensing my reluctance to continue, Hellion whined at my feet. Ignoring my audience, I turned to Mallory and, in a calm voice, instructed, "When you teach her to sit, make sure you use a commanding voice, otherwise she won't understand her cue. "Sit, Hellion!" I loudly commanded. At the same time, I pressed her rear into the floor, which forced her into a seated position. Then I praised her with a treat. It took four tries before she was sitting like a champ. Mallory and Ava clapped their hands.

"That was amazing. What else do you have in your bag of tricks?" Mallory asked, as she eyeballed the bags on the floor at my feet.

I held up the satchel full of fan mail. "Marcy said to give this to you," I directed at Grant.

"Fan mail?" he warily asked.

"Yep."

Grant pointed his finger at Chaz. "He'll take it."

"The fuck I will," Chaz snapped. The growl in his voice sent shivers up my spine. I'd tried to ignore him, but he was so… present, in his weathered jeans and Judas Priest t-shirt. Dark ink decorated his arms. I itched to take a closer look, but didn't dare. Truth be told, the guy kind of scared me.

"Yeah, I meant to tell you. We all voted and it's unanimous. You get fan mail detail for the next few months," Grant told him. I held my breath and waited for the explosion. Chaz had that lose-my-shit-at-the-drop-of-a-hat vibe about him.

"Fuck you," Chaz muttered as he took the bag from me. I had to admit; I was surprised he'd kept his cool. Our eyes briefly met but we both quickly looked away. Maybe I'd pegged him wrong.

"What are those?" Mallory asked.

I was so intent on tall, tatted, and scary that I'd almost forgotten my plan. "Oh, here," I sheepishly responded, and handed over a package of pee pads.

It took her a moment to register what they were. "Pee pads?" she asked, and broke into laughter. Then she tossed them to Grant.

"Do these things actually work?" he asked.

"You'd be surprised. Though outdoors is preferable, you have to start somewhere and those are the next best thing." Grant handed them to Evan. Evan promptly slapped Chaz on the stomach with them, and Grant and Evan both broke into laughter. Here I was, standing in Grant Hardy's living room, watching the members of Meltdown joke about pee pads. It was easy to forget that behind the music and the fame, they were real people. I slid my gaze to Chaz. The wary look on his face as he stared at the pee pads was kind of funny. Something told me he didn't find many things in life very funny. I mentally rolled my eyes. *Stop feeling sorry for the guy*, I thought. He certainly found the dog pissing on my shoes hilarious yesterday.

"Okay people, now that Dog Training 101 is over, let's say we get some music recorded!" Grant shouted. After accepting a cup of coffee from Mallory, I hoisted my bag over my shoulder and followed the motley crew down into the studio.

Three hours later, I was mulling over the budget, while the guys were behind the glass cutting tracks for a song that Grant and Nash had cowritten together. It had a harder feel to it than their usual sound, edging it more towards metal than rock. I liked it. I didn't, however, like the budgetary restraints that Marcy had placed on the upcoming tour. From the looks of it, more money was being allocated for the parties before and after the shows than the hotel. Sander and the guys used to bitch about how much they hated people in their dressing rooms before going on stage. They thought it was annoying and distracting. If we cut out the pre-party, we would have plenty of money for a nice suite of rooms and still be able to host an after-party. Half an hour later, when the guys were on break, I brought it up.

"Hey, guys." All eyes shot to me. I swallowed down my nerves before forging ahead. "I've been looking at the tour budget. It appears there is more than enough money put into the entertainment budget, but not near enough for lodging. I faintly remember how Indigo used to complain about having to entertain before their shows, and thought that if we cut out the pre-party, I could book you into some nice suites rather than smaller individual rooms. This would afford you more privacy and you would still have plenty of money left for a great after-party." When no one responded my heart sank. I opened my mouth to backpedal, and Grant cut me off.

"Do you know how long we've been trying to get out of having a pre-party?" I shook my head, no, because I really didn't have a clue. By the look on his face, though, I could assume it had been quite some time. "Forever," he answered. I glanced over at Evan and he winked at me. My eyes drifted to Chaz, who just stared at me as if he was wondering what planet I'd come from.

I was contemplating throwing my pen at his head when he asked, "You and Sander were close?"

"Olivia managed Indigo Road, a few years back," Grant told him.

"Road manager," I corrected. Chaz's brow shot up in question, so I further explained, "I was their road manager for a few years. Frank was my boss, and I was close to all of the guys in the band. I kind of had to be." I clamped my lips closed. Someone needed to shut me up.

"I'm sure they'll be psyched to see you," Evan chimed in. His eyes jerked to Grant. "That is still the plan, correct?" My stomach took a nosedive.

"What...plan?" I hesitantly asked.

"Didn't Marcy tell you? We're touring with Indigo Road," Chaz announced. I literally felt the bile rise from my stomach into my throat.

"Yeah, baby!" Evan bellowed, and the three of them bumped fists. Chaz just stood there staring at me with an indecipherable look on his face.

"Excuse me," I whispered, and all but ran from the room.

"Is she okay?" I heard one of them ask as I raced up the stairs. I bolted across the kitchen and into the bathroom, where I dropped to my knees and threw up my breakfast.

I was trapped in my own worst nightmare.

# CHAPTER SEVEN

## "Only a Memory"

*Chaz*

I mentioned touring with Indigo Road because I wanted a reaction. Well, I got one. The moment the words left my mouth, I saw her shoulders tense. I watched her smile disappear. I recognized the look in her eyes, but only because I'd seen it before, too many times to count. I'd been there. Done that. Invented the fucking t-shirt. Olivia Marshall was scared. Something happened. Was it Frank? Was it Sander? Whatever it was, it was bad enough to make her quit her job. Was it any of my business? No, but that didn't stop me from wondering. She intrigued me. Not in an I-want-to-stick-it-in-her kind of way, even though she was a knockout and I kind of did, but more in an I-can't-quite-figure-her-out kind of way. Talk about whiplash. Yesterday, we were introduced to a buttoned-up, heel-wearing, hot mess, who could barely string three words together without stuttering all over herself, and today we got a confident, dog-whispering control freak. So, which was she? A hot mess or a control freak? And why did she bring out every last fucking protective instinct in me? She was hiding something, and that something frightened her. Call me stupid, but I wanted to know what it was.

When Olivia returned from upstairs, she tried to play off her odd response with some lame excuse about having something in her eye. No one was buying it. She looked freaked. I'd done this to her. I was such a fucking dick. To get her out of her negative headspace, I tried taunting her. This got me nowhere with her, but sure did piss off the guys. Shortly after that, Grant called it a day and everyone went their separate ways. Before I could get out from behind my kit, Olivia was already halfway up the stairs. By the time I'd reached the top step, she'd made it to the car. I thought about stopping her, but then what? Apologize? She'd probably just knee me in the jewels, anyway. In the end, it really didn't matter, because she was gone.

"Marcy stuck her with the Beetle?" Grant asked. We watched from the front window as Olivia started Marcy's piece-of-shit car and began to pull away.

"Looks like it," I replied. Right as it rounded the bend of the driveway, the car expelled an ear-splitting backfire. Grant snorted. I shot him a dirty look.

"What?" he asked through his laughter.

"What in the world was that?" Mallory called out from the kitchen.

"That was Marcy's old Beetle backfiring," Grant responded, still laughing.

"Olivia drove the Beetle?" Hank asked. His surprised expression made me a little uneasy.

My eyebrow rose question. "Was she not supposed to?"

"Huh? Oh, no, I'm sure it's fine. I just wonder why she picked that over the Porsche?" Funny, I was wondering the same thing.

"Maybe she has a thing for shitty, old cars," Nash teased. I directed my scowl at him, and he laughed.

"You have to admit the Porsche is a bit much. Not everyone feels comfortable driving a flashy car," Mallory suggested. At this point, I was more worried about what had sent Olivia running more than what she was running in...

Evan stepped up beside me. "Olivia looked freaked when you mentioned the tour. I think we're missing something," he quietly stated. I didn't bother with a response. I knew she was freaked. Talking about it would only call it to everyone else's attention. I'd already done enough of that for one day. I heard him sigh as I walked away.

That night we ate Ava's famous spaghetti for dinner. Before Grant, Ava had worked for Dale's parents, and then for Dale after that. When Dale died, Grant took her in. When I came onto the scene, Ava was like a mother hen. At first, it made me all kinds of uncomfortable, but after a while, I'd gotten got used to it. It wasn't as if she was prying into my past or anything. She simply wanted to know my preferences. I loved Italian food. Spaghetti and meat sauce was one of my favorites. I hesitantly confessed this to her one afternoon, and from that point forward, she made sure to make it whenever I was in town. Very few people in this world were good to the core. Ava was definitely one of the best.

Grant and Mallory disappeared after dinner, probably to go bone in their bedroom. Hank made a lame excuse as to why he couldn't hang out with us, but we all knew the truth. He was dick dialing Marcy in Utah. Marcel, Sean, Evan, and I watched a movie and then Marcel and Sean took off for the back house.

"Do you need help going through the fan mail?" Evan's question jerked me from thoughts of crashing, to what I should be doing: reading fan mail. I glared ominously over at the bag sitting next to the fireplace, and wished that it would spontaneously burst into flames. I fucking hated fan mail. We all did. I mean seriously, could Marcy be any more archaic? No one still used snail mail these days. I made a mental note to talk to

Olivia about it. It's not like we couldn't afford to hire someone to do this shit for us.

"No, I've got it." If rifling through fan mail was my only penance for my bad judgment call with Chelle, then I'd happily take it.

"You sure? I've got nothing better to do tonight." As Evan followed me into Grant's office, his phone rang. "Be right back," he muttered. "Hey," his voice echoed out into the hall as he answered the call. I could tell from his tone that it was his wife. The bitch needed to either shit or get off the pot, but this constant back-and-forth limbo that she kept him in was seriously fucking with his head. Eventually, it would show in his playing. Hopefully, he wouldn't let it get that far.

Thirty minutes later, I was seeing cross-eyed. Letter after letter of drivel, whether it be naked pictures – some of indecipherable body parts – or fucked-up requests of lick this, suck this, sign this, and I was done. I'd barely made a dent in the bag, and was seriously considering burning the rest in the fireplace, when I saw a letter addressed to Charles Dunn. The hair on the back of my neck stood at attention. No one, except for my mother and her dick of a husband, Don, had ever called me Charles, and nobody…and I mean nobody, called me Dunn. I plucked the letter from the pile and inspected it. The penmanship looked sloppy, as if a child had addressed it. Carefully, sliding my finger into the fold at the top of the envelope, I eased it open and fished out the contents. It was a picture. My gut clenched with dread as I took in the red brick house, white picket fence, and smiling faces. Memories of that day, that exact moment in time, played through my head. The noose around my neck, born from childhood nightmares, tightened around my throat. Even though it was part of my imagination, it felt real. "Fuuuuuck," I hissed as I dropped my head to my hands and gasped for air. Once I'd gotten my shit together, I lifted my eyes back to the picture.

It was taken the morning I officially became Charles Dunn. I ran my finger over my mother's smiling face and thought about how happy she'd been that day. According to Mom, that was the day she'd gotten everything she'd ever wanted. Hell, so had I. Too bad it was one big, fucked-up lie. Try as you might, you never could forget the bad shit in your life, but if you tried hard enough, you could move past it and become a better person. Questions zinged through my head. Who had sent this? Where had it come from? What did it mean? I flipped the photo over and noticed writing on the back.

*"One big happy family."*

Bile shot from my stomach into my throat. Clearly, whoever sent it didn't know shit about me or my life.

The door handle to Grant's study rattled. Evan was back. The last thing I needed was him all up in my business. As the door swung open, I quickly ripped the picture up and shoved it in my pocket. My fingers fluttered a rhythmic dance over the pieces of torn picture as I watched him slump down into the chair across from me. He let out an exasperated sounding sigh.

"Trouble in paradise?" I asked. He rubbed his hands over his face. The poor guy looked defeated. What was it with women and their need to destroy? Mallory and Rowan had to be anomalies because, other than the two of them, I'd yet to meet a woman that didn't want to break balls and take names. Women were leeches, soul devourers…evil, fucking succubi. Evan muttered something, but I was so deep in my mental rant that I missed it. I was pretty sure it was something about his wife. If I asked him to repeat it, he would know I wasn't listening, which was nothing new, but definitely dickish.

"Did I tell you that we met in high school? God, I was such a player back then." A pained laugh escaped from his lips. Yep, it was definitely about his wife. I didn't want to pity the guy, but it was hard not to. He was clearly hurting. "She was my first…

everything." He kicked back in the chair and stared up at the ceiling. That's when I noticed the envelope. It was inches away from his left hand. Evan wouldn't know who Charles Dunn was, but I sure as hell did. His head tilted forward. He leveled his eyes on mine. I froze. "I didn't want a serious girlfriend, you know? I fought it, man, I really did, but we ran in the same circles." With a loud sigh, he dropped his head to the back of the chair, again. In one swift move, I plucked the envelope from the desk and shoved it inside my pocket. "She loved that I wanted to be a musician." His words surprised me. She sure as hell didn't appear to love it now. She probably never had. Like most women, she would have said anything to get the guy.

"What happened?" I found myself asking.

"I fell in love with her." His eyes looked haunted by memories as he stared off into the distance. "Aside from getting this gig with you guys, the day I married Amanda was the best day of my life."

"Let me guess, it wasn't enough, was it?" His eyes jerked to mine and flared in pained understanding.

"Music is in my soul. It always has been. Mandy knew this when she met me. She understood this when we said our vows. But now...she claims that I'm choosing music," he waved his hand in the air, "that I'm choosing all of this...over her." He let out a groan of frustration. "This is my dream. This puts a roof over her head and allows her luxuries she's never known. She wants it all, loves what it gives her, but only on her terms."

I shot him a questioning look. "Which are?"

"Come home. Gig locally. Give up the dream." I found the whole thing ridiculous, but I could see that he was struggling. It seemed simple to me. If she loved him, truly loved him, she wouldn't ask him to give up the one thing that made him who he was, but hell, what did I know? I'd spent the better part of a year sticking it to a murdering psychopath. I didn't want Evan to quit the band. He brought something to Meltdown that we'd never had before. He unified the group. Because of him, we were playing better than ever.

"What are you going to do?"

He slumped down into the chair, as if begging for it to swallow him whole. "I'm giving her what she wants. I'm signing the divorce papers." Relief rushed through me. I didn't know what to say. I felt bad for the guy, but I had to admit, his wife sounded like a grade-A bitch. He eyed the bag of fan mail. "You want help?"

"Nah, you go to bed. I've got it." As he stood to leave, I suddenly found myself wanting to impart wisdom. Normally, when this happened, I refused to act on it. I wasn't good with emotional shit. I hated anything touchy feely, but I considered Evan a friend, and I didn't have many of those in this world, so I gave it to him regardless of whether I should or not. "I don't pretend to know dick about relationships, but if she loves you, really loves you, she would support your dream instead of trying to take it away." His eyes glistened as he glanced back over his shoulder at me.

"I know," he quietly replied. Then he walked out the door and closed it behind him.

Three hours later, the bag was empty. I'd scratched out obligatory responses. I was toast. I barely made it to my bedroom before falling face first onto the bed. There was a reason why we all hated fan mail. It sucked ass. Not wanting to sleep in my clothes, I managed to strip off my t-shirt. As I pulled off my jeans, something fluttered to the floor. *A piece of the picture.* I picked it up off of the floor and pulled the remaining pieces from my jean pocket. Slowly, I put them back together on top of the dresser. I poured over the picture, as if willing it to give me answers. *Who sent it? What does it mean?* I wasn't sure, but something told me it wasn't good. I placed the pieces back inside the envelope. With a grunt of disgust, I flopped back onto the bed and closed my eyes. When sleep refused to come, I focused on another challenge: Olivia. The shock on her face when she discovered that we were touring with Indigo Road was stuck in my mind. Her scared expression bothered the hell out of me. My mind raced with all sorts of fucked-up scenarios.

Not able to stand it any longer, I snagged my laptop from my suitcase and cracked it open. I typed Olivia Marshall into the search engine and hit enter. Other than her affiliation with Indigo Road, I got nothing. Next, I searched Indigo Road. It appeared that Olivia Marshall vanished into thin air about three years ago. She was there and then she wasn't. Nothing was that cut and dried. Snagging my phone from the bedside table, I shot a text to their drummer, Gio:

*Hey, man. Are you ready for the tour? I can't wait to kick your asses all over the stage.*

A few minutes later, I got a reply: *Hey, dickhead, whatup? Good to see you're back. Ain't nobody gonna kick our asses. Didn't you hear? We're the best.*

His cocky response made me smile. It also brought out my competitive nature. Let's see what he has to say to this: *Yeah, we'll see. We've got an ace up our sleeves, someone who knows all of your dirty little secrets.*

*???* Gio immediately responded. For a split-second, I thought about playing it off, but curiosity had me by the balls.

*Olivia Marshall is our new road manager,* I typed.

After a long pause, he responded: *No shit?*

His response, or should I say lack of response bothered me. *Got any advice on how to handle her?* I typed.

After a long pause, his response came through: *Olivia was a sweet kid. Several of the guys enjoyed more than her company, if you catch my drift.* This was followed with a fist bump and two eggplant emogis. *Is he saying what I think he is?*

*She was a player???* I quickly responded.

*As I recall, that's what got her canned. Make sure you wrap it before you tap it. Gotta run. See your ugly mug next week.*

*Later,* I replied.

Why would Gio lie to me? Olivia Marshall was about as far away from a player as it got. Not only did I not get the answers I wanted, but I was now more confused than ever. One thing was for certain. It looked as if I wasn't the only one with secrets...

# CHAPTER EIGHT

## "Hit Me With Your Best Shot"

*Olivia*

I was frustrated. As in, *super-duper blow my cool* frustrated. I was panicked about seeing Sander again, weirdly attracted to Chaz Jones, and now Marcy's car was on the fritz. One backfire was so loud it nearly blasted the doors from the cars on either side of me. I blew out a huge sigh of relief as I pulled Shitty-Shitty-Bang-Bang into the garage and turned off the ignition. The engine puttered slowly before finally giving up the ghost. I dropped my head to the steering wheel and said a little prayer of thanks. *Marcy needs her head examined*, I thought as I bodily forced open the car door.

"Evil car," I muttered on my way to the house.

Once inside, I set my briefcase on the counter. It was days like this that I wished I still drank alcohol. All I wanted was to make enough money to survive for another year. Not like this. This was a train wreck, a free fall into Fuckedupville. I thought back to the last time I'd set eyes on Sander, and my stomach literally curdled. After everything I'd been through, all that I'd lost, how was I back here again?

My first few months working for Indigo Road were super exciting. They were also a bit of a nightmare. While I was learning how to do my job, I was simultaneously being tormented by their lead singer, Sander James. Every decision I made, he counteracted. Any ideas I came up with, he shot down. Sander pulled no punches about his dislike for me. I, on the other hand, was obsessed with him. The man had a voice of sin and the body of an Adonis. He was a god among men, and I was his number one groupie. I was smart, driven, and determined to succeed. My dream was to manage a band. Getting hired by Indigo Road was a huge step in that direction. Once I'd set my eyes on the prize, I never wavered. The goal was to make it to the top, and the proverbial icing on the cake, was to get there with Sander James. Too bad he didn't see it that way. In fact, he didn't see me at all. I was the hired help, and *hired help* was disposable. In my drive to be seen, to be noticed, I lost something invaluable. I lost me.

My phone rang from across the room. In my haste to retrieve it from the bottom of my purse, I nearly tripped over my own two feet. God, I was such a mess.

"Hello?" I finally answered, completely out of breath.

"Hi, Olivia. It's Marcy. Did I catch you at a bad time? You sound like you're exercising."

Biting back a humorous snort, I breathily replied, "Hi, Marcy. I just walked in from Grant's house. What's up? How's your dad?"

"He's the same. I was just calling to check in. How's everything going? Are the guys ready for the tour?" The guys were more than ready. I, however, was not.

"Why didn't you tell me that we were touring with Indigo Road?" I blurted. My voice sounded shrill and accusatory, but damn it, I was mad. I felt completely ambushed. I should have been among the first to know, not the last.

"I'm sorry. I didn't realize it was going to be a problem for you." Marcy's chilly response pulled me up short. *Shit!* This was a major problem for me. Only, I couldn't talk about it. Damn Frank and his contract. "Did something happen with Indigo Road that you're not telling me?" Marcy asked. If she only knew. My pulse raced as I scrambled for what to say.

"No, really, I was just taken by surprise. I should have asked more about the tour before I accepted the job." *Lame, Olivia,* I thought as I closed my eyes and mentally bashed my head against the nearest wall.

"Olivia?" she quietly urged, "you know this is part of the business. If you don't think you can handle it, you need to tell me now." There was a lot I needed to tell Marcy, but couldn't. Not unless I wanted to get nice and cozy with the inside of a jail cell, which I did not.

"I've got it, really. It just took me by surprise, that's all," I hastily repeated. Awkward silence stretched between us as I once again scrambled for something to say, something that would ease her mind and get me off the hook.

"Promise you will tell me if anything changes?" she asked in a skeptically wary tone of voice.

"You'll be the first to know. I promise," I told her. My eyes hit on the rack of keys by the door, and I suddenly remembered the next item on my list. "Not to change the subject or anything, but you really need to get someone to look at your car."

"What's wrong with my car?" Her panicked tone made me feel bad.

"Well, for one, it backfires." She didn't respond, so I kept going. "It won't accelerate past fifty miles an hour, which sucks on the highways, and it makes a constant squealing noise, as if one of the belts is loose."

"Olivia, are you driving the Beetle?" Her tone of panic was

now laced with humor, and I had a sinking feeling that I was about to be the butt of the joke.

"Uhhhhh...yes?" I half answered with a question, and she belted out a laugh.

"Do me a favor. Walk over to where the keys are hanging." I did as she asked. "Directly below the keys for the Beetle what do you see?" A snort of laughter spilled from my mouth as I stared at Porsche keys. "I keep a tarp on the Porsche when I'm not driving it," she humorously murmured. "There may be a few things on top of the tarp, but trust me when I say there's a pretty nice car underneath."

"I'm such an idiot," I whispered, and we both laughed.

"I'm surprised you're still in one piece," she managed to say, which prompted a recount of my ride to and from Grant's house. Once our laughter died down, she brought up Indigo Road again, and I assured her that everything was fine.

"You need to let me know now if this going to affect your job performance." My job performance, no. My life, yes.

"I promise not to let it affect the job I do for you," I reiterated for the third time.

"Are you sure?"

"I'm positive. Hey, before we hang up, there's something I wanted to talk to you about." I went on to discuss my budgetary ideas with her. When the call ended, I flopped down on the sofa. What an absolute mess I'd made of my life. It didn't matter how far I'd come or what lessons I'd learned, I always ended back at the same place.

After a dinner of grilled chicken and steamed vegetables, I tried to call my brother, Banks. I wanted to check on my place. I also wanted to see if Mom and Dad were still mad at me. Other than the occasional poop emoji, Mom hadn't spoken a word to me. I knew she was going to be mad. I did not, however, expect the silent treatment. When he didn't answer, I left Banks a message to call me.

As I got ready for bed that night, I tried to think of anything but the ridiculous situation I'd landed myself in. My mind wandered to Chaz. Talk about an enigma. The guy was a complete puzzle. He always seemed to be watching me. Like this afternoon, for example. When I found out about the tour and mentally freaked, it was like he sensed what was going on in my head. It almost felt as if we were somehow connected, but then he ruined it by taunting me. Why? Better yet, why did I care? What was it about him that intrigued me? I thought about him and, oh, what was her name? It was one word, like Cher. I would have remembered if it was Cher, though. What was she like? Did he love her? The more I thought about it, the more convinced I was that there was more to the guy than he let on. I fell asleep thinking about Cher and the backfiring Beetle.

I arrived at Grant's house the next morning in a better frame of mind as well as a better vehicle. Driving Marcy's Boxster was an exhilarating experience. Thankfully, the guys hadn't busted me driving the Beetle yesterday. Talk about embarrassing. Sometime between last night and this morning I'd made peace with the fact that Meltdown and Indigo Road were going on tour together. It was what it was. My contractual obligations to Indigo Road were no longer in effect. Sander no longer had a hold on me. Things were going to be fine. Hellion greeted me at the door with tail wags and doggy kisses.

"She's going to be heartbroken when you leave," Mallory called from the kitchen. She and Ava were having coffee. With them stood a familiar looking woman. It took me a minute to place her. *Rowan Burns.* She looked different in person. The red hair definitely fit her better than the black.

I smiled in greeting at the three of them. "You mean the hellhound isn't coming with us?" I teased.

"Have you been hanging out with Chaz?" The in-stereo

question pulled me up short. My surprised expression made all three of them laugh.

"The look on your face," Rowan howled. When the hilarity died down, she held out her hand. "You must be Olivia. Hi, I'm Rowan, Nash's fiancée." I instantly liked her.

I handed Hellion over to Mallory, before shaking Rowan's hand. "Nice to meet you." Now was my moment to find out more about Chaz. "About Chaz—" I started to say.

"What about me?" he asked.

"Shit!" Mallory screeched. We all four jumped in surprise. My heart skipped a few thousand beats as I turned to face him. I scrambled for something to say.

"Oh, uh, I was just going to ask if you were here today." I gave myself a mental pat on the back for maintaining my cool. The guy really did unnerve me. Chaz's skeptical expression told me he wasn't buying it.

"Grant told me to come retrieve you," he stonily replied. His gravel-coated voice sent shivers through my body. I didn't want to be affected by him. What I wanted didn't seem to matter, because whenever Chaz Jones was anywhere near my orbit, my brain shut off and my libido went into overdrive. With a disgusted huff, I excused myself and headed for the stairs. As I passed by him, he spoke in a low, sexy voice. "If you want to know something about me, ask me. Better yet, how about we have ourselves a little information exchange? I'll go first. What happened between you and Sander?" Our eyes met and held. His were a blue, so deep they appeared almost black. He had a darkness about him that called to me, but I couldn't dare answer, for fear that I would get lost in him...just like before. My body might want Chaz Jones, but I did not. I was here for the job, not this...whatever this was. I no longer had that fresh-faced, openhearted view about life. Thanks to Sander, I was jaded through-and-through.

"No thanks," I responded with a chilly smile. I felt him behind me as I made my way down the stairs to the recording studio. For three years I'd been in a hormonal funk. My internist blamed it on the antidepressants, but my shrink said that it was my body's way of protecting itself, and that it would respond when the time was right. Color me crazy, but I didn't exactly think this was the right time, nor did I feel that Chaz Jones was the right person to alleviate my...issue. Too bad my newly awakened libido seemed to strongly disagree. Grant's eyes lit up when he saw me enter the room.

"Great, Chaz found you. We're trying to decide which song to use as a closer for the album. Three of us have songs that would work. They're all good, but we can't seem to agree on which one best fits the tone of the album. You've heard the album up to this point, so we've decided to let you be the tiebreaker." My mouth flopped open in shock.

"Me?" I squeaked.

"Please?" Grant sweetly asked.

"Food and margaritas are your just reward," Nash coaxed. These men were beautiful to look at, but they were so much more. They were crazy talented, not to mention genuinely kind, at least most of them were. I could feel Chaz's eyes on me. *Don't look*, I told myself.

Finally, I threw up my hands in defeat. "Fine, but you might want to get a third opinion." Grant ushered me into the recording booth and placed me on a stool between him and Nash. I tried to keep my eyes off of Chaz, but it was as if they had a mind of their own. His energy filled the small space, rendering me breathless.

"You ready?" Grant asked.

"Hit me with your best shot," I cheekily replied. I watched him nod to each of the band members, and jumped when Nash's guitar belted out the opening chords. The song was exceptionally good, but slightly mellow. So far, my favorite song on the album was the one from yesterday, the edgier one that Grant and Nash had cowritten. The entire album had a similar vibe to it. It would be a shame to end it on a lighter note. When they were done playing, I thought about how to word my thoughts in a way that didn't hurt feelings.

"Well?" Nash asked.

"It's really good." Nash's hands shot up in the air in victory. "But," I continued, and felt bad when they dropped in defeat, "it doesn't have the same edge as the other songs in the album. Even the slower song, you know, the one you wrote for Rowan, has that certain raw feel to it. I'm sorry." I started to stand. "Mallory or Rowan should be doing this, not me."

"Sit," Chaz commanded. Without thinking, I plopped back down on the stool. My eyes snapped to his and my face flushed with heat as I glared defiantly at him. He looked so damn good sitting behind those drums. He responded to my glare with a slow, sexy wink.

"Next song!" Grant shouted. Evan nodded his head at Chaz, and Chaz began clicking his drumsticks together. I couldn't tear my eyes away from him as he began to pick up the tempo. One... Two...Three...Grant and Nash both came in with lead and bass guitars, and I knew that this was going to be the song. Chaz and Evan joined in, and Grant started singing. My eyes raked over his inked arms and the way his muscles flexed as they moved rhythmically over the drums. Chaz Jones was a force of nature. If I wasn't careful...very, very careful...I could get swept away.

From what I could gather, the song was called "Bitch-Slapped" and was about a million different types of betrayal. The line that hooked me in went something like:

*The world will do you no favors; so grab it while you can. Cause no matter how much you want it, you'll get bitch-slapped in the end.*

It was loud, dark, angry, and true…so true. When the song was over, I jumped off of my stool and screamed, "That's it! That's the one!" All eyes shot to Evan. Evan, however, was smiling at Chaz. When a smile appeared on Chaz's face, my heart stuttered in my chest. I'd never seen him smile like that. I had a feeling it wasn't a regular occurrence. I also had a feeling that the song we'd just heard belonged to Chaz, and not Evan.

"Fuuuuuuck," Grant groaned, "are you kidding me?" Evidently Grant had come to the same conclusion. Evan let out a bark of laughter and Nash had a few choice words to say. Clearly, I was missing something.

"You wrote that?" Nash asked, his voice filled with disbelief.

"Chaz wrote the lyrics. I helped get the sound down," Evan responded.

"Hot Mess declared it! You heard her. My song wins. Pay up, fuckers!" Chaz called out in obvious delight. My eyes shot to his, and I felt his wink where it counted. *Hot Mess?* Surely he didn't mean me. "Hot Mess," he mouthed, and I quickly looked away. Oh my gosh, he was talking about me! Is that how he saw me? I wasn't a hot mess. I was calm, cool, and very collected. If anything, he was the mess. My eyes dropped to my dancing unicorn flip-flops and pink painted toenails as I tried to reel in my spinning emotions. "Relax," his deep voice whispered in my ear. When I nearly catapulted off of my seat, his big hands settled at my waist to steady me. My eyes flashed to the guys, but they were busy counting their money. By the looks of it, Chaz had bet the house on this one. I wouldn't admit it out loud, but I was glad his song had won. I had a feeling he didn't win much with this group. "What happened with you and Sander?" he whispered in my ear.

"What happened with you and Cher?" I snapped back at him. His eyes flashed in surprised amusement.

"Cher?" he asked.

I dismissively waved my hand in the air. "You know who I'm talking about. I can't think of her name but it starts with a C."

"Let me know when you think of it, and I just might tell you," he murmured against my ear. He laughed when an involuntary shiver shot through my body, and suddenly I was furious. I jerked my head up to glare at him and wanted to kick my own ass when I realized that I'd just placed our faces inches apart.

"There's nothing to tell, so stop bugging me," I hissed through clenched teeth. My eyes dropped to his tongue as he licked his lips, and desire, like I'd never known pooled between my legs. I chalked it up to desperation, pussy confusion...temporary insanity.

"Chaz, quit harassing Olivia!" Evan called out. Chaz took a quick step back, and I felt as if I could breathe again. When he turned to address Evan's comment, I slid off of the stool and out the door.

Clearly, I needed to have my head examined, because I really, really wanted Chaz Jones.

# CHAPTER NINE

## "Redemption Song"

### Chaz

Olivia picked my song. I shouldn't have been surprised. It was clearly the best of the three, but that wasn't the point. The point was that she recognized great music when she heard it. The look on both Grant and Nash's faces when they realized they'd been duped, was priceless. If I'd known all I had to do was trick them to get them to play my songs, I would have done it years ago. I thought back to all the times they'd shut me down, and smiled. *Got you, fuckers.*

Stepping in as Meltdown's drummer was a dream come true, an all-time career high. It sucked balls that it took place under the shittiest of circumstances possible. Dale was dead, the band was one man short, and desperation had sunk in. Emotions were riding high and Meltdown was at a crossroads; hire a new drummer or walk away. I wasn't surprised they'd chosen me. I was a damn good drummer. If I'd had any idea of what I was up against, however, I might have chosen to go with a different band. That first year was hell. Plain and simple. Grant, Nash, and Luke had all three bonded over the loss of their fellow bandmate. They were an impenetrable fortress of anger and resentment. I learned pretty damn quickly that it was them against me. I wasn't their precious Dale, and they reminded me of it every time I took the throne. I had lyrics – they didn't care. I had suggestions – they didn't care. They wanted a drummer, not a friend, and certainly not someone who might add value. It wasn't until Luke tried to kill Grant that the house of cards came crashing down. The bond was broken. In another desperate moment, Evan was hired. I expected for them to flip him shit. I waited for them to stonewall his ideas. What did they do? They bent over backwards to welcome him into the fold. I should have resented him for it, but dammit if I didn't like him, too. In a matter of weeks, Evan did what no one had been able to do. He made us whole. And then I had to go and fuck it all up. Now we were back where we'd started. I was once again on the outside looking in. I hated that it mattered to me, but it did.

When Evan suggested that we try something different for the final song on the album, I had no clue what he had up his sleeve. But then Grant asked him what he had in mind, and he suggested a play-off. I knew exactly what he was doing. He was stepping up for me. I didn't know what to say. The only person to ever step up for me was my Uncle Bill, and that was over ten years ago. I never thought Grant would go for it. Not only did Grant go for it, but he bet money on it, and Olivia picked me.

*Olivia.*

When she was in the room, I tried not to stare at her, but there was something about her that made it hard to look away. She clearly wanted nothing to do with me. Because of this, I made it my mission to annoy the shit out of her. I was starting to really have some fun with it until she brought up Chelle. I shouldn't have been surprised. Of course, she knew about Chelle. It was her job to know our dirty little secrets, so why the fuck did it bother me so much?

My mind wandered to Chelle. The first time Grant brushed her off and she ended up in my bed, I fucked her out of anger. I thought it was funny when she paraded her naked ass in front of everyone the next morning. I knew exactly what she was doing, but couldn't care less. I got off. She certainly got off. What did I care if she panted after Grant like a bitch in heat? Grant was a dick and Chelle was a self-absorbed, manipulative slut. I was all too familiar with her type. In this business, they were a dime a dozen. Girls like Chelle used clothes and makeup like camouflage, yet wielded their words like weapons of mass destruction. Nash and I referred to her as a beautiful, destructive viper. My mother was a viper. I understood Chelle all too well because I'd spent years subjected to a razor-sharp tongue. In fact, I had a childhood full of scars to show from it. Chelle pulled no punches about using me to get to Grant, and I didn't care. She didn't land in my bed by accident. It was strategic planning at its finest. When one night turned into two, and so on and so forth, I knew exactly what I was getting myself into.

Along the way, though, something changed. She quit talking about Grant and started talking about us. She quit obsessing about Mallory and started making future plans...with me. Somewhere along the way, I began to believe that we could have a future together. Yes, she used sex to get what she wanted. I cannot lie, the fact that she wanted me felt good. She didn't dig into my psyche, ask personal questions about my past, or pester me. Did it surprise me when she asked to come on the road with me? Yes, but it also gave me hope, which was something I'd learn to never count on. Outside of sex, we really hadn't spent that much time together. When I told her no, it wasn't because I didn't want her there. It was because I knew that I couldn't have her there. She'd not only burned bridges, she'd blown them to hell and back. Grant and Nash would never have allowed it. Instead of accepting her fate, Chelle found a way to make it happen. Not only that, but she convinced her best friend, Paula, to help her. That was the thing about Chelle. She had this way of making you buy whatever lie she was selling. By the time she'd turned the tables on me, it was too late. I'd become like all the rest, a sucker, a fool...a dumbass. Did I realize she was playing me? No. While she was begging for my cock, did I know that she was planning to take out Mallory? No. When she crawled into my bed at night, did I know that she was crazy enough to poison some dude she didn't know for some fucked-up reason I still didn't understand? Fuck no. Even after I found the pictures and the vial of what I'd later learned to be poison, both of which she had viable excuses for, I still wouldn't have pegged her as a murderer. Shows how much I know. I honestly believed her. I believed her up until the moment she pulled the disappearing act. When I called Paula and she told me to look in my own back yard and that Chelle was finishing what she'd started, I knew that I'd become that guy - the one I'd made fun of, called pussy whipped...hated. I'd been played. The moment I realized that she was the person who'd hurt my friends, it was over. I can't be sure if it was ever love, but I sure as hell knew when it became hate.

"Why didn't you tell me?" Grant's question caught me by surprise. I'd been so deep in thought, I hadn't heard him approach.

"Tell you what?" I replied as I dug into the bottom of my suitcase for my swim trunks.

"That you could write lyrics like that." His answer stung. I'd tried a million times to tell him just that. What a dickhead.

On my way to the bathroom, I leaned in and whispered, "You're a dick." He was gone when I stepped out, and I kind of felt bad. Grant hadn't given me much of a chance, but it wasn't as if I'd been forthcoming either. Maybe it was time to bury the hatchet, so to speak.

Everyone but Olivia was already by the pool. A sliver of disappointment stole through me. Hot mess probably thought she was too good to slum it by the pool with us simple folk. Just the thought of seeing all of that virginal white skin in a swimsuit did funny things to me, like jumpstart my cock. The realization that I was getting a boner while wearing swim trunks made my lips twitch with humor, not to mention relief. It was good to know that he was back from the land of the lost.

"Oh my God, is Chaz actually smiling?" I heard Rowan whisper. I liked nursey. She and Evan were the only two who had actually made an effort to get to know me. I waited for my dick to settle, before turning to address her. When I caught sight of who was standing next to her, wearing a bikini, no less, my tongue literally stuck to the roof of my mouth. Golden haired and flawless skinned perfection stared back at me. Olivia shifted nervously from foot to foot under my scrutiny. Clearly, she was uncomfortable. I couldn't say why, but this bothered me. I thought back to my conversation with Gio. I wasn't buying it. There's no way that the woman standing in front of me, trying to hide her gorgeous body, was a band slag. No. Fucking. Way. Before I said something stupid, or she noticed that I was sporting a boner, I turned and walked away.

"Nice job on the song today," Nash commented as I passed by him in search of a bottle of water. For some reason, this pissed me off even more than Grant's earlier comment.

I couldn't help but say something. "You act as if this is something new, as if I've never come to you with a song I've written." His expression of surprise quickly morphed into one of anger.

"Why do you always have to be a tool?"

"Actually, I'm not being a tool. I'm pointing out a fact. Admit it. Had you known that was my song, you never would have agreed to Evan's terms."

"That's not true-" he started to protest.

"Bullshit," I snapped.

"Now isn't the time," Grant interceded.

"You lied to us all...about Chelle...for months...so excuse the hell out of me if I don't want to hear your song," Nash angrily spat out. And here it was, front and center, Nash's issue with me. Who was I kidding? Nash was never going to get over it. Rowan let out an exasperated sounding huff, but I didn't pay it much attention. I was done taking his shit.

"Fuck you, Nash. Clearly, you've never made a mistake before. Oh, I forgot, you have. In fact, your mistake got Rowan kidnapped. Hell, it almost got her killed. So, while you stand there on your perfect pedestal judging me, you might want to take a good hard look at yourself, you sanctimonious prick." I slashed my eyes to Grant. "You wanted me back? Well, here I am. Either you," I scanned over the crowd before continuing, "all of you, get the fuck over what happened with Chelle, or you can find yourself a new drummer." Before anyone else could comment, I was in the house and heading for my bedroom.

"Chaz, wait up!" Olivia called out. I halted mid-step. My mind screamed go, but my legs refused to move. My fingers drummed a nervous rhythm against the sides of my legs. One-two-one-one-two.

"You can't quit," she announced once she caught up with me. My fingers stopped mid-tap. As I lowered my head and narrowed my eyes on her, I noticed that she'd put on a white, lacy cover up. She really was a short little thing.

"I have a tall personality," she wryly commented. I hadn't meant to say that out loud. *What. The. Fuck?* I turned for my bedroom and she followed behind me.

When we reached my door, I stopped and asked, "Why can't

I quit?"

"You signed a five-year contract to play drums for Meltdown. Management can fire you, but if you decide to quit, you'll lose your shirt."

"Shit," I corrected.

"Shirt, and it's a pretty standard contract," she replied.

"I'll lose my shit, not shirt," I reiterated.

She smiled, and my cock responded with a happy jerk. "Well, hopefully you won't lose either."

*Focus,* I thought. "You read my contract?"

"I read all of your contracts." I didn't know how to respond to this, so I simply opened my door and waited for her to enter.

"Thanks, but no thanks. I just wanted you to know that it would be a horrible business decision for you to quit. Also, I wanted to tell you that your song today was really good. It will make a perfect ending to one of the best albums I've heard in a long time." The white, lacy getup was pointless because I could see right through it. Her tits bounced up and down with every word she spoke. I tried to ignore them, but I was a man, and she had a fine set of knockers. It didn't hurt that she was so damn animated. Chelle had been all angles and sharp edges. Olivia was rounded corners with a soft finish. A finish that my fingers ached to touch.

"Are you going to tell me what happened with you and Sander?" I quietly asked.

She stroked her tongue across her lips, and I felt it deep in my groin. When a woman had no clue as to her sex appeal, it only made her sexier. Olivia Marshall was one sexy woman. For a moment, I thought she was going to answer my question. When her full lips pursed and a look of annoyance appeared on her face, I knew the moment was lost. She took a step back.

"I should go. A word of advice from someone who knows. Don't let them get to you. You deserve to be part of the band."

As she turned to walk away, I scrambled for a way to get her to stay.

"I didn't know what Chelle was up to," I blurted. My confession stopped her dead in her tracks. Her head turned and her big, blue eyes peered back at me. A look of expectation materialized on her beautiful face. "If I'd known she was going to hurt them, I would have stopped her." I was like a runaway train. My mind screamed shut the hell up, but my lips kept moving. "I should have stopped her." Her eyes softened, not with pity as much as in understanding.

"From what I hear, you did stop her," she quietly replied. I shook my head. Her eyes seared into me as she searched my face. For what, I had no clue. "You stopped a woman from killing people you cared about, Chaz. Whether she meant something to you or not is now irrelevant. I'd say you did exactly the right thing at the right time, wouldn't you? You have a choice to make, right here, right now. You can keep beating yourself up, or you can get on with it. I suggest you get on with it. Now, it's a pretty day out. It would be a shame if you wasted it hiding in your room. Ignore Nash. Come join us by the pool."

I contemplated her words as I watched her walk away. Then, for reasons I couldn't begin to explain, I followed after her. Not because I wanted to hang with those fuckers, because I didn't, but because I couldn't seem to stop myself.

For better or worse, my sights were officially set on Olivia Marshall.

# CHAPTER TEN

## "Trouble"

*Olivia*

For the past two days, all I'd thought about was the conversation I'd had with Chaz outside his bedroom. I'd broken his words down, fully dissected them, and obsessed over my feelings about them. I'd always been this way. My shrink labeled it as highly introspective, but I felt it was more neurotic.

*Chaz.*

He was nothing like Sander. Whereas Sander was pathologically social, Chaz was a loner, a corner sitter, a brooder. It was hard not to compare the two of them as they were like night and day. For the first time since I'd walked away from my job with Indigo Road, I found that I was able to reflect back on my time with the band and my relationship with Sander with a new sense of clarity. The bitter heartache was no longer present. The bone deep feelings of betrayal were now faded memories of the past. I tried to recall when this had happened, but couldn't. It just…had. This job was a huge memory trigger, but the memories no longer hurt. It was as if they now belonged to someone else.

A few months into my job with Indigo Road, I caught a group of girls trying to break into Sander's hotel room. Sander was very specific about not wanting to be disturbed during his downtime. The girls shouldn't have been on his floor, much less anywhere near his room. Security should have been all over it, but they were nowhere to be found. This was back when electronic doors could be broken into with a simple swipe of a credit card. I stood there weighing my options. There were at least ten of them and one of me. They could easily take me if they wanted to.

When the girl on her knees in front of the door loudly whispered, "I've got it," and I heard the lock disengage, I panicked, and shouted, "Security! Stop and put your hands in the air!" Shrieks of surprise echoed through the hallway, and like a mob of wildebeests, they took off running the opposite direction down the hallway. As they rounded the corner, Sander's door flew open. His hand shot out and latched onto my arm.

"They can't get out that way. Quick, get in here," he whispered, and yanked me inside his hotel room. Once we heard them clatter back down the hallway and out the door, we broke into laughter. Sander offered me a drink. I chose water. We spent the next few hours talking about everything under the sun. When it was time for me to go, he kissed me. His breath tasted like the bourbon he'd been drinking all afternoon. Never, in my life, had I been exposed to something like Sander James. He was like a red-hot flame, and I... well, I was the poor, pathetic moth who was destined to get burned.

"Ready to go?" Marcel's question pulled me from my memories. Tour day was finally here. I was excited and nervous at the same time. Marcel and Sampson had strict orders to deliver me safely to the bus, while Hank and Sean were in charge of the guys.

"This goes to Chaz," I told him as I handed over the bag of fan mail. I made a mental note to talk to Marcy about transitioning fan mail to the computer. Once my bags were loaded in the car, we were off. Marcel and Sampson talked sports, while I thought about the upcoming tour. My mind drifted to Chaz and the way he looked in a swimsuit, all muscled and tatted. I'd been so tempted to throw caution to the wind. To forget about past mistakes, step inside his bedroom, and…I wasn't sure what came next, but that was just it. For the first time in what seemed like forever, I wanted to find out. I wanted to know what came next. I wasn't sure if it was the man or the circumstances. Either way, I would take it, because it made me feel alive again. We pulled into the parking lot and there it was…the bus. I waited for Marcel and Sampson to clear the area, before exiting the vehicle.

"What's next, boss lady?" Marcel asked.

Nervous tension roiled throughout my body. The guys had spent every second of the past month perfecting the new album, and tonight they were bringing it to their fans. Thank God Marcy had arranged things with Frank and Indigo Road prior to hiring me. I would still have to deal with them, but according to her, outside of the actual practices and shows, Indigo would be doing their own thing. That sounded like Frank, the pretentious ass. I was surprised that Sandor was still putting up with Frank's myopic bullshit. Our first stop was San Antonio. With Marcy's approval, I'd rearranged a few more things in the budget and had used the savings to have Meltdown's bus completely revamped. Linoleum and suede had been replaced with faux hardwood and leather. The bunks now had cushy mattresses, down comforters, and blackout blinds. Instead of one television, which was almost always commandeered by the gamers, there were now two. I also managed to slip in a new logo. Now, with the mere flip of a switch, the Meltdown logo on the side of the bus turned black, making the bus anonymous.

I chewed on the side of my nail as I stared up at my surprise. "Now we wait for them to arrive. Do you really think they'll like it?"

"Shiiiit, try love it," Marcel replied.

"And I thought cutting the pre-party for a better hotel room was genius. After this one, we should be worried about Marcy's job," Sampson teased. Marcel shot him a stern look, and he held up his hands. "I'm just saying..." his voice faded to a laugh. I really did love these guys. They were professional but nice. Respectful without being pushy. Indigo Road's security team was filled with a bunch of assholes who would betray one another at the drop of a hat. These guys truly seemed to like each other. More than that, they seemed to like me.

"Rest assured, that won't be an issue," I replied through my laughter. "I'm here for this tour, and this tour only. After that, I'm back to my regularly programmed life."

"You sure about that?" Sampson asked. Before I could answer him, the van carrying the guys pulled into the parking lot. Hank exited the van. He, Marcel, and Sampson had a pow-wow in the middle of the parking lot, before he headed back to let the guys out. Grant got out first, then Nash, Evan, and last came Chaz. Our eyes met from across the parking lot and my pulse fluttered. What was it about this man that made me feel like a weak-kneed girl? He was surly and direct, angry and demanding, but beneath all of this was a vulnerability that called to me. Today he was wearing ripped jeans and...I could be mistaken, but I was pretty sure he had on a Garth Brooks t-shirt. My lips twitched with the impulse to laugh. I would never in a billion years have pegged a tatted up, metal looking guy like Chaz Jones to be a country music fan.

"What the hell?" Grant asked. I jerked my head in his direction, and discovered him on the top step of the bus. He turned to me with a look of wonder on his face, and whispered,

"What did you do?"

"What?" Nash asked as he pushed by Grant to take a look. "Fuuuuuuuck," I heard him say from inside the bus.

"Since both of them are pussy whipped, can I assume there aren't strippers waiting for us inside?" Chaz asked. Just the sound of his voice made my stomach dip. I could feel the heat of his presence at my back, and I wished, for a brief moment, that I could lean back and absorb his warmth. That is, until I processed his question. He meant for it to be funny, but I found it to be rude and tasteless. Is that what he wanted? Strippers? Or better yet, prostitutes? And why did I care who the man screwed? He wasn't mine. As I moved to escape, he grasped my arm. "Hey, I was just kidding," he whispered in my ear. I turned my head and lasered my eyes at him.

"Sorry, but hiring strippers and prostitutes isn't a part of my job description. If that's what you want, you're on your own there, pal. Now, if you'll please let go of my arm, I have a job to do." He stared at me for a long moment. Then he dropped my arm and walked away. I wanted to call him back, to apologize for my immature reaction, but it was too late. The damage had been done.

"Two TVs and, oh my God, have you felt these beds?" Evan shouted from inside the bus.

"I'd say they like it," Marcel mused. I smiled at him, but deep inside I felt like utter shit.

It wasn't long before the roadies showed up with the convoy carrying the instruments. When all hands were finally on deck, I addressed the crowd. "For those of you who don't know me, my name is Olivia Marshall. I'm the road manager for this tour. This means all questions, concerns, and complaints come straight to me and not the band members. Do I make myself clear?" I waited for acknowledgement from the crew before continuing. "If I find out that you are harassing or bothering the members of the band in any way, shape, or form, you will be terminated on the spot. Is that clear?" Multiple heads nodded in understanding. "That being said, I think it's a great idea that we all get to know each other, so I've planned several crew parties along the way. These parties will be solely for the members of Meltdown and the crew. No Melties," my eyes found Chaz leaning against the bus, "and no outside entertainment will be allowed at these parties," I finished. Chaz shook his head and escaped into the bus. I wanted to kick myself. What was my problem? I didn't have to say that, but I couldn't seem to stop myself. I was acting like a jealous girlfriend.

"What about Indigo Road?" a voice called out.

I swallowed back a nasty remark. "Indigo Road has made their own plans, but I won't discourage the bands or crews from hanging out together." Several whoops and yips rang out through the parking lot. "Here's this week's schedule: Tonight, we are in San Antonio. Tomorrow and Sunday night we will be in Houston. We will be in Dallas Monday and Wednesday."

"What about Tuesday?" one of the roadies called out.

"Tuesday night, we will be having our first crew party around the hotel pool." I held my breath and waited for the onslaught. Fourth of July concerts were a huge moneymaker. Marcy and Frank, however, decided to forego the opportunity. I disagreed with their decision, but it wasn't mine to make.

"We're not playing on the Fourth?" Grant asked. I could tell from his tone that he was angry.

"We're not. Marcy and Frank," but before I could finish my sentence, he had his phone to his ear and had disappeared inside the bus. *Shit!* "That's all for now. We'll see you all in San Antonio!" I called out, and made my way towards the bus.

Grant apparently worked things out with Marcy, because he didn't mention the Fourth again. The guys loved the bus, that is, except for Chaz who wasn't speaking to me. Other than that, though, we seemed to be off to an excellent start.

We reached the hotel in San Antonio a little after three in the afternoon with just enough time to check in and get to the venue for a practice run before dinner and the show. While the roadies enjoyed a buffet style dinner with the Melties, the guys had chicken and beef fajitas catered by one of the best Mexican food restaurants in town. The Melties were livid when they discovered their access to the band had been cut off. A few of them decided to revolt, which got them a security escort out of the building. According to Hank, Indigo Road was hiding out on the other side of the venue. I was perfectly happy with this arrangement. In fact, I was downright giddy about it. Maybe, just maybe, I wouldn't have to deal with them at all.

The band got a hassle-free hour of peace and quiet before the show, which was something they seemed to really appreciate. That is, everyone but Chaz, who still wasn't speaking to me. I'd tried to apologize. I'd even gone so far as to utter those two magical words that I really abhorred saying, but he just stared blankly at me as if I wasn't there. The only indication that he'd heard me was that maddening drumming thing he did with his fingers. Over the past few weeks, I'd learned that his finger tempo was a direct correlation to his anxiety level. The more anxious he was, the faster he drummed. After what happened this morning, I was surprised his fingers hadn't fallen off.

"He's not worth it," Hank said from behind me.

"Who's not worth it?" I asked, knowing full well who he was referring to.

"Chaz. Marcy and I weren't kidding when we told you to keep your distance. That guy is trouble and has a mile-long list of issues." Hank's assumption was right on the mark. It was also completely unwarranted.

"Well, it's a good thing I'm not interested then, isn't it?" I snapped. Then I made a bee-line straight for trouble himself, and plopped my ass down next to him on the sofa. His head tilted down and his eyes landed on me. Midnight blue irises sucked me in. I could tell from his stiff body language that he was surprised to find me sitting there. His fingers drummed ninety-to-nothing against the back of the sofa, and for some strange reason, I found it comforting. I found him comforting. Go figure. We sat in silence for a minute or so before he made a motion to leave.

"I had a fling with Sander. Only, I thought it was more." The words got stuck in my throat, and I took a second to clear it, before continuing, "It was more than that…at least it was to me," I quietly added. "When I realized it meant nothing to him, that I meant nothing, I tried to walk away." I lifted my head. He was staring intently at me, and I wondered what he was thinking. Before I lost my nerve, I told him the rest. "Before Frank let me go, he made me sign a non-disclosure agreement stating that I wouldn't talk about anything concerning Indigo Road or my time with the band. I trust you not to say anything, because I really need this job. Now we're even." Before he could respond, I stood up and walked away.

I really hoped that I hadn't just made the biggest mistake of my life. If so, it wouldn't be the first time.

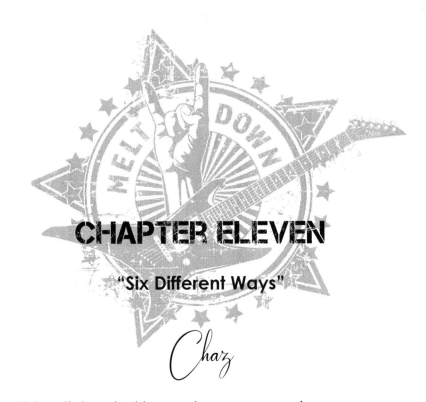

# CHAPTER ELEVEN

## "Six Different Ways"

*Chaz*

Olivia's little snit this morning over my stripper comment annoyed the hell out of me. She wasn't my boss. She wasn't my mother. She sure as hell wasn't my girlfriend. I could talk about strippers if I wanted to. After her spiel to the crew, we loaded onto the bus, where I immediately found a seat as far away from her as I could get. I tried to ignore her, but what I mostly did, was stew. I mean, seriously. Chelle could have cared less if I fucked a stripper, much less talked about one. Olivia flipped her shit at the mere mention of one, and then wouldn't even give me a chance to explain. Fuck her. The more I thought about it, the more pissed off I got. I felt trapped...by her, by my memories, by my life. I wanted to bend her over my knee and spank her ass. My cock liked that idea. Five minutes into the ride and I was sporting a boner. Great. I contemplated reading through fan mail, but quickly decided against it. For all I knew, there could be another letter. When Evan asked if I wanted to play video games, I jumped at the idea.

Thirty minutes later, Evan was kicking my ass in Call of Duty. We had another forty-five minutes to go, and I was distracted. The more I tried to ignore Olivia, the more aware of her I became. It was as if suddenly I could sense her every move, which pissed me off because I was trying so damn hard not to.

"Fuck it. I'm done," I told Evan, after he'd killed me for the fifth time in a row.

"You can't quit in the middle of a game," he whined.

"I just did." I tossed my controller onto the chair next to him, and made my way to the refrigerator, where I snagged a bottle of water.

"You okay?" Grant asked. He and Nash were sitting at our new kick ass media table looking at their computers.

"Fucking perfect," I snarled as I dropped down onto one of the cushy leather sofas. I could feel Olivia's eyes on me as I pulled my headphones from my bag and plugged them into my phone. I inserted them in my ears and hit play. As "Machinehead" filled my ears, my fingers drummed to the beat of the song. Slowly, I began to relax. And then I felt her, or rather, I smelled her. Her scent reminded me of the flowers my mother planted in her garden when I was a kid. Gardenias, I think they were. The sofa shifted with the weight of her body as she sat down next to me. Her smell was intoxicating. I closed my eyes and soaked in her nearness. The song transitioned from Bush to Weezer, and I tried to focus on the lyrics, but all I could think about was her. When she called my name, I turned my head. Eyes so blue they were almost transparent stared up at me. She was right there, so close that I could see each mascara coated eyelash. Her peach scented lips begged to be tasted. I wanted to taste them. I wanted to taste her. Olivia Marshall was flawless. She was also a giant pain in my ass. Her lips moved, but I couldn't make out what she said. I pulled out an earbud and cocked my head, but all I got was a lame-ass apology. Whatever. I was still pissed. I waited for her to finish. Then I shoved the earbud back in my ear and resumed listening. A long minute passed before she stood up. With a loud huff of annoyance, which I heard over my music, she stormed off. I felt bad, which pissed me off. Why should I feel like shit when I didn't do anything? What in the hell was this woman doing to me? I didn't want to care. I sure as hell didn't need to care, but for some very twisted reason, I did.

I managed to keep my distance for the rest of the day. That is, until Olivia blindsided me with that shit about Sander. Now I was all fucked in the head. Gio had lied to me. I didn't know what pissed me off more, the fact that Sander had been with Olivia or that Gio had lied about it. I thought about this afternoon's practice, and how Gio had acted all concerned when he'd asked about Olivia. Hell, Sander was right there with him, the fucker. The subject of my thoughts suddenly popped her head into the room. Our eyes met for a brief second before she dismissed me. I hated when she did that.

"Alright, boys, Indigo is wrapping up their final set. You're on in fifteen. The security team is in place, but since the hallway is a bit rowdy tonight, we've added extra security for your protection. It's show time," she announced.

Grant and Sander had agreed that they would alternate which band would take the stage first on this tour. To our disappointment, Indigo Road was first up at this venue, which meant that we'd go second tonight and first tomorrow night. I tapped my sticks against the chair in front of me and tried to focus on tonight's performance, but all I could think about was the hot mess standing across the room trying her damnedest to ignore me. She'd changed clothes. She'd also put on more makeup. I couldn't help but wonder if it was because of Sander. Just the thought pissed me off. Her black jeans fit her ass like a well-loved glove and her button-up shirt was tied at the waist. A small strip of bare skin between the top of her jeans and the tied-off shirt was on full display. What the fuck was she thinking? I had the sudden urge to call her out on her outfit. Marcy wouldn't have been caught dead wearing that. Clearly, someone needed to fill her in on proper dress code. Hank said something to her and she gave him an award-winning smile. A twinge of pain pierced my jaw as I ground my back teeth together. Good fucking thing Hank was involved with Marcy, or else we'd have a big problem. Olivia glanced in my direction, and I quickly looked away. Eventually, my eyes wandered back to her. She was once again talking to Hank, and I noticed that her hair was longer than I'd realized. It was probably because she preferred to wear it up. I liked it down. A laugh trickled from her shimmery, peach colored lips, and the pain in my jaw increased. Fucking Hank. My eyes wandered back to that damn shirt. It looked as if it belonged to some dude she'd nailed. Whatever. Now, I was mad because I was pissed about something so damn stupid. Was it wrong that I wanted to kiss her peach lips and chew her a new asshole at the same time? Probably.

Grant stood and clapped his hands together. "Okay, boys, this is it," he soberly stated. Evan, Nash, and I circled around him. "A lot of shit has gone down, but we're here, and it's a damn good place to be. We're united. We're better than ever. We're fucking indestructible. This album is our best yet. Now, let's go out there and blow their fucking minds!"

Adrenaline lit up the room as we loudly replied with a, "Fuck yes!" Hank and Marcel took the lead, while Sean and Sampson flanked our sides. A few hired security guards brought up the rear.

As we passed by Olivia, I leaned in and whispered, "Just so you know, we are far from even." When she narrowed her eyes and pursed her pretty, peach lips at me, I smiled.

"What was that about?" Evan asked.

"Noneya," I snapped.

He shot me a confused look, and asked, "Huh?"

"Noneya fucking business," I told him, and tried not to smile when he rolled his eyes at me like a girl. Yep, tonight's show was going to be epic. I could feel it in my bones.

The venue we were playing had a rising stage. It was cool, because we could get situated without having a million eyes on us. There was only one drawback. The moment we appeared on stage, we had to be ready to play. No delays. No fuckups. Four beats and go.

"Burn it Down" was the first song on our playlist. It was a favorite from Meltdown's first album, which was recorded before I'd come onto the scene. One by one, Grant nodded to each of us as the stage began to rise. "We've got this," he mouthed. Blinding lights followed by a deafening roar of screaming voices greeted us as the stage clicked into place. After a lightening quick four-count, we were off and running. From "Burn it Down," we dove straight into "Avalanche." "Avalanche" used a mixture of snare and bass drums, and was one of my all-time favorite songs to play. After "Avalanche," Grant introduced the members of the band. When he got to me, I did my normal routine, and held my sticks high in the air. The roar of the crowd flowed through me. Not only did it fill me up, it made me whole. These were the times I lived for. Nothing but the music could make me feel this good. As the cheering went on and on, I took notice. Something was different. Why wasn't Grant introducing Evan? That's when I realized, the crowd was chanting my name.

"Chaz Jones, Chaz Jones, Chaz Jones," they chanted over and over again.

I shot Grant a questioning look, and he shrugged. "Give them a bow," he mouthed.

*Fuck it,* I thought as I stood and circled around my drum kit. When I reached the front of the stage, I scanned over the mass of screaming people. The crowd began to quiet down, as if waiting for me to say something prolific. I waited for silence, and then I flipped up my middle finger and tossed my sticks as far as I could into the mass of humanity. The crowd went absolutely ballistic.

"They're paying homage to you, man," Evan said in my ear. It was awkward and awesome at the same time. As I turned to make my way back to my throne, I spotted Olivia standing off to the side of the stage. She'd pulled her hair up and I could see a sheen of sweat glistening on her chest at the 'V' of her collared shirt, or should I say Sander's shirt. A mental image of her riding Sander's cock popped into my head, and I growled in disgust. Sander was a pussy. In a moment of anger, I ripped off my sweat-soaked shirt and lobbed it out into the sea of screaming people, which managed to rile them up all over again. With a chuff of humor, I shook my head and headed back to my throne. I searched for Olivia, but she was gone.

Pretty soon, the show was over and we were being lowered back down into the pit.

"That was fucking amazing!" Evan shouted. I had to agree. The crowd was insane. We'd given an unprecedented three, instead of our usual two, encores before finally calling it quits. I stunk like a mother fucker and was in dire need of a shower. We all were.

"Hold," Hank ordered, and waited for us to get into proper formation. As security lead us into a packed hallway, Hank shouted, "Clear the hallway!" We held tight and waited for the hallway to clear before proceeding to our empty dressing room, where we were greeted with bottles of ice water, beer, and Gatorade. Grant threw me a spare t-shirt. I nodded in thanks and pulled it on.

"Where is everyone?" Nash asked. Screw everyone, where was our manager?

"Where's Olivia?" I asked Hank.

"Olivia thought you might need a moment of downtime in order to change and grab something to drink," he responded.

"Oliviaaaaaaa," Evan teased.

I shot him a scathing look. "What are you, three?" He laughed and I tried not to punch him in the face.

"The last I saw, she was in the next room over talking with Sander," Marcel told me. *Fuck!* I thought as I beat feet in that direction. Sure enough, that's where I found her...with Sander. The fucker had her cornered. She looked like a frightened animal, and suddenly, I was furious. Olivia's eyes widened in surprise when she caught me stalking in their direction. Sander turned as I approached the two of them.

"There you are. I've been looking everywhere for you." A cute little squeak escaped from her lips as I pulled her into my arms. "I missed you," I murmured just loud enough for Sander to hear. Her fingernails dug into my back in warning, and I smiled. I should have stopped there, but the possessive look in Sander's eyes really pissed me the hell off, so instead of pulling back like I should have, I lowered my mouth to hers, and did something I'd wanted to do since the moment I'd laid eyes on her. I kissed her. At first, she just stood there, but then slowly, she opened up. Invitation accepted. I went all in. Her lips tasted as good as the fantasy, but her tongue far surpassed my wildest dreams. I swallowed down her sexy-as-shit moan, and damn if I didn't almost drop to my knees. I was about to lay her out on the table in front of us, strip her bare...feast on her, when Sander, the fucker, cleared his throat. Olivia's entire body went rigid. Her nails dug deep. With a growl of frustration, I released my hold on her. She pulled back, but she didn't jerk away like I expected.

"I didn't realize the two of you were together," Sander commented.

"It's new," she retorted.

"Yep," I said at the same time, ignoring her piercing glare.

After a long, very uncomfortable pause, Sander muttered something about his bandmates, and excused himself from the room.

Once he was completely out of sight, Olivia turned and in a very hushed voice, hissed, "What in the hell was that?"

"That was me saving you," I dryly responded. By the look in her eyes, I'd say she didn't like my answer.

Pointing her finger at my chest, she gritted her teeth, and said, "I don't need for you or any man to save me...ever." Then she turned on her heel and stormed off.

Before she reached the door, I called out, "You're welcome." Her middle finger shot high into the hair, and I let out a bark of laughter.

Challenge accepted.

# CHAPTER TWELVE

## "Lies"

### Olivia

It was inevitable that I would run into Sander. I'd mentally planned for it. I knew exactly what I was going to say when the time arrived. Only, it didn't happen. When I made it through the day without seeing hide nor hair of anyone from Indigo Road, I began to let down my guard. Meltdown was my number one priority. Not Indigo Road. Not Sander. As for Chaz Jones, well, he was a distraction I neither wanted nor needed. The moment he ripped his shirt from his body and threw it into the crowd of screaming women, I was out of there. If he wanted to place his toned, tatted torso on full display, who was I to judge? I was not a jealous person by nature. I just...wasn't. So, why was I seeing green? Why did I let it bother me? The answer was pretty damn simple. My attraction to Chaz was getting out of hand. I had to find a way to shut it down. After making sure the dressing room was ready to go, I slipped into the adjacent room to regroup. That's where Sander found me.

"It's good to see you, Olivia. You're looking gorgeous as ever." The sound of his voice, a voice I'd once loved beyond all reason, washed over me. Then the realization that I'd been ambushed hit me full force. *Damnit! Why now?* I thought as I slowly turned to face him. My mind scrambled to recall my rehearsed speech from earlier, but all I got was a blank slate of nothing. *No!* I screamed inside my head as panic threatened to take hold. I thought about what my therapist had told me, and grasped for something, a mental weapon of sorts, to help me regain control. The image of Chaz's smiling face popped into my head, and suddenly I could breathe again. "Are you okay?" Sander asked. He reached for me, but I quickly dodged his hand.

"I'm fine," I curtly replied.

We stood there, like two strangers, staring at each other. The first thing I noticed was how much he'd aged. The past three years had not been kind to him. Gone was the fresh-faced boy. In its place was a weathered looking man with crows-feet and laugh lines, most likely caused by rough living. His reddish-brown hair was streaked with blond hilights. Underneath it, however, I saw traces of gray. The memories swept in like a tidal wave.

Everything changed the day Sander James kissed me in his hotel room. Suddenly, I was his go-to girl. To the band, the crew...Frank, we'd finally set aside our differences, learned how to tolerate each other. Little did they know that when I wasn't playing manager, I was being stalked, cornered, and controlled. When Sander snapped his fingers, I was there. When he said jump, I asked how high. He owned me and I let him. I let him, because finally, I'd gotten what I'd wanted. Kisses were snuck when no one was looking. The sex was hard, quick...stolen. Sander was demanding. Sander was controlling. Sander was...a liar.

After a long moment staring at each other, he broke the

silence. "I couldn't believe it when Gio told me you were managing Meltdown." Of course, he would have to mention Gio. "I hope they know how lucky they are to have you," he added. Here I was, standing face-to-face with the man who had completely devastated my world. I waited for the pain to hit, but all I felt was numb. The revelation was exhilarating. As I studied his mouth, a mouth that I'd once wanted, lips I'd once begged for, I was engulfed with an overwhelming sense of sadness. My obsession with this man had nearly destroyed me. I'd waited years for this moment. I'd gone through hell to get to this place. Yet, here I was, and all I wanted to do was to walk out the door and never look back.

"What, you're not going to talk to me?" Sander's abrupt tone yanked me back to the situation at hand. It also irritated me. He wasn't the only one who had changed over the past three years. If he thought I was still his pathetic little pet, he'd better think again.

"What do you want, Sander?" I finally asked. His face turned a light shade of pink.

"What do I want?" he dramatically gasped. "I want to know why you left? I want to know why you refused my calls? I want to know what the fuck you're doing here," he circled his finger in the air, "managing them, and not us? That's what I want." His words infuriated me. He knew damn well why I wasn't managing his band anymore.

"Are you kidding me? Y-you know why I left," I angrily stuttered.

"I have no clue why you left, Olivia." His dark eyes bore down on me. I hated to break it to him, but I was no longer afraid of him. Of his controlling nature...his volatility.

"Your signature was on the agreement, Sander. Nice try." His head cocked and his eyes seared through me. I stared back at him with a blank expression on my face.

"You and I both know I sign at least ten things a week for the band," he angrily huffed. I knew this and I also knew that nine times out of ten, he had no clue as to what he was actually signing. A sinking feeling came over me. *What if Frank never told him?*

"Frank never told you then?" I wasn't sure I wanted to hear the answer, but I had to ask.

"Told me what, that you left? Yeah, he told me. He told me that you had a family emergency and had to go home. After a few days, I tried calling you, but your phone went straight to voicemail. When you still weren't back after a few weeks, I tried calling your parents' home. Your mother gave me the runaround. Frank told me that you wanted out, but he never said why. After everything we had, everything we'd been through together, you owe me an explanation." I didn't owe him a damn thing. If anything, he owed me. When I didn't respond, he changed directions. "What agreement exactly are you referring to, Olivia, and what does Frank have to do with you leaving?" I didn't know whether to laugh or cry. I'd wanted this. Dreamt about this. Prayed for this. In my lowest of lows, I was willing to forgive all indiscretions for one more chance. Now, all I felt was confused. Right as I opened my mouth to respond, the door opened, and in stepped the man I'd been trying not to think about all day. *Chaz.* Before I could stop him from interrupting, I was in his arms and he was kissing me like his life depended on it. We'd been dancing around each other for the better part of two weeks, and at the absolute worst possible time, he decided to set a match to my smoldering libido. His lips touched mine. His spicy, sweaty scent swirled around me. His tongue tangled, licked, devoured. Sander no longer mattered. What I'd lost no longer mattered. All that mattered was this amazingly perfect kiss.

Before I did something massively stupid, like stick my hand

down his pants, or climb him like a tree, the reality of the situation slammed into me. I tried to pull back, but he had a death grip... on my ass, no less. As if sensing that I was about to knee him in the jewels, he reluctantly released me. Sander said something, I wasn't quite sure what, and then he was gone. As much as I'd enjoyed the kiss...never had one like it...wanted more - so much more...I couldn't. I'd gone down that road once before. I had scars. Soul deep, jaggedly ugly, forever-there scars, and I knew, I knew that if I let Chaz Jones in, he wouldn't just leave scars. He would destroy me. So, I turned on him, threw up my defenses, and did what I did best. I ran.

Now I was stuck at an after-party I'd planned, watching the man I couldn't let myself have flirt with anything with two breasts and a vagina. At the moment he was actually scowling, but I'd learned to read his scowls. This one was his I'm-moderately-interested scowl. Personally, I preferred the you're-a-complete-idiot scowl. Thank goodness Indigo Road had decided to cut out early. I wasn't sure I could deal with both Chaz and Sander in the same place after what happened earlier. Why did he have to kiss me? I couldn't decide who I was more furious with, Sander, Chaz, or myself. What was wrong with me? I had a job to do, and here I was, acting like a possessive hussy over a man I didn't even know, when I should be worrying about what the man who'd practically destroyed my life was going do next.

The air shifted beside me as Hank suddenly appeared. "Are you going to stand here sulking all night?" he arrogantly asked. When I didn't answer, he laughed. "I warned you," he said in a singsong voice.

"Aren't you supposed to be protecting somebody?" I pointed my finger in the direction of the band members, who were busy drinking beer and signing body parts, and tried not to growl when he laughed again. I was too tired to find humor in anything. If I didn't get to bed soon, I was going to curl up on one of the sofas.

"Don't lie. You care about him, don't you?" His smug tone made me want to punch him where it counted.

"Who are you, Dr. Phil? Even if I wanted to, I couldn't, so the answer is no. Now drop it." I was out the door before he could say another word. What was it with these guys? They were like nosy teenage girls. As I rounded the corner for the bathroom, I ran smack into Frank. *And the day just keeps getting better*, I thought.

"There you are," he said with a toothy grin.

"Yep, here I am," I dryly replied. Not only had Sander aged, but so had Frank. His salt and pepper hair was now all salt. He looked as if he'd shrunk a few inches.

"Can we talk?" he asked. The last thing I wanted to do was talk to Frank right now. I was dead on my feet and completely out of patience. If pushed, there was no telling what I would say.

"I don't think that's a good idea."

He took a step back and scanned me from head to toe. "Look at you. You look...really good." He sounded surprised, the jerk. "Look, Livie-"

"Olivia," I corrected. He didn't get to call me Livie anymore.

"Olivia," he said. "We left things on a bad foot. I-"

I cut him off before he could finish. "Why didn't you tell him?"

He stared at me for a long moment, and I could tell that he was weighing his words before they left his mouth. This, right here, is what made Frank an excellent manager. It's also what made him a shitty friend. "What happened was unfortunate. Sander was most unhappy that you left. It would have caused a rift, which was not in the best interest of the band." I blinked, and then I laughed right in his craggy old face.

"Who do you think you're talking to? You don't give a shit about the band. You're out for you and only you, Frank." By the way he narrowed his eyes and curled his upper lip, I knew I'd hit home.

"What did you think was going to happen, O-liv-ia?" He broke my name into three syllables. Yep, he was pissed. "You saw with your very own eyes what I'd been seeing for years. You weren't the first to get caught in Sander's web, darling, and you certainly aren't the last. This is who he is – what he does. You were a momentary thrill, collateral damage. Sander knew it. Gio knew it. I knew it. The only one who didn't...was you. If anything, you should be thanking me. I saved you." His words stung, even if there was some truth to them. Frank had no idea what he'd done, what I'd been through, how I felt. Tears burned the backs of my eyes, but I refused to let them fall.

"Fuck you, Frank," I spat.

"Olivia-" he started to say, but I held up my hand to stop him.

"I think it's a good idea if we steer clear of each other during this tour, don't you?" His mouth puckered, as if he'd just sucked on a lemon.

"Yes, Olivia, I think that's a wise idea, except for the fact that Sander wants to see you. He's asked me to arrange a meeting between the two of you."

"Are you kidding me? Bad idea, Frank. Sander talking to me is not for the good of him or the band, and you know it."

"It's a good thing you signed that contract, isn't it?" he snarled.

"Yes, a contract that Sander knows nothing about. Sander. Knows. Nothing. Frank." I slowly enunciated each word. "Imagine when he finds out the truth? Trust me when I say you do not want that to happen." Before he could reply, I marched my ass past him and into the bathroom, where I sunk to the floor and burst into tears.

That's where Chaz found me. Sitting on a filthy bathroom floor, bawling my eyes out over a guy who was once my world and a past that once meant everything. He didn't ask questions.

He didn't pester for answers. He dropped down beside me and gently placed his hand on the back of my head in silent invitation. I took it. I leaned my head on his shoulder and cried for everything I'd lost and what it had cost me. When I was all cried out, he slid his hand to my scalp, and began massaging.

"You want to talk about it?" he asked.

"I can't," I thickly replied. The hand massaging my scalp suddenly froze in mid-motion.

"Look at me." His gruff tone sent a spear of apprehension through me. I lifted my head and was immediately lost in the depths of his deep blue eyes. "Can't or won't?" he asked.

"Both," I breathily replied. He nodded his head in acceptance, and suddenly I wanted to. I wanted to spill all of my secrets. Every. Last. One. Because I knew, in my gut of guts, that he would keep them...me...my heart, safe. His eyes darted away for a second before settling back on mine.

"I didn't love her, but I cared." At first, I didn't know what he was talking about, but then it hit me. He was talking about Chelle. "I..." he took a second to gather his words. I held my breath and waited for them. "I knew she was up to something and I ignored it. I ignored it because I wanted to keep feeling good, even if it was a lie." His words made my heart hurt. I understood all too well what this was costing him. His eyes drifted from his lap to mine, and held. "And because I didn't want for it to end, I lied to everyone I cared about." My heart broke for him. We were more alike than I had realized. "It was all one, big, fucked-up lie," he quietly confessed. I was absorbed by his velvet blue, pain filled eyes. "I know what it's like to have secrets. I know what they can do to you. I'm definitely not the right person to give advice, but if you ever need to talk..." He shrugged off the rest of the sentence. It didn't matter. I knew what he was trying to say. Tears trickled down my face and he gently wiped them away. Everyone else might consider Chaz Jones an asshole, but not me. To me he was special.

"Thanks," I whispered. His eyes dropped to my mouth, and I waited for it, braced for it... wanted it like my next breath.

"Uh, you have a little booger." He did an air circle around half my face with his finger, indicating just how not small the booger actually was. I sucked in a shocked breath, and let out a gush of laughter. After a short minute, he joined in.

Yep, Chaz Jones was definitely something special.

# CHAPTER THIRTEEN

## "Waitin' for the Bus"

*Chaz*

Anger seared through me when I found Olivia crying on the bathroom floor. Red hot, fighting mad anger. I struggled with what to do. A part of me wanted to walk away, to leave her and her bullshit tears in my rearview mirror and never look back. Another part of me wanted to kiss her and bury myself so deep inside her that she wouldn't know where I began and she ended. Instead, I gave her the last thing I wanted, but what she really needed. I gave her a shoulder to lean on, someone to talk to... my friendship. Had it been Chelle, I wouldn't have given two shits about the tears, the bathroom floor...anything. This was definitely a first for me.

While she cried a river on my shirt, I thought about what had brought us to this moment. One thing was for sure. Something bad had happened between Olivia and either Frank, Sander, or both. I'd passed Frank in the hall. If he was the reason she was sitting on the floor crying, Olivia wasn't talking. She was smart not to tell me, not to trust me. Hell, I didn't trust anyone. Why should she? Still, it didn't stop me from wanting to know. The closer I got, the more I wanted from her. I knew this was a self-destructive path, but I couldn't seem to stop myself. To be honest, I wasn't sure I even wanted to.

"You better?" I asked, once we'd stopped laughing about an imaginary booger that I'd made Oliva aware of in order to break the tension.

She lifted her gorgeous eyes to mine, and I was relieved to see that they were dry of tears. "Please tell me you were joking?" She pointed to her nose, and I swallowed down another bark of laughter.

"I never joke about boogers," I managed to reply with a straight face. Olivia let out the cutest sounding huff and smacked me on the arm. I couldn't help but laugh. If this was anyone else, I would take her. Right here. Right now. Nasty bathroom floor or not, I would bury my cock inside her, but Olivia Marshall deserved more. She deserved more than this and definitely more than me. I held out my hand, and tried not to react to the rightness of her touch as she slid her hand in mine. Once she was on her feet, I let go. There was an instant void. I could see it in her eyes. She felt it, too. I quickly looked away, and thought, *fuck me, what am I doing?*

As we neared the dressing room, she slowed almost to a stop. Every time she looked at me, I was struck dumb. Even with swollen eyes, a red nose, and a splotchy face, she was crazy beautiful. "Thanks, Chaz," she quietly said. Before I could respond, she was swallowed up by the crowded room.

Two hours later, I was back in my hotel room. I should have been exhausted, but I was still riding high on adrenaline from the show. I was also still thinking about Olivia and her magic touch. Still wishing for things that would never be. My eyes wandered to the bag of fan mail. Evan had offered to handle it for me, but the thought that there might be another letter addressed to Charles Dunn somewhere inside, stopped me from letting him. When Marcy checked in with us earlier this afternoon, I took the opportunity to suggest going paperless. If Grant and Nash hadn't immediately jumped on board with the idea, she would have never gone for it. Marcy was a good manager, but she was definitely old school. As it stood, she'd promised to consider it. That didn't stop the fact that I still had to deal with the bag sitting across the room from me, but at least it was progress.

I expelled a groan of frustration and manned up and dug in. About halfway through the bag I spotted it. This time the envelope was light blue instead of white. Charles Dunn was written in the same childish handwriting as the previous letter. I held my breath as I ripped it open and fished out the contents. It was a picture, same as before. This one was of me and my stepdad. I was eleven years old. We were standing on the steps of the YMCA, me in my Y Guides shirt and Don in his police uniform. I remembered the moment it was taken, and how embarrassed I was that, even though all of the other fathers were wearing jeans and t-shirts, Don insisted on wearing his police uniform. Nausea roiled in my gut when I read the note on the back.

*Must have been nice.*

Nice, my ass. I stared down at the picture in my hand. The best part about Y Guides was the father/son weekend camping trip. I'd looked forward to it for months. Little did I know, but the week before the trip, Don had gotten into trouble at the station and had been placed on temporary leave. To say that he was unhappy was an understatement. He lied to us, told us that he was dealing with a stressful case. I told Mom that I didn't want to go on the trip with him in such a bad mood, but she ignored me. We went. The weekend was a nightmare. I didn't fit in. I was too hyper. My finger tapping was annoying. What the fuck was wrong with me? You name it, Don said it. As long as I lived, I would never forget that weekend. Not only did my friends discover what an epic tool my stepdad was, but I learned what it felt like to be on the other side of someone's fist. "It was a mistake, an accident," he'd claimed, when in truth, it was just the beginning.

I set the picture aside, and tried not to think about its implications as I quickly sorted through the rest of the bag. Just when I thought I was home free, I found another one. Same envelope. Same handwriting.

"You've got to be kidding me?" I growled. For a second, I considered ripping it up, but quickly decided against it at the last minute. No matter how I sliced it, this was evidence. I tore open the top of the envelope and fished out the picture from inside. "Fuck," I whispered. It was another picture of me. I was alone in the photo, staring at something off in the distance. I tried to recall when it was taken, but couldn't. The t-shirt I was wearing was a fourteenth birthday present from my best friend, Marco, so it had to be sometime after that. I swallowed back a stomach full of sour bile. Sticking out from under the t-shirt was a row of perfectly symmetrical cigarette burns. Sometimes, when I closed my eyes, I could still smell the stench of burning flesh. The pain was awful, but that smell was horrific. The side of my face was an array of brightly colored bruises. The timing made sense, because it wasn't until right after my fourteenth birthday that I started fighting back. I flipped the picture over.

*Not so great after all, was it?*

The only person who could possibly have sent these pictures was my mother, but that made no sense. The bitch had over ten years to get in touch with me. Why would she do so now? I pulled out the first photo, that I'd subsequently taped back together, and one-by-one, lined all three up on the foot of my bed. They ranged from bad to worse. I hated to see what she was going to send next. I was pretty sure this wasn't my mother's doing, but maybe it was time for Mommy Dearest and I to have a little chat? I snatched my phone from the side table, dialed the last number I could remember her having, and was not surprised to receive an out-of-service recording. The only other person I could think to call was my Uncle Bill. I bet he would know where my mom was. Bill was my stepdad's younger brother. He and my cousin Earle were the reason I was here and not buried six feet under. They saved me when no one else would. Sadly, Earle died from cancer when I was in my early twenties. Bill's voicemail picked up and I left him a quick message to call me. I thought about tracking him down at the police station, but as it was the middle of the night, it would have to wait until morning. Before crashing for the night, I slid the photos back in the envelopes and placed them in my bag. They would be safe there for now.

The next day was crazy busy. Not only did I not get an opportunity to find dick out about the Olivia-Sander-Frank situation, but I had no time to follow up on Bill. As we were first to play that night, we spent an extra hour in practice, where we played like complete and utter shit.

"What the fuck!" Grant shouted, after we fucked up for the tenth time.

"You know, there is such a thing as overworking it," I shared.

"Yes, and there's also such a thing as being unprepared and looking like idiots," Grant shot back.

"So, break it up. Do something different," Evan suggested. We all stared at him as if he'd lost his mind. "No, seriously. We're in our heads right now, so let's shake it up."

"What do you have in mind," Nash skeptically asked.

"Name a song." No one said anything. "Come on, give me a song. Chaz, what were you listening to earlier, and don't say Country."

"Foo Fighters," I answered.

"Song! Give me a song!" Evan shouted.

"'Everlong!'" I shouted back.

"Chazzy's listening to love songs," Nash teased, and laughed when I flipped him both middle fingers.

"Play it!" Evan screamed. Nash started playing. Grant jumped in with bass a few beats later. Evan rolled in with keys, and shouted, "Beat Chaz!"

"Fuck," I muttered, and gave him what he wanted.

After a few minutes of playing, Evan screamed, "Who knows the fucking words?"

"Chaz does!" Grant shouted.

"Fuck," I muttered again. Evan scowled over at me, and I flipped him off. Then I gave them what they wanted. "Alright, you pussies, I'm going to rock your world. Take it from the top, dickhead!" I shouted at Grant.

By the middle of the song, the kinks were gone and we were all singing. Evan was right. We just needed to get out of our heads. Grant rolled from "Everlong" straight into "Machinehead," and Grant absolutely crushed it. Nash took us out with "Killing In The Name," which was one of my all-time favorite Rage Against the Machine songs to play. We were having such a good time playing that we didn't see the audience gathered off to the side of the stage. That is, until we'd finished and were rewarded with cat calls, hand clapping, and cheers.

Olivia caught up with me on the way back to the dressing room. "I didn't know you could sing, she said in a breathy make-my-cock-hard voice.

"I can do a lot of things," I told her, and was surprised when she took my bait.

"Oh yeah, like what?"

"How about I show you later?" I half-joked. She smiled, and I could see it in the sparkle of her eyes. She totally wanted me.

Right before we hit the stage, I ran into Gio in the hallway.

He tried to talk to me, but I had nothing to say. Nothing good, that is. As far as I was concerned, he was a lying piece of shit. They all were. Just like San Antonio, the show was brilliant. We were at the top of our game and the crowd was on fucking fire. While Indigo took the stage, we partied in our dressing room with our VIPs.

That night we headed to Houston. After only five hours of sleep from the night before, spending half the day doing promotional shit and the other half practicing and performing, I was wiped. Evan wanted to play video games and Grant and Nash wanted to watch movies. I didn't give a shit what we did. Grant wanted to watch a comedy and Nash wanted a drama. Evan was too busy arguing with his wife to weigh in and Olivia was doing computer shit. Finally, sick of listening to the two of them bitch, I grabbed a leftover drinking straw and a knife. I cut one side short and pretended to shuffle the pieces around in my hands, before holding them up in front of me. Nash picked the long straw and immediately started gloating.

Just to piss him off, I said, "Short straw wins."

"What? No it doesn't. The long straw always wins," he argued.

"My game. My rules. The short straw wins." I glanced over at Olivia, who was staring intently at the three of us with an amused expression on her face, and winked at her.

"You heard him, I win!" Grant proclaimed, and that was that.

All it took was a dark bus and a slow movie to knock me out. I awakened when I felt the sofa shift beside me. At first, I thought it was one of the guys, but then I smelled her. Olivia Marshall was the only thing on the fucking planet that could take me from zero to rock hard in mere seconds. I slowly cracked open my eyes. She was curled in a sideways ball with her head close to me and her feet pointing toward the opposite end of the sofa. Her eyes were closed. Without even thinking about it, I shifted closer and settled her head against my shoulder. I slowly began to massage the back of her neck. A sexy little moan slipped from her lips, and I felt it all the way to my cock. We stayed like that for the longest time, me rubbing her neck, and her firing off groans of appreciation. My balls ached like no one's business, but it didn't matter, because for the first time since I was a kid, I felt centered, as if this was exactly where I was supposed to be. The realization that I would be perfectly content to sit here, boner and aching balls included, massaging the back of Olivia Marshall's neck for the rest of my days, should have scared the shit out of me. So, why didn't it?

The next thing I knew, the bus was pulling to a stop. We'd arrived in Houston. Olivia was nowhere to be seen. For a moment, I thought that I'd dreamt the entire incident, but as I was leaning down to grab my bag, I smelled the scent of gardenias on my t-shirt.

If tonight told me anything, it was that I needed to steer clear of Olivia Marshall. I needed to, but I wasn't going to.

# CHAPTER FOURTEEN

## "It Wasn't Me"

### Olivia

Houston was an absolute disaster. It started when we arrived and discovered our hotel reservation had been canceled and our rooms rebooked. The manager refused to give any information on what had happened, but I could see the truth. I'd watched him scramble behind the counter and witnessed the panicked expression on his face when he realized he'd screwed up. He called his employees to task, but no one knew where to point the finger. The guys took it pretty well. I, however, was furious. I wanted for someone to pay. In the end, the hotel came through and figured out a way to accommodate us. It wasn't the executive suites, but at least we had rooms.

Next, the soundboard cut out in the middle of Indigo Road's practice. One of Indigo's roadies told their security he thought he'd seen one of Meltdown's roadies tampering with the equipment. This led to Indigo's security team interrogating Meltdown's roadies, which royally pissed off Hank, and nearly led to a brawl between the two security teams. Frank and I had to jump into the middle of it, which resulted in the bands practicing acoustically. Frank and I were left to handle the security teams and the sound engineers. As if all of this wasn't bad enough, Frank took our close proximity as an opportunity to hit me up for a meeting with Sander.

"Now is not the time," I quietly responded. Indigo was currently on stage, while Meltdown stood off to the side waiting their turn. I could feel both Sander and Chaz's eyes on me.

"I told Sander what you said, but you know Sander. He's not going to give this up. He's furious with me right now, and wants answers," he murmured under his breath. For more reasons than one, I did not want to talk to Sander. Frank thought he knew the whole story, but he didn't know the half of it. No one did. As far as I was concerned, my past with Sander was dead and buried. Nothing anyone could say or do could change that. Digging the past up now would only hurt us both.

"I've already spoken with Sander, Frank. I'm not under contract with Indigo Road, therefore, I owe you nothing. What's done is done. I signed your contract. I abided by your rules. I left well enough alone. Now, back the hell off." Before he could respond, I turned and walked away. On my way back to Meltdown's dressing room, my phone dinged with a text message from my mother.

"Excuse me," someone said. I stepped to the side to let them pass, and quickly skimmed over Mom's text.

*We need to talk.* What was it with everyone wanting to talk all of the sudden? I sent her a poop emoji in response.

*Funny girl. Call me,* she shot back. My parents were good people, but they could be seriously annoying. *Kind of like Chaz.* He was avoiding me. I didn't mean to fall asleep on his shoulder last night, but when he pulled me in, it felt so right. Then he started rubbing my head. That felt more than right. That felt...I shuddered at the memory of his hands on me. We both ended up falling asleep. When I woke, I was entwined in his arms. As much as I wanted to stay there, I couldn't. Before anyone saw us, I escaped to the front of the bus. I didn't mean to hurt his feelings. I didn't want to lead him on. The more I was around him, the more I wanted to be around him, which was dangerous. Chaz Jones was dangerous for me. Sander wanted to talk. Chaz wanted to...I wasn't really sure what he wanted from me, but I had a good idea. One was a controlling nob, while the other was a grumpy introvert. I thought about what Chaz would do in my shoes, and bit back a snort. He would give Sander the middle finger and tell him to fuck off. Maybe I should consider ripping a page from the Chaz Jones playbook. It would serve Sander right.

The caterer was waiting for me when I arrived in the dressing room. While Indigo Road was on stage, Meltdown was hosting an event with what Marcy referred to as "friends of the band." This consisted of reporters, radio hosts, and magazine affiliates, all who had shown deference to Meltdown during their time of distress. It was supposed to be a casual meet and greet. Intimate, yet informal. No personal questions. Only talk of the current tour.

"I unloaded twelve trays of food and now there are ten!" the caterer loudly exclaimed as I walked through the door.

"You must be Caitlyn. I'm Olivia. What seems to be the problem?" As she explained how two trays of food had vanished into thin air, I tried not to panic. Two missing trays meant not enough food. Caitlyn was beside herself, but as bad as felt for her, it didn't change the fact that we now had a problem that required fixing. In the end, there was nothing she could do but apologize and refund me for the missing trays. My previous management experience had taught me that if something could go wrong, it would. In other words, always have a contingency plan. I had cash. Now, all I needed were a few roadies to do my bidding.

I found the bulk of our crew hanging out behind the loading dock. At first, I couldn't see what they were doing, but then one of the bigger guys turned and I spotted him shoveling down appetizers from a catering tray. My stomach dropped. It appeared that the crew was thoroughly enjoying the missing food, my missing food, to be exact.

"Where did you get that?" I asked. A few of the guys eyed me warily, but most of the group just ignored me and continued eating. "Where did you get these?" I repeated more firmly.

Finally, someone answered, "Dunno, some guy brought them out to us and told us to enjoy." *Are you kidding me?* I was livid, as in stomp-my-foot, lose-my-shit livid. Someone walked into Meltdown's dressing room, stole two trays of food, and handed it to the roadies. Who would do that? Better yet, why?

"Where's Larry?" I asked. Larry was Meltdown's roadie captain. All bands had a go-to guy. Larry was ours.

"Probably inside," someone answered.

I bit back a rude comment as I whipped out my phone and texted Hank. In a brief message, I told him where I was and what was going on. Five minutes later, both he and Larry appeared. Through gritted teeth, I explained the dilemma, and in no time at all, we had the story: Some unidentified guy suddenly appeared out of the blue with two trays of food, told them what a great job they were doing, and to enjoy, courtesy of management. Did it never occur to them to ask? When asked what happened to the guy, they said he just walked off. After scolding the crew, Hank and Larry said they'd look into it. In the meantime, we were still short on food. Larry enlisted a few guys to make a run to a nearby sushi restaurant to grab some quick takeout for me. The mystery wasn't solved, but at least now we would have enough food for the gathering.

As it turned out, only half the people who showed up ate

anything and we had plenty of leftovers, all which was hand delivered to the roadies by yours truly. I managed to make a few friends in the process, but still wanted to know who'd taken the trays.

Regardless of the day's fiascos, Meltdown rocked the stage that night. I'd give it to them, they were making Indigo Road look like amateurs. Not only was Sander looking old, he was sounding old. I thought about what Marcy had told me, and couldn't help but wonder if Sander had been using the whole time we were together. Maybe that's why...

"Your boyfriend is a decent drummer," a voice behind me spoke. *Gio.* I wondered when he would search me out. *Today just really isn't my day.* Not only did I not respond to Gio's comment, I didn't even bother to acknowledge his existence. As usual, he failed to get the hint. "You're looking good, Olivia." I glanced over my shoulder and made a point to scan my eyes up and down his body. Then, without saying a word, I turned back to the stage.

Gio Andrews was the drummer for Indigo Road and Sander's best friend, or so I thought. When I first started working for Indigo, and Sander was so horrible to me, I tried to enlist Gio's help. It didn't take me long to figure out that Gio was nothing but a two-faced asshole. Everything I told him, he repeated back to Sander.

"Soooo, are you going to talk to him?" he asked. And here is was, the real reason for Gio's impromptu visit.

I turned and gave him my full attention. "Tell me something G. Do you know why I left?" I knew he did, but I wanted him to confirm it. After a long pause, he nodded his head yes. "Then you know why I'm not going to answer your question." With that being said, I turned on my heel and walked off.

"Olivia?" he called after me. I glanced back to see what he wanted. "San..." I watched him struggle with his words, but

I really didn't care. None of it mattered anymore. Not Frank. Not Sander. Not Gio. I was sad for what I'd lost, but I was no longer heartbroken. These people no longer had a hold over me. I wasn't walking away because it mattered. I was walking away because I no longer gave a damn. "You weren't like the rest," he finally managed to say. That's where he was wrong. I was just like the rest. With a shake of my head, I continued down the stairs and out the door. I heard him call my name again, but I had no intention of letting him stop me a second time.

The after-party was off the rails that night. For one, everyone but Chaz seemed to be falling down, stumbling drunk. Evan kept making the crowd shout the words, "Hey, ho," while Grant and Nash challenged anyone who passed by them to a game of Whist. It didn't matter one iota to them that no one knew what the game was, much less how to play it. Chaz stood in the corner the entire night with his eyes glued to the woman standing in front of him. He wasn't touching her, but he sure was hanging on her every word. No matter how much I tried to play it off as no big deal, it bothered me. As in, really, really bothered me. I tried not to obsess, but the woman wore way too much makeup. And why did she even bother wearing a skirt? She could have just worn panties...red panties from the looks of it.

I had a moment of déjà vu when Hank suddenly appeared beside me. I waited for him to tease or taunt me about Chaz. Instead, he stood there with a scowl on his face, while perusing the crowd.

"What's wrong?" I asked.

"There are too many people here." I scanned the room and noticed it did seem unusually crowded.

I lifted my brow in question. "What are you thinking?"

"I think we've got a security breach." My eyes snapped to his.

"How?" This was not good.

"That's what I'd like to know. You stay here and check VIP badges of everyone entering and exiting the room. I'll grab the boys and do a perimeter check."

An hour passed before Hank and the rest of the security team returned. By that time, I'd discovered twenty people without badges and ten without tickets period. Hank and the guys discovered that one of the doors leading to the loading dock had been propped open.

It appeared that someone was trying to sabotage us.

While Sampson and Sean shepherded the band members to the bus, Hank and Marcel stayed behind to question the party crashers.

Evan promptly sequestered himself in the bathroom, while Grant and Nash passed out in their respective bunks. Chaz disappeared to the back bedroom. I was worried about him, or so I told myself. Truthfully, I wasn't sure exactly what I was, but I wanted to find out.

"Knock, knock," I called out as I barged into the room.

"I could have been jacking off," his deep voice responded. The light from the hallway spilled across the bed, and I could see that he was lying down.

"And what a sight that would have been," I teased.

"Go away, Olivia." I tried not to let his growly words or the fact that he didn't want me there hurt my feelings, but it kind of did.

"Are you okay?" I quietly asked.

"I'm fine, and if I wanted company, I would ask for it."

"Awww, sure I'll keep you company, sugar bunches. Scoot over." I pushed him with my hip and smiled when he let out an aggravated sounding huff. Once I'd settled onto the bed beside him, the room got strangely quiet. "Talk to me," I whispered.

"Has anyone ever told you you're a pain in the ass?" he asked. Laughter bubbled to the surface. I couldn't help but let it out. He was just so damn...grumpy.

"Coming from you, that's a downright compliment." He didn't respond, so I kept going. "I... saw you talking to that woman tonight. She was...cute."

"Jealousy is an ugly trait," he gruffly responded. I smacked him on the arm, and the bed vibrated with his laughter.

"I'm not jealous. I was simply making conversation."

"You're going to have to do better than that."

"Is she your girlfriend?" I partially teased. The other part of me was dead serious.

"No, Olivia, she's not my girlfriend. Either give me something or get out." God, he was such an ass. However, he was right. He'd given me depth last night. It was my turn to reciprocate. He'd been asking about Sander for weeks now.

*Here goes nothing*, I thought as I took a cleansing breath, and jumped in, "Five years ago, I got a job with Indigo Road as their road manager. Keep in mind, road manager was a loose title back then. What I really was, was Frank's assistant." I smiled when I felt the vibrations of his fingers as they thrummed against the mattress. For a moment, I got lost in the beat, but then he nudged me to continue. "My dream was to manage a band like Indigo Road. I loved their music. I loved everything about them." The drumming stopped.

"You didn't even know them," he commented.

When I felt it start back up, I continued, "You're right, I didn't. Sander hated me on the spot. He wanted a male manager. He called me all kinds of names, tormented me...God, how he tormented me. I could do no right." After a moment of silence, he nudged me again. Someone was impatient. "One day, I saved him from a pack of girls who had somehow figured out the location of his room. I busted them trying to break in and scared them off. Sander invited me in and we...talked." The drumming halted again, and I waited for him to comment.

"Bullshit," he rasped. I laughed, and he nudged me again. I liked the playful side of Chaz. Who was I kidding, I liked all of his sides, even the grumpy one.

I waited for his fingers to start back up, before replying, "We did talk, but we also kissed. I thought I'd died and gone to heaven."

"Let me guess, you became lovers after that," he dryly responded. His tone was calm, but his fingers told the truth.

"I don't think I like your tone," I teased. I felt his head turn in my direction. I couldn't see his eyes, but I knew they were staring at me.

"Am I wrong?" he asked. His breath smelled like cinnamon, which made me really self-conscious about mine. I tried to recall what I'd last eaten. "Am I wrong?" he repeated with a nudge.

"No, you're not wrong. We became lovers, if that's what you want to call it." The words floated between us.

"What would you call it?" he quietly asked.

"I don't know, his dirty little secret?" His fingers stopped, and I eagerly waited for his response.

"There ain't nothing dirty about you, sweetheart." His words sent shivers up my spine. If my nipples got any harder, they would be able to cut glass. Here I was, talking about Sander, while lusting for Chaz. "Let me guess, Sander told you that you were his one true love. You believed him, but later found out that you weren't the only one getting his rock star cock. Does that about sum it up?" he asked. Yep, that about summed it up.

"You have no idea." It might have been the way I said it. Who knows, maybe he was intuitive enough to feel the pain in those four words. For whatever reason, his warm hand found mine, and I gladly accepted it. His thumb rubbed back and forth across mine and I found it both comforting and arousing.

"Tell me," he urged. As if sensing my hesitation, he added, "It doesn't leave this room. I promise."

I stared up at the ceiling and sighed. Then I told him the rest, at least I told him most of the rest. "One afternoon, I needed to talk to Sander, but couldn't find him. One of the roadies told me they'd seen him get on the bus. When he wanted peace and quiet, he would sometimes escape to the bus to take a nap. I remember bounding up the steps of the bus. It took me a minute to grasp what I was seeing. In broad daylight. Right there, for anyone to walk in on, to see, was Sander...and Gio." Chaz's head jerked in my direction. I could feel his eyes on me. I could feel them lasering in on my shame.

"No shit. Sander was fucking Gio?" His shocked tone mimicked how I'd felt that day. I never saw it coming. It bowled me over. It destroyed me.

A self-deprecating laugh whooshed from my lips. "Yeah, apparently they had a thing. I would have never believed it had I not see it in action."

"Sorry, but I fail to see the humor," Chaz growled. That was just the thing. It was funny. Okay, it wasn't then, but it was now. Another burst of laughter escaped, and the next thing I knew, he was towering over me, caging me to the mattress with his body. "Sander's an idiot," he whispered. He was so close. So. Damn. Close.

"I was the idiot," I corrected. "I never knew. I didn't even suspect. What does that say about me?"

"You were young, dumb, and in love. That's what it says." He lowered his body down to where I could feel every hard inch of him hovering, touching, pressing against me. "From where I see it, you have a choice to make, right here, right now. You can keep beating yourself up, or you can get on with it. I suggest you get on with it." I was thoroughly impressed that he'd remembered word for word what I'd said to him that day in Grant's hallway.

"I'm getting on with it," I breathily replied.

"Are you done with him?" he asked.

"Are you done with her?" I shot back. He sealed his mouth to mine and swallowed down my gasp of surprise. He dropped his full weight on me and I welcomed it by opening my legs, by inviting him closer, by wanting to feel every inch of him on me, near me...in me. His hands wrapped around my hips as my fingers found purchase in his hair. He growled. I whimpered. We both wanted more. I ate up his kisses, while he moved in a rocking motion against my core. Long, hard, painfully erotic strokes against my center. If he didn't stop, I was going to come, and embarrass the hell out of myself.

Someone knocked on the door. We both froze. In a matter of seconds, he was off of the bed and out the door.

"Oh my God," I whispered, after finally catching my breath. My second "Oh, my God," was accompanied by a fit of silent laughter. Chaz Jones was an animal, and I - well, I was in deep, deep shit.

# CHAPTER FIFTEEN

## "One Step Closer"

*Chaz*

Hank stood at the door with a less than thrilled expression on his face.

"Problem?" I asked as I pulled the door shut behind me.

"Do you think that's wise?" He nodded his head at the closed door. His possessive tone pissed me off.

"Do you think it's wise to be boning your boss?" I shot back.

"This isn't about me," he snapped.

On my way past him, I paused. Our chests were practically touching. I didn't care. Hank was a big dude, but so was I. If he pushed, I could take him. I didn't necessarily want to, but I could. I didn't like the way he looked at Olivia. I hated how she was always smiling and joking around with him. Fuck him for judging me, and fuck him for thinking that he needed to save her from me. "What I do, and who I do it with, is none of your business," I warned, before making my way to the front of the bus. If Hank was smart, he would back the hell off.

"I saw you with Paula tonight!" he called after me.

"Goody for you," I replied over my shoulder as I exited the bus.

Tonight was all kinds of messed up. One minute I was being confronted by Paula and the next my tongue was down Olivia's throat. I pushed aside my feelings for Olivia for a moment and focused in on my earlier confrontation with Paula.

After all of the shit went down with Chelle, Paula disappeared. She wouldn't answer her phone. She wasn't at her apartment. She was in the wind. The police wanted her for questioning. I simply wanted to make sure she was okay. The authorities eventually found her hiding out at her grandmother's place. She had information, but not enough to land her ass in a jail cell. If any good came from the Chelle fiasco, it was Paula getting exonerated. I didn't blame her for not answering her phone. We'd both been burned. The after-party was in full swing when she suddenly popped up in front of me.

"Hey, Chaz. How's it hanging?" she slurred. "You wanna sign my tits? You know, for old time's sake?" She lifted her shirt and shoved her tits in my face. As it turned out, the main reason Paula went along with Chelle, was because she had a thing for me. Chelle knew it. Paula knew it. I, however, did not. If I'd known, I never would have played along.

"Put your shirt down," I snapped. With a loud huff, she slowly lowered her shirt. I shook my head in disgust. Her eyes were glassy and her nose was running. She was clearly high on something. I patiently listened as she slurred her way through an apology. She said she had no idea about what Chelle was doing and had been played like the rest of us. She had my full sympathy until she offered to blow me if I would pay for a hotel room for her. She had apparently snorted her last dollar. Chelle may have had a hold over me, but she had a death grip on Paula. With Chelle out of the picture, Paula had a chance to turn herself around, to figure herself out. Yet, there she stood with her painted face, skimpy clothing, and snotty nose...wasting it. I wanted to shake her, to show her she could have a better life, but she was too gone to listen. That, and I wasn't exactly the poster boy for clean living. In the end, I gave her money for a hotel room and told her to stop wasting her life. Sean stepped up right as she mumbled something about Chelle and my backyard, and thankfully escorted her from the building before she made a scene.

Eyes turned to me as I entered the hotel lobby. I quickly fished my room key out of my back pocket and made my way to the elevator. Hank was going to chew my ass when he realized I'd failed to follow security protocol, again. Fuck Hank. I pressed the elevator button, and waited. People were staring, but no one dared approach. *Smart people*. As I rode the elevator to the fifteenth floor, I thought about Olivia. I wanted Olivia Marshall more than I'd ever wanted anyone or anything. Whether I should or not was irrelevant. The feelings she evoked whenever she was near...the way she demanded all of my attention. I wanted her, plain and simple. Last night, I gave her more of me than I'd ever given anyone. I left the ball in her court. She'd avoided me today. Then again, I didn't exactly make myself available. When she flopped down beside me on the bed and shoved me over, I didn't know what to think. I wanted her there, but a part of me didn't. A part of me was still holding out, but then she made me laugh with her silly remarks and her funny comments. She made me forget about all of the shit in my life. She gave me her secrets and stole my black heart. Once she'd bared her gardenia scented soul to me, it was game over. Olivia Marshall was mine.

My bags were waiting for me inside my room. After downing half a bottle of water, I dropped onto the bed with a tired groan and mulled over what she'd told me. Sander and Gio. Talk about an unexpected twist. Gio's text now made sense. Olivia wasn't nailing the band. She was nailing Sander. She was the competition. Sander was a dickwit. No wonder she was twelve shades of fucked up about seeing him. It didn't take much to connect the dots. She'd caught the two of them together and had most likely spilled the beans to Frank. The question is, did Frank push her out or did she quit? Either way, he stopped her from talking. I sure as hell hope she'd gotten hush money in exchange for that silence. If the world found out those two were boning, it would be all over the tabloids. Talk about bad press. I stared at the ceiling and thought about what almost happened with Olivia tonight. I contemplated visiting her room in order to finish what we'd started, but I didn't want her to think that's all I wanted from her. I paused at my last thought, and laughed. I was so whipped.

"Fuuuuuuck," I moaned as I rose from the bed and went in search of my toothbrush. I knew nothing about relationships. I'd had a handful of girlfriends in my life, all who'd eventually gotten a clue and dumped me. The rest were just one-night stands or stray fucks. Chelle was the closest I'd come to a commitment, and we all know how that turned out. Chelle and I didn't talk. We screwed. Olivia was different. She made me want things... things I didn't know how to give.

I fell asleep listening to music and woke the next morning to someone banging on my door. My first thought was, *Olivia*. I sprang from the bed, vaulted across the room, and flung open the door, only to discover Marcel standing there with a toothy grin on his face.

"Morning, Chazeroo. We've got an all hands meeting in conference room one in approximately fifteen minutes," he announced. I blinked. His eyes dropped to my crotch and a smirk appeared on his face. "You might want to take care of that before the meeting." Before he said another word, I slammed the door in his face. His laughter echoed in the hallway. I glanced down at my cock bulge and sighed. Then I headed for the shower to stroke a quick one off before the meeting.

I arrived at conference room one a few minutes late. Hank shot me a dirty look as I walked in. I returned it with a smile. Of course, he was sitting next to Olivia, the fucker. Olivia's eyes locked on me the moment I entered the room. Instead of taking the empty seat on the opposite side of her, I leaned against the wall by the door and scanned the room. Grant was sipping coffee, while Nash and Evan both had their heads down on the table in front of them. I was pretty sure Evan was asleep. Sean, Marcel, and Sampson lined the opposite wall like sentries.

"Now that everyone's here, let's get started," Hank announced. I shouldn't let Hank get to me, but the guy really crawled up my ass.

Marcy's voice suddenly belted from Hank's cell phone speaker. "I received a very disturbing call from Frank Ingles last night. He's claiming that Meltdown and their security team is trying to sabotage Indigo Road and the tour. I assured him this wasn't the case, but I wanted to hear it from you firsthand. What in the hell is going on?" she angrily hissed. Grant's eyes found mine and rose in question. I shrugged. Hank started to explain that the Indigo Road security team had been very pushy and had accused some of Meltdown's roadies of breaking the soundboard but Marcy interrupted. "What do you have to say about all of this, Olivia?" Olivia's eyes widened in surprise.

She gave Hank an apologetic look, before answering. "Actually, I have a lot to say. If anyone's being sabotaged, it's Meltdown. Not only have we had issues with our hotel reservations getting canceled and some of our event catering getting diverted, but we've also had security issues as well." She hadn't mentioned anything about this to me last night.

"All of which we're looking into it," Hank added.

"From what I hear, all you're looking into is each other,"

Marcy snapped. Evan's head shot up in surprise. Nash's jaw dropped.

"Whoa," Grant cut in. Olivia looked as if she'd been slapped.

"Everyone clear the room," Hank ordered. No one moved.

"We're not done," Marcy snapped.

"Out!" Hank shouted. He didn't have to tell me twice.

Olivia's phone rang as she was rushing out the door. I thought about going after her, but decided against it. Instead, I waited for Marcel and Sean to give the all clear before grabbing a cup of coffee and heading back to my room. By my estimation, I had just enough time to call the police precinct, check emails, and work out before practice. Somewhere in there, I would pay Olivia a visit.

Two hours later, I was still in my hotel room. According to Bill's partner, Mario, Bill had taken an early retirement a few years back. He didn't go into detail, but suggested I call the house. I'd been avoiding that option, mainly because I didn't want to talk to Bill's wife, Darlene. Darlene and I had a mutual dislike for each other. Darlene was a fucking bitch. My laptop had been open for less than a minute when my email notifications began pouring in. The first dozen emails were spam. The next few were bills. The subject line of the next email caught my attention. My eyes froze on the name Charles Dunn. The email was from someone called ghstr8@gmail.com.

"You've got to be fucking kidding me," I muttered to myself as I opened the email and scanned its contents. It was a picture, similar to the letters I'd received. This one was of my profile. Same burns. Same bruising. Different words.

*Looks painful.*

*Fuck you*, I thought.

Rarely did Don go for my face. He knew better. As an upstanding member of the police force, he knew exactly where to focus his aim. He knew how to cause the most pain, yet inflict the least amount of damage.

I closed out of the email and checked to see if there were others. My gut twisted when I noticed two more emails, also with Charles Dunn in the subject line. All three had been sent this past week from the same gmail account. The second and third emails bothered me the most. For one, the person sending them had no fucking idea what they were talking about, but that's not what stuck in my craw. What bothered me was the fact that there was photographic evidence to begin with. Photographic evidence that I had no clue even existed...until now. The picture in the second email had been taken while I was asleep. I was lying on my stomach. My face was turned toward the camera, my eyes closed, and my entire torso was on display. Each bruise, welt, and cigarette burn was exposed for the world to see. The third picture was also taken while I was sleeping. This time my back was facing the camera. From the looks of the damage, it had been taken after one of Don's episodes with his belt. He had a thing for belts and handcuffs. He also had a thing for helpless boys. *Is this what he did while I was sleeping? Did he creep around and take photographic evidence of his fucked-up handywork?* My stomach churned at the sight of my twisted past. With just a click of the mouse, whoever sent these could expose me, my ugly childhood, and my dirty secrets to the world. I scrambled for a solution. I didn't know dick about computers. I could contact Bobby or Cas at LASH, but then I would have to explain. I could hire an unknown, but I could never trust them not to tell. That I'd hidden my fucked-up past for this long was a miracle in itself. At first, I thought the sender might be my mom, but letter number three ruled that out. My mother was the queen of denial. To send those pictures would be an admission of guilt, which was something that would never happen.

After Don was demoted, he started drinking. He'd been known to drink a beer or two after work, but this was different.

He took up drinking hard liquor. Liquor made Don a mean mother fucker. His newfound love for the hard stuff didn't only change him. It also changed my mother. The happy sparkle in her eyes slowly began to fade. She offered to get him help, but officers of the law didn't need help, because officers of the law didn't have problems. The first time Don beat me with a belt was the weekend my mother went to visit her sister in Pennsylvania. I was twelve years old. I forgot to add ice to his drink. That was all it took. No ice, and he was on me. Before I knew what was happening, I was face down on my bed with my hands and feet secured to the posts, and my ass bared for all the world to see. I hid in my room for two days after that. No food. No water. Just scared out of my mind. The night my mother returned, I showed her what Don had done to my back, butt, and legs. She flinched. Then told me I needed to watch my smart mouth from now on. That was it. She knew what was happening. She heard it, saw it, knew it was happening...and chose to ignore it. My mother wouldn't have pictures, because my mother refused to acknowledge it ever happened. Whoever sent these wanted something. I just needed to figure out what that something was.

By the time I'd closed out of my emails, it was time for practice. Olivia was not on the bus. She'd hitched a ride to the venue earlier with Sean. I tried not to let it bother me. It did. The ride over was eerily quiet. Nash, Grant, and Evan still looked green from last night and Hank, well, Hank just looked downright pissed. I can't say I blamed him. Marcy was out of line this morning. Hopefully, he'd put her in her place. I strummed my fingers against the sofa and thought about Olivia. At some point, we were going to have to talk about last night. If I had anything to say about it, we were going to do a hell of a lot more than talk.

Practice went surprisingly well. As I was coming off of the stage, I nearly ran into Gio and Sander. Gio patted me on the back, while Sander shot me a worried look. I smiled at them both. I would never betray Olivia's trust, but I can't say I wasn't tempted.

Dinner was sandwiches with homemade potato chips fried right on the spot. After they were placed on my plate, the chef sprinkled Old Bay seasoning over them. With Marcy in charge, we ate potluck and mystery meat. I liked Olivia's style better. I liked Olivia better. From what I could tell, so did everyone else. When Marcel gave the fifteen-minute nod instead of Olivia, I was disappointed. I hadn't seen her since this morning. I should have gone looking for her this afternoon instead of obsessing over those damn emails.

The walk to the stage was low key. The entire night had been low key. None of us seemed to be feeling it at the sound check. It was as if a fuse had blown. Our morale had taken a hit. We reached the bottom of the stage, and there she stood. There they all stood; Mallory, Rowan, and Olivia. Grant and Nash were suddenly on cloud fucking nine. My eyes met Olivia's over the kissing couples. I winked. She smiled. I wanted to touch her. I could see it in her eyes, she wanted it too. The girls hugged me as I made my way up the steps to the screaming audience.

When I passed by Olivia, I leaned in, and whispered in her ear, "Tonight you're mine." I didn't wait to see her reaction. I didn't need to.

In the blink of an eye, the switch had been flipped. We were back. On fire. At the top of our fucking game. Olivia had seen it coming and had stopped it at the pass. Call it intuition. Call it excellent management. Whatever it was, she was on top of it.

After the show, we made our way back to our dressing room, where Grant and Nash played catch up with their women. Evan sucked down a bottle of water before crashing for a few minutes on the sofa. I quickly changed my shirt and went in search of Olivia.

With the help of one of Indigo's roadies, I found her. She was with Sander. They were alone in a room together. Fucking great. I paused with my hand on the door. Olivia's voice rang out, as clear as day. Her words pierced through me.

"You have no idea. I was pregnant!" I took a step back, but that didn't stop me from hearing the rest. "I came to tell you I was pregnant. I walked in on you and Gio. I saw you. Why didn't you tell me? Why were you even with me?" I could practically taste her pain. "God, do you know how stupid I felt? Everyone knew but me!" Sander's response was too low to hear. I stepped back up to the door. I was going in, but before I had the chance, she tossed the grenade.

"Fuck you, Sander! I had your fucking baby."

Pulled the pin.

"By myself. All alone. I gave birth to your son!"

And blew my world to hell.

# CHAPTER SIXTEEN

## "Wrecking Ball"

*Olivia*

I didn't plan on telling Sander the truth about why I'd quit my job. As far as I was concerned he didn't deserve to know, but after this morning's conversation with my mother, followed by his badgering, I was tired of fighting it...him...the whole damn situation. We had unfinished business and it was starting to interfere with my job. So, when I found myself once again cornered by him, I snapped and, straight up, no holds barred, let him have it.

"I left because I was pregnant," I told him. He stared at me with a blank expression. I was beginning to wonder if he'd heard me, when he finally spoke.

"What do you mean you were pregnant?" He may have sounded calm, but I knew different. I could tell by the wild look in his eyes and the way he kept clenching and unclenching his fists that he was anything but. A knot of tension sitting in the pit of my stomach rocketed to my throat and wrapped around my vocal cords. Sander had always been larger than life, and he had a temper to match. A temper that I'd been on the receiving end of on many occasions. The desire to abort mission and walk away, to leave Sander and all of his bullshit behind was overwhelming. The only thing stopping me was the knowledge that if I didn't tell him, I would never truly be free. I hated that he still had the power to make me feel this way. "Olivia," he warned.

A long, uncomfortable moment passed. It was a moment filled with expectation and angst, where I continued to mentally beat myself up over a man that wasn't, and truthfully had never been, worth it. Somehow, I managed to pull my head together enough to explain. "I started feeling sick around Kentucky. At the time, I was worried that I might have mono, but the tour was moving so fast. There wasn't time to see a doctor, so I waited until we had two days in the same city before visiting an Urgent Care. Pregnancy was the last thing I expected." My pulse jumped when he took a step in my direction. Being that I wasn't sure if he was going to hug me or lay into me, I erred on the side of caution and took a step back. His lips thinned with disapproval, but at least he stayed put.

"You were pregnant?" he finally asked.

"I was," I carefully admitted.

"And you aborted it?" The words came out as more of an accusation than a question. At first, I was shocked, but the shock quickly turned to hurt, and then anger.

"Fuck you, Sander." He scowled. I laughed. Once upon a time, those words never would have left my mouth. I was a good girl...his good girl.

"I'm glad you find this funny, Olivia, but excuse me if I don't see the humor. You're standing here telling me that I had a child, that we had a child...a child in which I knew nothing about. Now, I repeat, why didn't you tell me?" His words, his tone, and the fact that he thought he could stand here and scold me was beyond infuriating. Fear and trepidation took a back seat to anger and hurt – years of anger and hurt, and I was suddenly hit with a moment of clarity. Sander only had power if I gave it to him. I'd already given him enough power over me. No more.

"I tried to tell you. In fact, I came looking for you as soon as I found out. You see, I had this fantasy in my head that you were going to sweep me off of my feet, that we would get married and raise our child together in wedded bliss." Again, I laughed, because really, how stupid was I? "You weren't in your hotel room. On my way to Frank's room I ran into one of the roadies and he said he thought he'd seen you on the bus." The memories skated through my head. His eyes followed me as I moved to the other side of the room, and I was reminded of a time when I would have done anything for him. Truth be told, I was grateful for every awful thing that had happened between us because it helped to shape me into the woman I was today. This, right here, right now, was the final chapter in our story, and I was more than ready for it to end.

"I came to tell you I was pregnant and walked in on you and Gio. As you can imagine, it was quite a shock." His eyes widened in surprise. "Why didn't you tell me the two of you were lovers? God, do you know how stupid I felt? Everyone knew but me." He dropped his head and took a few deep breaths.

After a long, very awkward moment, he spoke. "I wish you would have told me. I didn't know. Gio and I... what you walked in on... meant nothing. You have to believe me. It's complicated - just...something we do when we need to blow off steam, that's all." I couldn't believe what I was hearing.

"Please tell me you're kidding? Not even a week after we'd made our relationship exclusive, I caught you balls deep in a man, and that's all you have to say, that you were blowing off steam?"

"I was messed up back then. I was hooked on pills and had let it get out of control. Gio was the only one who knew. He helped me to control it," he stammered.

"I bet he did," I snorted in disgust. His eyes narrowed dangerously in on me. That look used to scare the hell out of me. Not anymore. When he realized I wasn't cowering, he changed tactics.

"So, what? You just bailed? And then what? Aborted my kid out of spite?" Years of pent-up, red hot fury surged through me. How fucking dare he? He wasn't there. He had no idea what I'd gone through.

"Fuck you, Sander. I didn't have an abortion. I had our child." Tears threatened to spill as I placed my hands protectively over my stomach.

"You did?" His voice was suddenly upbeat. God, the pain. It was like I was living it all over again. I needed to shut it down. Biting back the tears, I straightened my shoulders and gave him the rest.

"There were complications. The baby died in utero in my seventh month. It was a boy. I had to deliver him. With the help of my family, I... we, buried him." As the memories of that day swept in, I had to look away to keep from losing it. I closed my eyes and took a deep breath. Now was not the time to fall apart. When I opened them back up, he was staring off to the side with a look of regret and sadness etched across his face. It was too little, too late. He could have come for me, but he didn't. He didn't know I was pregnant, that I'd delivered his child, because he didn't care enough to find out. His eyes slowly drifted back to mine.

"Olivia-" he whispered. I shook my head at him. Story time was over. I didn't hate Sander James, but I no longer loved him and I sure as hell didn't respect him.

"Now you know why I left. In case you're wondering, his name was Sander." A heart wrenching groan shot from his mouth. "What you considered blowing off steam...nearly destroyed me."

He reached his hand out to me. "Olivia, please," he whispered.

"No," I said out loud, more to myself than to him. "I loved you, Sander. It was an obsessive, all-consuming, dangerously self-destructive love. Now, it's nothing." In the flip of a switch his pain morphed into anger.

"So, what now, Olivia? You've picked yourself up and dusted yourself off? You're back in the saddle and ready to have a run at it again? And with Chaz Jones, to boot, please..." he scoffed. "Talk about self-destructive. That guy is a ticking time bomb." Maybe he was right. Maybe he was wrong. Either way, it was mine to discover.

"Chaz Jones is more of a man than you'll ever be. We're done. This," I circled my finger in the air, "is done." I leaned forward and landed my final blow. "If you try to corner me again, better yet, if you so much as speak to me again, I will talk. Trust me, you don't want that to happen." Before he could reply, I turned and walked out the door. After a quick cry, I pulled myself together and made my way back down the hall. It was finally over. Sander knew the truth. A myriad of emotions stole through me, but I mostly just felt relieved.

Meltdown's dressing room was filled with people when I returned. I was so not in the mood for this right now. All I wanted was to find Chaz. I scanned the room and found Grant and Mallory in the back left corner. Grant appeared to be signing autographs. Nash and Rowan occupied one of the sofas, while Evan was busy scribbling his name on some girl's stomach. Chaz was nowhere to be seen. After a minute more of searching, I drifted over to Sean and asked where everyone was. He told me Hank was in a meeting with Indigo's security and Marcel had driven Chaz back to the hotel. I turned to ask him why, when Hank appeared in the doorway. He looked tired. Marcy wasn't only gunning for me. She was also gunning for Hank. As I made my way over to where he was standing, I thought back to this morning's events.

Right after Hank booted us out of the meeting this morning, my phone rang. Without thinking, I answered it, only to discover my enraged mother on the other end. Apparently, baby brother, Banks, spilled the beans and told our mother that, not only was I on the road with Meltdown, but that Indigo Road was also part of the tour. To say that my parents despised Sander James was an understatement. If it wasn't for my contractual obligations, she and my father would have gone after him years ago. It took me a good half hour to calm her rant and an additional few minutes to convince her I had the situation well under control. I didn't blame her for being upset. She'd been my rock through the worst time in my life. She was there when I got the news about the baby. She was in the delivery room when I gave birth. She was able to hold her grandson just long enough to kiss him goodbye and cried a river of tears when we buried him. After that, she'd watched her only daughter completely self-destruct. No, I didn't blame her one bit for worrying, but it was time for her to let it go. It took some fast talking on my part, but once she realized I was standing strong and not going to fall under Sander's evil spell again, she let me go, but only if I promised to check in on a daily basis.

With my Mom dilemma taken care of, I was off to my next task. I needed to find Hank and make sure I still had a job.

Hank arched a brow when he saw me standing outside his hotel room door. "Are you sure you want to come in? I might feel the need to jump you." He chuckled at my snort of disgust.

"Are you okay?" I gave him a friendly pat on the shoulder and took his lack of response as a big fat no. I didn't blame him for being angry. Once we'd settled, me in the chair and him on the foot of his bed, I addressed the elephant in the room. "Not to talk bad about Marcy or anything, but talk about unprofessional. She called us out... in front of everyone. I mean, really, one minute we were talking about a security breach and the next she was accusing us of...what exactly?"

"You're right, it was unprofessional. I told her as much. I also told her she was grossly misinformed, but she wouldn't listen." He scrubbed his hands over his face and let out a groan of frustration. "It's like she wants to believe the worst of me. She's always been that way. I thought with time she would get past it, but if anything, she's only gotten worse. This time she's gone too far." I could see the hurt in his eyes. He was in love with Marcy, the poor guy.

"I'm sorry, Hank. Maybe I should talk to her." He shook his head.

"She's threatened by you. She's ready to hire someone to take care of her dad, just so she can come back and reassert control over the situation. I tried to talk her out of it, but I'm pretty sure she's got the wheels already in motion. I'm not sure what that means for you or your job, but she mentioned it at least three different times." I hated to admit it, but I wasn't surprised. It was a good thing my contract was airtight through the remainder of this tour. Marcy could make my life hell, but she couldn't fire me without a damn good reason, and even then, she would have to get Meltdown's consent.

I explained this to Hank. At least, I explained the part about my contract being secure. Our conversation drifted from Marcy to the tour and the noticeable drop in Meltdown's morale over the past few days. I brought up the idea of getting the girls involved. Hank agreed it was worth a try, so I shot a quick text to Mallory, who immediately responded with a, "Hell yes."

I had to return several phone calls after my meeting with Hank. By the time I was done, it was time for Marcel and I to leave for the airport. Grant and Nash were going to freak when they discovered what we'd been up to all day.

It turned out that our surprise was just what the doctor ordered. The guys took one look at their women and everything changed. Meltdown played better than ever, and I had a much anticipated date with Chaz. Only, Chaz wasn't here. He'd gone back to the hotel room and I had not a clue as to why.

"The perimeter is secure and everyone is accounted for," Hank informed me as I approached. One of the wait staff passed by and I told him that we needed more ice added to the tubs of cold drinks. When I turned back, Hank was watching me with a knowing look in his eye. "Did you need something?" he asked, and smirked when I casually mentioned Chaz. When he realized he wasn't going to get a rise out of me, he told me that Chaz had gone back to the hotel. Yes, I was well aware of this.

"Did he happen to mention why he was leaving early?" I asked. He grinned and laughed when I smacked him on the chest.

"You wore him out," he teased, and laughed harder when I smacked him a second time. "If you want to go, I can hold down the fort." His offer was generous, but there was no way I could leave right now. What if something went wrong? I wanted to be with Chaz, but I needed this job. The last thing I wanted was to give Marcy a reason to fire me.

Two painfully long hours later, we were finally back at the hotel. I'd thought about texting Chaz, but something stopped me from following through with it. That something was called fear. What if he'd gotten cold feet? What if he wasn't alone? After my talk with Sander, my head was all over the place. One thing was for sure. I wanted Chaz Jones. I couldn't stop thinking about him. Sampson escorted me to my room, while the rest of the security team took care of the rest of the band members and their significant others. After thanking Sampson, I slipped inside, where I quickly changed into sweats and brushed my teeth. On my way out the door, I flipped over the do not disturb sign. For fear of being caught, I bypassed the elevator for the stairs. Chaz's room was located on the floor above mine, two doors down from Grant's room, to be exact. When I found the hallway empty, I power walked my way to his door and quietly rapped my knuckles against it. My heart was thrumming nervously inside my chest. *Please be alone*, I thought. Finally, after what seemed like forever, he answered the door.

*Oh. My.*

I was too busy swallowing my tongue to see the scowl on his face. Bare chest. Chiseled abs. Low riding sweatpants. *Chaz Jones.*

"What do you want?" he growled. His terse tone caught my attention and I jerked my eyes from his gorgeous body to his face. What did I want? What did he mean what did I want?

"You left early," I whispered.

His brow arced. "Yeah? I was tired." Something was clearly wrong.

I glanced nervously up and down the hall, before asking, "Is something...wrong?"

"Why are you whispering?" he all but shouted. My face flamed with embarrassment.

"Shhhhh," I hissed, and quickly shoved him inside his room and closed the door behind us. We stood in the entry to his suite staring at each other. Clearly, he was angry. All kinds of crazy thoughts flitted through my head. "Why are you mad at me?" I finally asked.

"To be mad, I'd first have to give a damn," he snapped. I felt as if I'd been slapped.

"I don't understand."

"I just bet you don't. You told me quite the tale last night. Too bad you left out the most important part." *Oh God.* My stomach did a free fall. *He knows.* My eyes dropped to something on the floor and that's when I noticed the mess. Pieces of broken lamp littered the floor. A chair was turned over. The drapes were strewn across the carpet.

"Chaz-"

"How old is your kid, Olivia? Three, or is it four, now? Does he or she look more like you or Sander? No wonder you freaked when you found out we were going on tour with Indigo Road. You were going to have to face your baby daddy. Tell me, were you ever going to tell him? I mean, shit, that's a pretty big secret you've been sitting on. I take it the reunion didn't go so well?" His tone deepened from anger to downright pissed off.

"Chaz-" I tried to explain, but he cut me off.

"I was made a fool of once. I'm not looking for a repeat performance. There's the door. I suggest you use it." He gave a sharp nod towards the door.

My heart painfully twisted in my chest as his venomous words scored through me. I would gladly leave, but first I was going to set the record straight. Not because he needed to hear it, but because I needed to say it. Tears spilled from my eyes. I didn't bother wiping them away. I had nothing to be ashamed of. I hated Sander James, and right this moment, I hated Chaz Jones, too.

"My son would be two and a half years old...had he lived." His brow creased in confusion. "You want to know why I'm here? I'm here because no matter how hard I try, I can't seem to stay away." When understanding hit, his eyes jerked to mine, but by that time, it was too late. "You," I jammed my pointer finder into his rock-hard chest, "just made that easy for me. Fuck you for judging me, Chaz, and fuck you for making me care. I thought you were different." I turned to leave, but he was in front of me, blocking my way. "Move," I ordered, and gasped in outrage when I found myself pressed against the wall. With his hands on either side of my face and his front to my back, he had me caged in.

"I'm sorry," his deep voice rasped in my ear.

"Let me go," I whispered through my tears. I tried to duck out of his grasp, and found myself face-to-face with him. I refused to look him in the eye because I knew if I did, I would give in. "Let me go," I repeated through clenched teeth. I was seconds away from ramming my knee into his groin.

The tips of his fingers grazed against my chin as he gently forced me to look him in the eyes. "I'm sorry," he repeated. "I stayed long enough to hear you tell him about the kid. I freaked and bolted after that." He pressed his body against mine. "I'm a dick," he rasped in his sexy, deep voice. His pelvis tilted. Fire ignited where our bodies touched. My heart raced. He groaned and I gasped. "Forgive me," he murmured against my ear, right before he sucked the lobe into his warm mouth. As he gently bit down, every nerve ending in my body shot to attention. "Forgive me," he whispered a second time. He was hard. Hard and big. Bigger than I'd imagined, and I had quite the imagination. A groan ripped from my lips as he rocked his pelvis against mine. Shockwaves of pleasure dance up my spine and pooled between my legs.

"I don't like you," I breathily told him. "I-" He released my ear, only to swallow down the rest of my sentence with the sweetest kiss I'd ever known.

Midnight blue eyes, drunk with desire, held me captive as he pinned me against the wall. "Forgive me," he ordered. Before I could respond, I was in his arms and we were on the move.

"Chaz!"

"You forgive me," he muttered, and laughed when I responded with a loud huff.

# CHAPTER SEVENTEEN

## "Everlong"

*Chaz*

After overhearing Olivia's confession to Sander, I had to get the hell out of there. I felt duped. Once again, I was standing on the outside, the last to know...the sucker. Olivia had been pregnant. She and Sander had a child together. No wonder she was so fucked up over him. I couldn't compete with that. Hell, I didn't want to compete with that. By the time I made it back to the hotel room, I was a mess. I'd been a mess over Chelle, but this was different. This mattered. Olivia mattered. Since the very first day she'd walked through Grant's door in her tight skirt and pantyhose, she was all I could think about. Each day after that had presented a new challenge, a challenge I looked forward to. Olivia made all of the shit with Chelle seem inconsequential. She made me realize there was something bigger, better...more. She made me feel things. She made me want things. She was nothing but a fucking liar. And I was nothing but a fool. I let go, lost my cool, and destroyed the hotel room.

Then, suddenly, she was there, standing outside my door in sweats and flip-flops with a come-hither smile on her face. I didn't want to want her, but I did. The faint scent of gardenias wafted through the air as she pushed past me and my traitorous dick jumped to attention. Olivia was right here in my room, and I wanted her, but I couldn't have her. Not anymore. So, I gave into my anger, unleashed my frustration, and what did she do? She took it and gave it right back, which only made me want her more. She gave me the truth...forced me to listen, and in return, I did something unprecedented. I apologized. Not only had I hurt her, but I hurt for her. Olivia Marshall was a warrior.

I dropped us both onto the bed and she stared up at me with lust in her eyes. Lust and trust. I wanted her to trust me, but I also wanted for her to know what she was getting into.

"If you want pretty words and gentle touches, I'm not that guy. As witnessed earlier tonight, I don't always listen. I make snap judgments." Her gaze followed mine to the broken lamp on the floor. "I'm destructive." Her eyes shifted back to my face. "I want you. I want to fuck you into next year. I want to make you forget Sander James ever existed." Her eyes sparked with humor as she placed her hand over my mouth.

"Yes," she said, and that was all it took. The gloves were off. As I rose up onto my knees, little miss fast fingers latched onto my johnson. Her eyes bugged when she realized he was wider than her five-fingered grip. This was with sweatpants on. Wait until she saw him in the raw.

"Ah-ah-ah, not yet," I told her. Her eyes jumped from my painfully hard cock to my face, and wrinkled in confusion. "I want to see you. All of you. I want to touch you, taste you, lick you, suck you, memorize you. If you get your twitchy little fingers on me before I get the chance to do all of this, I will shoot like a rocket. Don't get me wrong, that would feel great, but in the end, it would really suck for you." I closed my eyes and absorbed the sound of her laughter. It was better than any music.

"Well, we can't have that, can we?" she asked in a very cocky tone. No, we certainly couldn't. I felt like a kid in a candy store who was finally getting to unwrap his favorite piece of candy. I started with the bulky sweatshirt. I'd seen Olivia's tits. Not totally bare, mind you, but close. I knew how epic they were going to be. I nearly swallowed my tongue when I discovered she wasn't wearing a bra. Nothing could have prepared me for the perky perfection spread before me. A gasp of pleasure shot from her lips as I circled my tongue around her tight little nipple. The gasp turned to a moan when I sucked it deeper into my mouth. My cock screamed for completion, my balls were on fire. If it was anyone else, I would forego the formalities, but this was Olivia. She deserved everything I was about to give her and more.

"Chaz," she groaned as I switched to the other perky peak. Her fingers pulled at my hair while she practically rammed her tit down my throat, and I almost shot my load. Olivia was a closet dirty girl. My every fantasy come true. I released her tit and smiled when she let out a mewl of disappointment. *Dirty girl needs to learn a little patience.* Her eyes shifted to my straining cock as I sat back on my heels. Before she decided to go for it, I slid both hands up her thighs, wrapped my fingers around the elastic waistband of her sweatpants, and slowly pulled them off of her body. Big tits. Slim stomach. Curvy thighs. No panties. Completely bare pussy. Fuck, she was perfect. She reared up as I ran my finger through her slit. She opened her legs in invitation and I lowered my head for a taste. Tangy sweetness danced across my taste buds.

"Oh, God," she whispered as I dug my hands under her body, gripped tightly onto her ass cheeks, and sucked her clit deep into my mouth. As I worked her into a frenzy, she vacillated between chanting both mine and God's name over and over again. The moment she exploded with a scream that sounded like "Rubber duck," but I'm pretty sure was "Holy fuck," I jerked down my sweatpants, slid the condom on, lined my cock to her entrance, and powered in. Tight, wet heat engulfed me as spasms of bliss wrapped around my nuts and skittered up my spine.

"You're sooooo biiiiiiiig." Her awestruck tone would have been funny if I wasn't balls deep inside her and busy focusing on trying not to prematurely blow my load. Gardenias mixed with pussy wafted through the air. Olivia Marshall was finally in my bed, under me, and I was in fucking heaven. I pulled out and slowly pushed back in. She groaned. I moaned. I picked up the pace. The pressure built with each stroke. Spine tingles morphed into waves of sizzling hot pleasure. I was close. From the look of raw ecstasy on her face, she wasn't far behind me. Out of the blue I felt it. At first, I thought I was imagining it, but then I felt it again. Dirty girl was apparently also a contortionist.

"Fuuuuuuuuuck," I hissed in one elongated breath as her fingers gently grazed across my balls. Her breaths sounded more like gasps for air.

"I'm going to come," she panted. With her fingers on my nuts, so was I. Yep, Olivia was a dirty, dirty girl. Two could play that game. While she strummed my nuts like a finely tuned fiddle, I slid one of my hands up to her nipple and the other down to her clit. I was the master, the king, the fucking ruler of finger play, which I proved as she screamed out my name, clamped down like a vice on my cock, and shattered around me. The top of my head exploded as I shot like a cannon into the sweetest pussy I'd ever known. Olivia Marshall was scalding hot perfection. She was my hot mess, my dirty girl, and I was a fucking goner.

After, we lay there in satisfied silence while trying to catch our breath.

"Holy wow. That was..."

"Epic? The best you've ever had? Fucking revolutionary?" I

finished for her.

"I was going to say interesting," she murmured into my chest, and broke into laughter when I dug my fingers into her ribs.

"Hold that thought," I said as I took a quick minute to discard the condom. She was still sprawled on the bed when I returned. Her head was tilted to the side, her eyes closed, her gorgeous body on full display. The thought that Sander had seen this... touched this, that he'd been the first to explore, experience, and conquer this bugged the fucking shit out of me. Olivia's head turned. Her eyes found me. Her pupils dilated with lust as she took me in... as she took all of me in.

"God Chaz." Her reverent tone made my cock swell. I wanted her again, but first, we needed to have a little chat.

"Tell me," I said as I crawled onto the bed beside her. Her head tilted in my direction.

"Tell you what?"

"Tell me about your son." Her eyes darted away. I ran my fingers across her perfectly symmetrical collarbone, and smiled when she shivered at my touch. "Tell me," I whispered.

After a long moment, she gave in. She told me about carrying her son, about losing him, and about how it felt to bury him. She explained how she then sunk into a depression so deep that she no longer wanted to live and how her family had saved her. When she was all talked out, I held her in my arms and gently rubbed her back as she fell asleep. I watched her sleep for what felt like hours, and when I couldn't stand it any longer, I slid between her thighs and woke her with my mouth. She came whispering my name and, as she wrapped her legs around my waist, I slid inside. In my head, I told her how beautiful she was, how brave she'd been as I surged in and out of her body, but I couldn't make my mouth say the words. Afterwards, she rubbed her hands over my tattoos while I shared what I could of myself...my secrets with her. I told her that I never knew my real dad. I told her about Mom marrying Don and how I was diagnosed with severe ADHD shortly after that.

"Is that what the finger tapping is all about?" Her question caught me by surprise and it was my turn to look away in shame. "Oh no you don't. You know my worst, now." She laughed when I scowled at her. As far as I was concerned, nothing about this was funny. "Relax, hot pants. Your finger tapping is how I read your moods. Fast means you're happy. Slow means you're thinking or worried about something. Hard means you're angry. Believe it or not, I find it comforting." Her words shocked me. No one had ever said anything like this to me before. Ever. In less than a month, Olivia Marshall had managed to do what no one else had ever done. She'd broken in and laid claim to my heart.

# CHAPTER EIGHTEEN

## "Somebody Told Me"

*Olivia*

Chaz woke me before dawn in the best way possible; with his mouth between my legs. After bringing me to the brink of orgasm over and over again, he finally slid inside. Last night, we couldn't get enough of each other. The sex was fast, hard, and dirty. This was something entirely different. This was slow, sensual, and intense. It was by far the best sex I'd ever had. Of course, I didn't tell Chaz this. He would gloat. Actually, he would probably say, "I know," in his cocky matter-of-fact way.

"What are you thinking?" he murmured. He was lying face down on the bed with his head in the crook of his arms. Somewhere along the way, the sheets had disappeared from the bed. I'd gotten my fill of his amazing body last night, but had yet to fully explore. I traced my finger over the tattoos adorning his back, and thought about the answers I wanted to give, but couldn't. It sounded crazy, but I felt as if I'd always known him, as if everything I'd been through was meant to lead me right here, to this place and this person. Something under my fingertips caught my attention. It felt like a ridge or maybe even a scar. A second later, I discovered another one. When I traced across a third one, the realization of what I was actually feeling slammed into me.

"What are these?" I asked. His body tensed beneath my fingers right before he flipped onto his back. The bathroom light spilled into the room, casting a warm glow around us. He lowered his head to my hand and stroked his tongue across my fingers. My core instantly melted into a giant puddle of lust. I knew what he was trying to do, and as much as I wanted him and everything he had to offer, I wanted answers more. He entwined our fingers together. "Stop trying to distract me." My warning melted into a gasp when he lifted our entwined fingers and slowly feathered them across my breasts.

"Has anyone ever told you that you have a killer rack?" His naughty words, his sexy, deep tone, and the way he looked at me when he was deep inside equaled one giant turn on. He released my hand long enough to snag my phone from the night stand. "Password," he commanded.

"Uh, no," I playfully responded, and grabbed it from his hands. There was no way he was getting a picture of my tits. My phone lit up with a text. Without thinking, I punched in my four-digit password. He snatched it back right as the screen popped up. "Nuh-uh!" I shouted, and dove for it. A deep chuckle shot from his mouth as he lifted it high above our heads.

"You better cover those beauties, because they're about to be commemorated. In fact, I think this moment should be immortalized in the history books. We'll title it, *The Day Chaz Jones conquered Oliva Marshall*. He held up the camera, and we were instantly bathed in light.

"Oh my God!" I gasped, "You did not just do that."

"Fuck, that's bright," he exclaimed, when the camera flash

blinded us both. Instead of handing over my phone, he started punching buttons.

"Wait, no, stop that!" I scolded.

"Relax. I'm just sending it to myself." I should have been mad, but it was hard to be angry with him when he was like this. I loved this side of Chaz. I loved even more that I was the one who got to experience it.

"Let me see." He held the picture up for me to see. Other than the fact that we were clearly naked in bed together, it really was a good picture. "My boob is showing and look," I pointed to his partially hidden groin, "you can see your happy trail."

"Pshaw, you can barely make out the side of your boob." He brought the phone in close to his face, and added, "And maybe like three of my pubes, if that. Who's this?" he asked as he slowly began scrolling through my photos.

"That's my younger brother, Banks." Pretty soon I was giving a dissertation on each of my family members. That led to a discussion about music.

"Do you really like country music, or do you just like to wear the t-shirts?" I teased.

"Every t-shirt you've seen is from a concert I've attended," he answered. I don't know why, but this surprised me. In my mind, Chaz was famous, so to discover him doing something like attending someone else's concert seemed so...normal.

"How does that work? Do you buy a ticket and just show up?"

"I used to just show up. Now I get Marcy to handle it." My breath hitched with excitement.

"Marcy handles it?" I whispered. He smiled, and I knew he saw right though me. If Marcy had an in with other agents, did that mean I also had an in, because that would be epic.

"Do you have a particular show you'd like to see?" he asked. I started to list my top five, but then decided to mess with him instead.

"Oh my God, I would love to see Michael Bolton, or Pussycat Dolls. Wait, no, I really want to see is Vanilla Ice."

His head jerked and his eyes landed on me. "You kidding me?" he asked, and I couldn't help but laugh. His facial expression was too funny for words. Eventually, we drifted into a comfortable silence. I knew I should go, but didn't want to. I wanted to ask what this meant, but wasn't sure I wanted to hear his answer. I had yet to define it myself, so it didn't seem fair of me to expect him to.

"I should probably go," I announced. The bus was due to leave for Dallas at nine. As it was, we were looking at a maximum of three hours of sleep.

Warm, muscular arms banded around me. "Stay," he whispered in my ear. I wanted to, more than I could say, but I didn't want to lose my job.

"I want to, but Marcy is on the warpath right now. She's looking for someone to blame and I don't need that person to be me," I tried to explain.

"Marcy's hands are tied. She can't do shit, Olivia." I was about to ask him to clarify, but was distracted by his next statement. "And while I disagree with how she's handling things right now, I can't fault her for being paranoid about her relationship with Hank."

Swiveling my head around, I leveled my gaze on him. "What? Why? Hank is totally faithful to her." A skeptical look appeared on his face.

"If you'd knocked on Hank's door instead of mine last night, he would have taken one look at you in those sexy sweats and cute flip-flops and would have forgotten all about Marcy." I had no idea what to say to this. He was wrong.

"Hank and I are just friends, Chaz." His arms tightened around me. As I relaxed back into his chest, I contemplated his words. Was I missing something? I really didn't think so. "Hank's totally in love with Marcy," I said more to myself than to him. I didn't realize his fingers were thrumming against the side of my leg until they stopped.

"Hank's done with Marcy, especially after the way she's been acting. He's at the end of his rope, which is why he's been making suck-my-cock eyes at you for the past few weeks."

"He has not."

"Trust me, he has." I had no idea what to say to this, so I chose not to respond. Instead, I did exactly what I shouldn't have. I settled back into his arms, and drifted to sleep.

The sound of my phone ringing jerked us both awake. Right as mine stopped, Chaz's started up.

"Shit, it's after nine," he groggily announced, before answering, "Lo?" After a long pause, he said, "I'll be there in five." After another pause, he snapped, "How am I supposed to know where she is? I'm not her fucking keeper." His eyes drifted in my direction as he said this, and he nodded his head toward the door. Shit! We were going to get so busted. I tossed off the covers and scurried around the room searching for my clothes. I was in deep shit. I was supposed to be the first on the bus, not the last. As fast as humanly possible, I pulled on my clothes and made a mad dash for the door. Chaz stopped me midway across the room.

"I have to go," I panted. Hot, naked, hardness pressed me flush against the wall. Hard being the operative word. I was now panicked and turned on at the same time. If he stripped me down right here and took me against the wall, I wouldn't stop him. That's how much of a goner I was for him.

"Don't you dare leave this room without giving me a proper goodbye," he warned. My entire body tingled at his raw, possessive tone. Before I could respond, his lips were on mine, his tongue swept in, and I was once again consumed by all that was Chaz Jones. Right as I was ready to throw down my shoes and climb him like a tree, he murmured, "See you on the bus," against my lips. When he turned and walked away, my eyes dropped to his naked ass. I had firsthand knowledge of his amazing body. I knew exactly what it felt like to be dominated by Chaz Jones. Once he was safely out of sight, my brain came back online, and I raced from the room like a bat out of hell.

All it took was one look in the mirror to know I was going to be late. My hair was a mess. My eyes were puffy. I looked rough and I smelled of sex. There was no way I was getting on that bus like this.

Half an hour later, I barreled out the door and paused when I saw Hank and Marcel waiting outside the bus with their arms crossed. With my wet hair twisted into a knot on the top of my head and no makeup on, I powered across the parking lot in their direction.

"You're late," Hank observantly pointed out.

"Sorry! My alarm didn't go off," I called out as I dropped my bag at their feet. I ducked my head to avoid Hank's glare and started up the bus steps.

"I tried to call you," he growled from behind me.

"Yes, and I was asleep. Keep your pants on, we can still get there on time," I nonchalantly replied as I stepped inside the bus. "Sorry!" I called out to everyone as I made my way to one of the chairs. "I accidentally overslept." Thank God no one paid me any attention. Grant and Nash were busy talking to Mallory and Rowan, Evan was playing a video game, and Chaz appeared to be fiddling with his phone. About that time, my phone dinged with a text message. I waited until I slid into my seat to read it.

Chaz – *You're late.*

I shot off a quick response. *Gee, I wonder why?* When he returned it with a fist, three eggplant emojis, and two coconuts, I shook my head.

A few minutes later, the bus took off with a jerk. I mentally groaned when Hank plopped down next to me. I could tell from our earlier confrontation that he was grumpy and looking for an argument. After the amazing night with Chaz, I was not in the mood.

"I think we should talk," he firmly stated.

"Good morning, Hank." I gave him a beaming smile. He scowled back at me. He really was awfully crabby this morning. "Did you ride the bus simply to interrogate me, because if so, I'm not in the mood," I told him as my phone dinged with another text. Chaz's name popped up on my screen. He would have to wait.

"You're giving Marcy a damn good reason to fire you, Olivia." Hank's words, not to mention the scathing manner in which they were delivered, were slightly irritating. I thought about this morning's conversation with Chaz and wondered if he might have a point. If so, I needed to nip it in the bud. Hank was a nice guy, but that was it. I was no more interested in him than I was in Sander. My phone dinged with another message. Chaz's name popped up again, and again, I ignored it.

Turning in my chair, I gave Hank my full attention. "I'm doing no such thing and you know it. Look, is there something you know that I don't, because by my recollection, I've done everything that Marcy has ever asked of me. In fact, I've gone above and beyond the call of duty." I arced a questioning brow at him.

"Where were you this morning?" he asked. "I knocked on your door. When you didn't answer, I called...several times, in fact. I'm surprised after our conversation yesterday and in light of everything that has happened, that you would act so careless."

"What are you, my keeper?" I snapped.

"Someone should be," he snapped back. "We both know where you were this morning. Marcy and I both warned you." I tried to think of how to respond. When my phone dinged a third time, I let out an irritated sigh. Thank God Chaz was behind me instead of in front of me. Otherwise, I would be glaring at him right now. I glanced down at my text messages. All three were from Chaz. All three telling me in no uncertain terms to ditch Hank. When I refused to reply, a loud bang erupted from the back of the bus. Hank scowled and jerked his head around to see what had caused it. I, however, did not. I knew exactly what it was. Chaz's temper tantrum gave me just enough time to focus on a proper reply.

When Hank's head finally swiveled back in my direction, I asked, "What is this really about? Marcy hired me to do a job. I'm doing that job. Nowhere in the contract does it say I can't fraternize with other employees or members of the band. Marcy can try and fire me, but on what grounds? Jealousy? Pettiness? Insecurity? Chaz and I are friends. You and I are friends. I consider everyone on this bus...a friend. Marcy is angry and feeling out of control. I don't blame her. Odd things are happening. However, instead of trying to solve the problem, she's looking for someone to blame. If she would listen to me, I could explain, but she won't. That's not my problem. My problem is making sure that nothing else happens on my watch. Where I spend my time or who I spend it with when I'm not working is my business, not yours and certainly not Marcy's."

"It's more than that, Olivia," he cut in. "Marcy is afraid you're doing a better job. Hell, you are doing a better job. Blane was a good front man. Marcy is better behind the scenes. You're good at both, which scares the shit out of her. She's threatened and you need to watch your back." He leaned close, and whispered, "I'm not trying to mind your business. I'm just trying to watch out for you, that's all." Just as I was about to explain that I didn't need for him to watch out for me, Hank's phone rang. "Excuse me," he said as he moved off to take the call. Relieved that the conversation was over, I glanced over my shoulder to check on Chaz, only to discover he wasn't there. *Crap!* Evan was still playing video games. The sound of Grant's laughter rang out from one of the bunks. That left Nash, Rowan, and Chaz unaccounted for. On the way to the back of the bus, I passed by the bunks. No Chaz. When I was flush to the bathroom door, it opened. Chaz pierced me with an angry glare and my stomach tensed. I opened my mouth to explain and found myself inside the bathroom with my back against the wall and a very unhappy man looming over me.

"Tell me, Olivia, is this a thrill for you? Are you trying to see how far you can push before I break?" He leaned in and, in a harsh tone, whispered, "Because I'm here to tell you, I'm at my breaking point." The warmth of his breath rushed over my ear, making me shiver.

"Hank is a colleague and a friend, Chaz. Nothing more. Nothing less," I whispered back in an equally harsh tone.

"I don't like the way he looks at you. I don't like how he demands so much of your attention. I. Don't. Like. Him." He stressed each word one at a time. "And you, you just make me crazy. All I can think about is getting inside you. Do you feel this?" He pressed his hard cock into my stomach and liquid fire pooled between my legs. I not only felt it, I wanted it. My desire for him was overwhelming. He was quiet, broody... misunderstood, one hundred percent man where it counted, yet soft when it mattered, except for right now. Right now, he was angry. "Turn around," he growled. A jolt of excitement blazed through my body. Then it hit me where we were and what we were about to do.

"Chaz-" Before I could get another word out, he lifted me up and turned me around. The bathroom wall was at my front and Chaz's fingers were on the button of my jeans. "Chaz, we can't!" I gasped as he flicked it open and began lowering my zipper. "Chaz, seriously," I begged as he pushed my jeans and my panties to my knees. The realization that he was about to fuck me in the bus bathroom with the entire band and security right outside the door, should have scared the shit out of me, but instead, it only heightened my arousal. "Oh, God," I breathed when I felt a hand on the back of my neck and another on my hip. In one fluid motion, he had me bent over with my face smushed against the bathroom wall and my ass in the air. A moan slipped from my traitorous lips when I felt his fingers part me and slip inside. "We can't," I faintly protested and nearly bit my tongue off when he slammed inside me. In punishingly hard, rough, angry strokes, he let me have it, and I loved every single second of it. My breath hitched as my orgasm began to peak. As if sensing the enormity of it, Chaz covered my mouth with his hand to stifle my scream. A short second later, I felt him tense behind me. A sexy grunt shot from his mouth as he powered through his finish. As fast as he was in, he was out. His weight lifted from my back and I could finally move. I thought he was being stealthy. I thought we were on the same page. The toilet flushed and I started to pull up my pants. His head dropped to my ear and his words seared through me.

"Last night...this morning...just now...I don't do shit like this. I don't like games and I don't like people who play them. I'm warning you, Olivia, either you stop fucking toying with me, or you need to walk the hell away. It's your choice," he stated in an angry, clipped tone of voice. Then he was gone. Tears spilled from my eyes as I attempted to put myself back together. *What a jerk!* I cursed him to the moon and back as I angrily brushed away the tears. I'd show him playing games, the giant ass.

And I did just that. For the remainder of the ride to Dallas, I ignored him. I could feel his eyes on me. I didn't care. I could feel him glaring at me whenever I spoke to Hank. I didn't care. I'd humiliated myself. I let him fuck me out of anger. Even worse, I wanted it. I'd practically begged for it. What did that say about me? Nothing good, that's for sure.

We arrived in Dallas with very little time to unpack before the guys needed to be at rehearsal. Since it was the Fourth of July weekend, I spared no expense on the hotel suites. Everyone got their own suite, except for the security team who had to share. My room was located on the floor below.

When Marcy failed to schedule a Fourth of July show, she'd incurred Grant's wrath. To make it up to him, she arranged a special firework display at tonight's performance and placed me in charge of all of the details. Last week, when I'd spoken to the pyrotechnist in charge of both purchasing and setting up the display, all was in order. Today, however, when I called to confirm, he claimed the order had been canceled. To say I lost my cool was a mild understatement. After drilling the man for details, I hung up and immediately called Marcy. I explained how someone posing as me called two days ago and canceled the order. Among other things, Marcy accused me of trying to make her look bad. I assured her this wasn't the case, but she refused to listen to reason. After all, none of this had occurred on her watch, had it? I thought back on my earlier conversation with Hank. He was right. Marcy no longer viewed me as an ally, but as a rival. Clearly, she was looking for someone to blame. The hell if that someone was going to be me.

If my experience working for Indigo Road had taught me anything, it was to always be proactive. Enough was enough. This wasn't a fluke. This was intentional. Someone was trying to make a statement, and they were using me to do it. I sat back in my chair and thought about what I would do if I was Marcy. I would go straight to Grant. If she got to him first, I could kiss my job goodbye.

"Shit!" The word barely left my mouth before I was up and on the move.

One look at Grant's missing shirt and wild hair and I could pretty much guess what he'd been up to.

"We've got a problem," I announced. Without saying a word, he stepped aside and ushered me in. Then he patiently listened while I outlined what had been happening. From the missing platters of food to the canceled fireworks, I told it all. When I was done talking, he asked two questions: Why hadn't I come to him before now and was Marcy aware of what had been happening. The first, I had no good answer for. His eyes flashed with anger when I told him Marcy knew everything. I wasn't necessarily looking to get Marcy in trouble, per se, but after the way she'd treated me, I also wasn't looking to protect her. He was worried. So was I. Before letting me go, he thanked me, told me none of this was my fault, and not to worry about the fireworks. Then he walked me to the door and promptly dismissed me. I stared longingly at Chaz's door, before making my way back down to my room. I was still mad at him. I wasn't playing games. I was simply doing my job. If he couldn't see that, then this was never going to work. I tried not to think about how much I wanted him in my life. I tried not to think about how secure he made me feel, or how each time he smiled at me, I felt as if I'd won the lottery. I tried, but I lost, because Chaz Jones was officially under my skin. That didn't mean I wasn't still mad, because I was.

While the boys were busy practicing, I ushered in the caterers and helped them set up. I then stole a few minutes with Mallory and Rowan. The girls made me feel welcome, like I was part of the group. Our conversation slid from wedding plans to my relationship with Chaz, and in no time at all, we were discussing what happened with Chelle. I was shocked to learn the details around the poisoning. My heart ached for Chaz. The conversation veered off the rails somewhere between Mallory's comment about Chaz being an animal in bed and Rowan questioning whether Chaz's penis was as big as Nash claimed.

The guys returned right as Mallory was describing Chaz's brilliant rendition of "Downtown" the night they'd played Shout-a-Song at Grant's house. Grant and Nash wanted to know what we were laughing about, while Chaz did his best to ignore me. Eventually, the laughter died down. As the girls made their way over to their guys, I stood there with my heart on my sleeve. How had I gotten in so deep so fast with these people? This was nothing like my experience with Indigo Road. With Indigo, I'd been chasing a foolish dream. I knew nothing about Sander James, but wanted him nonetheless. Being a part of a team held no value. All that mattered was my touchdown with fame. Back then I would have taken any of them. That it was Sander was nothing more than a fluke. It was a matter of being at the right place at the right time. I was a foolish girl, playing adult games, and I got burned.

This was different.

I never planned for this. I didn't have the first clue as to how to navigate these waters. Chaz and I had both been burned. It was because of this that I was drawn to him. I liked who I was when I was with him. He made me feel secure, which was something I never felt when I was with Sander. I liked everything about Chaz...except for his inability to trust me. He hurt me this morning. I cared, but I was no man's doormat. So, when Grant asked me to stay and eat with them, I had to decline. Not because I wanted to, but because I wanted to a little too much. I wanted to be a part of the group...this group. I didn't just value the job, I valued the people. Grant was an amazing leader. Yes, he had mad musical skills, but so did the rest of the band. Nash was super funny and Evan was such a sweet soul. This was supposed to be about a job. I wasn't supposed to care and I sure as hell wasn't supposed to fall in love.

"Olivia, wait," Chaz called out as I stepped from the dressing room into the hallway. I paused, hoping he would come after me.

When he didn't, I was once again reminded of my past mistakes and how I never seemed to learn from them.

At the fifteen-minute mark, I slid my head back into the dressing room and shouted out a warning. I made sure to avoid any and all eye contact with Chaz. While Meltdown lined up to take the stage, I ushered Mallory and Rowan down the crowded hallway.

"Can I just say how much I love you," Mallory shouted over the loud voices.

"Thanks, but why?" I called out over my shoulder.

"You're making this stress free for the guys. They can't say enough good things about you and this tour." Her kind words meant more than she would ever know. I was about to lead them up onto the stage, when I suddenly decided against it. If we stood at the bottom of the steps, they could grab a quick hug or kiss before the guys hit the stage.

Mallory turned to me and let out a squeal of excitement when the decibel levels in the hallway shot through the roof. They were close. Grant came first. He spotted Mallory and his face lit up with an award-winning smile. She jumped him like a spider monkey and he caught her with a laugh. Rowan let out a peal of laughter when Nash swept her up into his arms. I felt something brush against my arm. My pulse skyrocketed and my stomach fluttered when I discovered that something was Chaz. Our gazes locked. It was too much. He grabbed my arm as I turned to leave.

"This is far from over," he growled into my ear. His cinnamon scented breath reminded me of last night and the crazy, off-the-charts chemistry between us. Goose bumps erupted when I felt his hand brush against my ass. Long, tapered fingers...fingers that had the ability to give blistering hot pleasure, trailed up my spine and found their place on the back of my neck. Slowly, he reeled me in. I would be a liar if I said I didn't want his mouth, his breath...his words. They were all I wanted. "Fuck, Olivia,

I'm a jealous prick. I admit it. I"- His words were drowned out by a deafening noise. It sounded like a cannon had gone off right beside us. The next thing I knew, Chaz jerked me tightly to his chest and we were on the move.

"What was that?" I shouted over the screaming crowd.

"Dunno, but security is evacuating. Hold tight." His voice was muffled by the ringing in my ears. People jostled us as we made our way down the crowded hallway. I wrapped my fingers around his belt loops as security ushered us out of the building and onto the bus.

"What the fuck happened?" Grant shouted, once we were all accounted for. Chaz dropped into one of the chairs and pulled me down with him. So much for discretion.

"The rigging collapsed," Sean answered. We all stared at him in horror.

"As in the ceiling?" Rowan squeaked. Nash pulled her in and kissed the side of her head.

"What about our instruments?" he asked.

"We'll know when Hank returns." I could tell by the tone of Sean's voice that he wasn't feeling very optimistic.

A few minutes later, the bus doors opened, and Hank and Marcel appeared.

"What's the status?" Grant asked.

"The rigging fell," Hank clipped.

"The whole thing?" he asked.

"The whole thing," Hank confirmed.

"What's the status on our instruments?" Nash asked.

Hank swallowed, and I knew what he was going to say. "They're gone. Everything on that stage is gone."

"Was anyone hurt?" Chaz's voice rumbled against my back. I dropped my hand to his leg and squeezed.

We both relaxed when Hank responded, "Lucky for us, no one was on the stage."

"Do they have any idea what happened?" I asked.

"They're looking into it," Hank vaguely answered. His eyes drifted to Grant when he said this.

"Say it," Grant commanded. I had no idea what he was asking, until Hank responded.

"The cables looked frayed. I think it was intentional." Grant's eyes shot to me and I felt Chaz tense underneath me. I was right. Someone was trying to sabotage us.

"That's it. I'm calling in LASH," Grant announced.

On the ride back to the hotel, Grant told everyone what had been happening behind the scenes for the past few weeks. Hank and I filled in some of the blanks, but by the time we arrived, everyone had a pretty clear picture.

As the bus entered the hotel parking lot, Chaz pulled me close, and said, "You've been holding out on me."

He was not wrong, but something deep in my gut told me I wasn't the only one holding out.

# CHAPTER NINETEEN

## "Keep on Fallin'"

*Chaz*

On the bus ride back to the hotel, all I could think about was how good it felt to have Olivia in my arms again. I could tell by her erect spine and tense jaw she was still angry, but at least she was no longer fighting me.

I fucked up.

My good mood evaporated the moment Hank followed Olivia onto the bus this morning. The way he looked at her, practically panted after her, irritated the shit out of me. I knew what he was thinking because I was thinking the same thing. She was gorgeous, unbelievably cool - the whole package. Olivia Marshall was the shit. What she wasn't, was available. Hank's failure to understand this was about to cause some serious problems. Olivia was clueless. She considered him a friend. If she realized what he was doing, what he was really thinking, she would tell him to get lost. As it was, she didn't see the dirty looks or hear his snide comments. Hank was sly. I'd give him that. He made sure to hold back the competitive gleam in his eye whenever she was near. Like a fucking fox, he was hiding behind his relationship with Marcy, a relationship we both knew was circling the toilet. He may be slick, but I was slicker. The game was over, he just refused to throw in the towel. This morning, right before he cozied up next to Olivia on the bus, he shot me a challenging look. *Challenge this, motherfucker,* I thought, but didn't dare say out loud. I wasn't stupid. He was baiting me, just waiting for me to mess up, so he could swoop in and save the damsel in distress. That he did it just moments after I'd been balls deep inside her was uber dickish. Olivia, being the nice person she was, welcomed him with a gold-medal smile. The fact that she was smiling at him and not me, sitting next to him and not me, was enough to send me over the edge. I texted her. She ignored it. I heard him scold her for being with me and lost my fucking cool. It was as if suddenly I was back there again; my childhood...my place in the band...the hospital with Chelle, back where I had no control. Back in that place where my feelings didn't matter, where I didn't matter. My dirty girl was playing games and didn't even know it. If it was anyone else but Olivia I would cut my losses and walk away.

When the overwhelming urge to kill Hank became too much, I hauled my ass to the bathroom, where I attempted to gain some perspective. Prison wasn't high on my list of places to visit. After splashing cold water on my face, I felt calm enough to deal. *Keep cool and don't react,* I told myself as I opened the bathroom door. There she stood, my savior and my downfall. I snapped. I pulled her into the bathroom with me and, even though she said no, I took her. Screw consequences. Screw Hank. I was obsessed by my need to possess her, to stake my claim... to own her. A part of me knew I was messing up, but I couldn't seem to stop. The next thing I knew, I was inside her, fucking her, punishing her. I wanted to fill her full of me, to ride out my anger. I punished her, all right. The damage was done. As if that wasn't bad enough, I then gave her an ultimatum and walked away.

Minutes later, Olivia reappeared. As she walked past me, I saw traces of tears on her face. My chest constricted. My gut twisted. She'd clearly been crying...because of me.

I did that.

I hurt her.

Olivia avoided me for the rest of the day, and with good cause. I didn't blame her for keeping her distance. I needed to stay away, but no matter how hard I tried, I couldn't. I was a dick, an asshole, a motherfucker, a moron – I was out of control.

Tonight, as we marched down the hallway to take the stage, my head was filled with thoughts of the bus ride, of Olivia's tearstained face and the pain I'd caused. If I didn't understand me, how did I expect her to? Suddenly, she was there, standing at the base of the stage, my beautiful hot mess, my dirty girl. Her eyes ghosted past me, as if I wasn't there. The ache in my chest was back, only worse. I fought the urge to grab her. To carry her off and fuck some sense into the both of us. At that moment, I would have given anything to go back and do this morning over again. I had to say something, but what? I wanted to apologize, but I needed to make her understand. I had demons...fucked-up, out of control demons. Before I got the chance to explain, the rigging fell, and suddenly, the opportunity to hold her, to touch her, was right in front of my face. Like a starving man, I took it.

As the bus pulled into the hotel parking lot, Olivia tried to escape from my lap. When she realized that wasn't happening, she swung her head around and pierced me with a fiery stare.

"We need to talk," I calmly stated.

"Tomorrow," she spat back at me. Yep, she was still pissed.

"Tonight," I sternly replied.

With narrowed eyes and pursed lips, she said, "Tomorrow,

Chaz." This clearly wasn't going in my favor, so I changed tactics.

"What happened tonight was seriously messed up. You're upset. Let me take care of you."

A hiss of air shot from her lips as she reared her head back and widened her eyes in mock surprise. "What? Like you did this morning? No thanks." She twisted back around and gave me the back of her head. Her words burned. So much so that I lifted my hands and let her go. Like a wild animal cut loose, she bounded from my lap. I called her name in warning. She turned to blast me, but I beat her to the punch.

"You have a choice. Either I drag you to my hotel room and fuck some sense into you or you let me walk you to your door." One way or the other we were going to talk. With a loud huff, she snatched up her purse and her bag.

"Fine," she said, "you can walk me to my door." As I followed her off of the bus, I couldn't help but smile.

"Group meeting tomorrow morning in my suite at ten o'clock sharp," Grant said, once we were in the elevator.

"When are you calling LASH?" Evan asked.

"After we talk to Marcy. You good with that?" Grant directed the question at Hank, but Hank was too busy watching us to respond.

"Do you need me tonight?" Olivia asked.

"Yes," Hank snapped.

"No. We can fill you in tomorrow," Grant answered at the same time. Hank scowled at him and he responded with a questioning look.

"Stop trying to get rid of me," I whispered into Olivia's ear. Her hand shot back and slammed into my leg, barely missing my nuts. A grunt of surprise burst from my mouth, and all eyes snapped to me.

"Dude, please tell me you didn't just fart!" Nash exclaimed.

I shot him an evil grin and tried not to laugh when everyone scrambled to the opposite side of the elevator. Olivia's eyes swiveled around and landed on me. She glared. I winked. She rolled her eyes. I smiled.

The elevator hit Olivia's floor first. Hank made a move to get off, but since Marcel was closer to the doors, he beat him to it. I waved my middle finger at Hank as I followed Marcel and Olivia off of the elevator.

"You're not coming in," Olivia whispered as we waited for Marcel to clear the room.

"We need to talk," I repeated for the third time.

"We can do that tomorrow," she stressed.

"All clear," Marcel announced.

"Goodnight, Marcel," Olivia sweetly replied.

"Night Olivia," he responded, and slapped me on the back as he started back down the hallway toward the stairwell.

"Inside now," I commanded, once he was out of sight. With a huff, she flounced inside the room. She was disgusted with me. I didn't blame her, but before I left this room tonight, we were going to talk. As she turned to lay into me, I was on her.

"Chaz," she hissed. Finally, I had her exactly where I wanted - face-to-face, with my knee wedged between her thighs, one hand on her chin, and the other on the back of her neck. She was trapped. My prisoner for the taking. Her eyes darkened with anger, anger and lust. If looks could kill, I would be a dead man right now.

"I need you to listen. If you want me to leave after you've heard me out, I will," I calmly stated.

"Talk," she haughtily ordered. God, she was cute. She narrowed her eyes at my twitching lips, and I fought back a full-blown smile. Then I got down to business.

"I fucked up this morning. I saw you with Hank and lost my cool. In the bathroom...you asked me to stop. I didn't." Anger turned to puzzlement as I tried to find the right words to explain. "You didn't want it. I was angry. You don't see what I see." I dropped my forehead to hers, and whispered, "I should have stopped." Her body tensed and I jerked my head up in time to witness another impressive eye roll.

"You're kidding, right? If I hadn't wanted it, I would have screamed the bus down," she responded in that same haughty tone that made my hands itch to spank her ass. "I said no because we were in a bus bathroom and I didn't want to compromise my job. I was angry and hurt because you clearly don't trust me. I don't want Hank. We work together, that's all. You accused me of playing games. This isn't a game to me. My feelings for you are real. I'm not Chelle. You aren't Sander and you're certainly not Hank. If you can't see that...if we can't figure out how to let our pasts go...to move on, then you're right, we should walk away before one or both of us gets hurt." It took me a moment to process her words. She didn't want Hank or Sander. She wanted me. Chelle might have laid me low, but Olivia had the power to completely take me out.

"What happened today wasn't about Chelle or Sander. It was about me. Hank is playing games. You don't see it, but I do. I let it get to me and I shouldn't have. I took it out on you. You tell me I don't need to worry about Hank, well you sure as hell don't have to worry about Chelle."

"For your information, Hank isn't exactly my type. As for Sander, this may sound strange, but it feels as if it happened to someone else. I was a stupid girl who mistook ambition for love. I was young and foolish and it almost broke me. I look at him now and I feel absolutely nothing. I'm probably not making any sense..." She shrugged off the rest of the sentence, but I got what she meant. It made perfect sense, because I felt the exact same way about Chelle.

"I get it," I told her.

After a long moment of us staring at each other, she let out a cute little snort. "God, that period in my life was really messed up."

"Babe, I'm not trying to one up you here, but Sander was nothing but a bad decision. You'll never go through that again because I won't let you. As far as fucked-up pasts go, mine has yours beat by a long shot."

"Whatever," she huffed, and I found myself wanting to confess all of my sins. I'd already told her more than I'd ever told anyone. I wanted her trust. In truth, I wanted so much more than that, but something told me that would never happen if I didn't gain her trust first, so I slowly released my hold on her and took a step back. Her eyes widened with surprise when I pulled off my shirt, and darkened with arousal as it dropped to the floor at my feet. I would never get tired of seeing that look on her face. Lust turned to confusion when I took her hand in mine.

"This morning, you asked about the raised spots on my back." I lifted her fingers to my chest and began dragging them over my torso. Her brows came together in question. "They're scars," I told her. Her eyes jerked to mine.

"What?" she asked, her voice no more than a whisper.

"They're scars," I repeated more slowly.

"Scars from what?" Goose bumps erupted on the backs of my arms as she reverently traced her fingers over each indentation. Fuck, this was hard.

"My stepfather, Don, was a mean drunk. He thought it was cool to burn me with his cigarettes." She inhaled a strangled breath, and I continued before losing my nerve. "Occasionally, he used a cigar, but mostly it was cigarettes." Her mouth dropped open in shock. I waited for it; the look of pity, the conciliatory words. Her eyes lifted to mine, but there was no pity. There was fire.

"Are you kidding me? How old were you? Oh my God, who

173

does that? Please tell me you kicked his ass. Better yet, please, tell me the man is dead, because if he's not, I'm going to fly home and get my dad's rifle. Then we're paying Dan a visit!" she all but shrieked.

"Don," I corrected. Only Olivia could make me want to laugh, while talking about my fucked-up childhood.

"I'm being serious," she growled.

"I can see that. Rest assured, wildcat, Don is dead."

She leaned in, and I thought she was about to lay one on me. I wouldn't accept her pity, but I sure as hell would take her mouth. When she got within kissing distance, she snarled, "I hope you fucking killed him," and gasped when I jerked her the rest of the way in and sealed my lips to hers. Enough with story time. I was done with this trek down memory lane. I was done with Hank, Chelle, and Sander.

I pulled back long enough to say, "Come on, Wildcat, we have a date with your bed." A cute squeal shot from her mouth as I lifted her over my shoulder and tossed her onto the bed. Before I got my hands on my zipper, she had her jeans off and was working on her top. All day long I'd worried. I thought I'd taken something from her, that I'd ruined this thing we'd been building, when all along, she'd wanted it. Even though I'd acted like a fucked-up, out of control, jealous idiot, the realization that she still wanted me was indescribable. Olivia's eyes followed my fingers as I lowered my zipper and stripped out of my jeans. They remained glued on my cock as I neared the foot of the bed. The moment I dropped a knee to the bed, she was on the move. The next thing I knew, her hands were on my ass and her lips were on me, sucking, licking, taking me in. Holy fuck, if I wasn't careful I would drown in her. Warning tingles erupted at the base of my spine. As much as I wanted to let go, to shoot my load down her throat, I wanted to finish inside her more. She gasped in outrage when I disengaged from her mouth.

"You like that, huh?" I asked. Eyes hooded with lust raked over me as I rolled on a condom and moved between her legs. "Hold onto the headboard, dirty girl." She quickly complied, and I slammed inside. Her head dropped back on the pillow and her mouth opened in a silent scream. This time I wasn't punishing her. I was branding her. Olivia Marshall was mine. I held back nothing. I gave her everything I had, and in return I got her heels in my spine, her nails in my ass, and my name on her lips as she screamed out her orgasm. Life didn't get any better than this.

As planned, we met in Grant's suite at ten the next morning. Spirits were at an all-time low. Someone was messing with us... again. This time, I took a seat next to Olivia. It wasn't lost on me how quickly things had changed in the past twenty-four hours.

Marcy was being less of a bitch today. She actually managed to listen to both Hank and Olivia's recount of the situation before making judgment. She was worried. We all were. Missing sandwiches and canceled hotel rooms were one thing, but wrecking an entire stage filled with thousands of dollars' worth of instruments was something else, and that something was criminal. Hank and Marcel filled her in on what the police had discovered, which pretty much amounted to nada at this point. She agreed that LASH should be involved. From there the conversation moved to Indigo Road and their plans. According to Marcy, she'd already spoken to Frank, and Indigo wasn't planning to perform without Meltdown. Our replacement instruments would be waiting for us when we arrived in St. Louis. In the meantime, we were on a break. As there was a crowd gathered outside the hotel entrance, we were told not to leave the grounds. Marcy also wanted for us to include Indigo Road and their team at tonight's party. She felt it would be good if both bands bonded together in a show of solidarity and wanted for Olivia to make it happen. When she asked to speak privately with Grant and Hank, Grant hit the mute button and told us he'd catch up with us later.

Sampson escorted Olivia and I back to her hotel room, where she had a minor freak out. I didn't have a clue as to what to say, so I simply wrapped my arms around her and pulled her in for a hug.

"She's out to get me, Chaz," she murmured into my chest. I felt bad. Normally, I would agree with her, but in this case, Marcy was right. We needed to band together. I told Olivia as much and she managed to calm down long enough to form a plan. Then she said she had shit to do and kicked me out of her room.

On my way up to my suite, my phone rang. I answered thinking it was Evan calling to work out and was surprised to hear Uncle Bills' voice on the other end.

"Charles, it's Bill. Or, would you prefer I call you Chaz now?" His abrupt tone immediately put me on the defensive. I told him I preferred Chaz. After unsuccessfully trying to make small talk, I cut straight to the chase and asked about my mother. After a long pause accompanied by a few coughs and a good phlegmy throat clear, he told me my mother had passed away. What. The. Fuck? I asked him to explain and he told me he didn't have any real details, just that he knew that she'd died. That was it. Bill hated my mother, and with good reason, but still, I expected more from him. I asked why he didn't call, why no one called, to inform me. Hell, she was my mother. He mumbled some bullshit about me being a big rock star and being hard to reach and all. I countered that I'd had the same cell phone number since I was eighteen. This seemed to irritate him, because he suddenly snapped, "I don't know, son. I wasn't there when she died, therefore, I don't have the answers you're searching for." Bill was my uncle. He'd been in my life for as long as I could remember. He helped save me from Don and my mother. Not only that, he helped save me from myself. The elevator opened with a loud ding. As I stepped onto my floor, I tried to process his words. My mother was dead. I would have pushed harder, but shock and the fact that Marcel, Hank, and Sampson were standing in the middle of the hallway staring at me, stopped me. "I wish I had answers for you, but I don't. Did you need something else?" he asked. I told him no and we hung up. Something was wrong, as in seriously fucked up. Not only was my mother dead, but my uncle, one of the few people who mattered in my life, was acting like he didn't even know me.

"Grant's looking for you," Sampson said as I approached. Ignoring Hank's glare, I stepped into Grant's suite to see what he wanted. Nash, Evan, Rowan, and Mallory were all there.

"Good, you're here," Grant said, when he saw me walk in. He nodded to Marcel and the door snapped shut behind me.

"Marcy is on the warpath. She's looking for someone to blame and right now that someone is Olivia." His eyes hit on me when he said Olivia's name. "She thinks Olivia is trying to make her look bad."

"Marcy doesn't need Olivia to do that," I calmly stated. Inside, my gut was twisting.

"Do you think Olivia had something to do with the rigging?" Nash asked. *What a stupid fucking question,* I thought.

"Absolutely not," I responded.

His brow shot up. "You sure about that? Where was she yesterday morning? Hank tried to play it off, but it was apparent he was looking for her. How do we know she wasn't at the venue fucking with the rigging? For that matter, how do we know she didn't call and cancel the hotel and the fireworks?" His eyes darted wildly around the room before coming back to me. "Other than the fact that she worked with Indigo Road years ago, we don't know anything about her."

"Nash-" Rowan said.

"I'm serious!" he exclaimed. It was apparent he'd had a little bit too much drama in his life. Talk about barking up the wrong tree. Olivia was playing with something, all right, just not the rigging.

"Why would she do that?" Evan asked.

"Who knows? Maybe Marcy's right. Maybe Olivia is after her job?"

Cutting through his stupid ass tirade, I asked, "Marcy actually said that?" As if sensing I was about to come unglued, he took a deep breath and slowed his roll.

"Look, I like Olivia. I think she's a damn good manager. I'm just worried. Too much isn't adding up," he answered. Rowan and Mallory both scowled at him.

"You can absolutely count her out," I snapped. He scowled. I glowered. Finally, I shared, "Olivia wasn't sabotaging the band or trying to hijack Marcy's job. She was with me yesterday morning. We both overslept. That's why she was late for the bus." No one said a word. Scowls immediately turned into smiles, which apparently hacked Nash off.

"You knew?" he directed at Rowan.

"We didn't know, know, but we had our suspicions," she answered.

"I think you and Olivia make such a great couple," Mallory announced.

"Thanks," I dryly responded. Evan slapped me on the back and laughed when I shoved him away. Grant just stood there staring at me. "Don't even think about passing judgment right now," I warned.

He held up his hands. "No judgment here. Olivia is a good

girl. It's your life. Your business. Just be careful."

"You've got to be kidding me," Nash growled. "Wasn't Chelle enough? Haven't you done enough damage?" All eyes shot to him, but he didn't heed the warning glares. "Can't you find someone not affiliated with the band to fuck? I mean, really?"

"Nash," Rowan hissed.

I saw red. Nash had been baiting me for months. I'd held my temper time and time again, when what I wanted to do, dreamt about, was to beat the living shit out of him. This was no longer about Chelle. This wasn't about the woman he loved and what I'd done to her. This was about me and him. This was about Olivia. This was about trying to start over, but always getting stuck in the past. Fuck Nash. I was done being his whipping boy, done taking his shit, and done with him. Without warning, I cocked my arm back and plowed my fist into the side of his face. Mallory and Rowan screamed as Nash dropped his head and tackled me to the ground. Fists flew as adrenaline fueled by pent-up rage coursed through us. This was a long time coming. He nailed me in the ribs and I jabbed him a good one in the lip. By the time Grant and Evan pulled us apart, we'd done some serious damage to the room as well as to each other. Rowan cursed like a sailor at the two of us before storming out the door. Mallory shook her head before escaping to the bedroom. Evan and Grant just stared at us as if we'd lost our minds. After what seemed like forever, Grant found his voice.

"This is done. You," he directed at Nash, "need to get the fuck over it."

"Me?" Nash asked, clearly surprised he was being called on the carpet for his stupidity.

"Yes, you!" Grant shouted. "If I was Chaz, I would have beaten your ass well before now. This ends here! Everyone has let it go but you!" His eyes roamed over the mess we'd made. "Either learn how to deal with each other, or quit, and don't bother coming back. Now, get the fuck out of my hotel room!" he shouted. Evan helped us both up off of the floor. I was pretty sure one of my ribs were cracked. Not only that, but my left eye had started to swell. If I didn't get ice on it in the next few minutes, I wouldn't be able to see out of it.

"That was epic," Evan muttered on the way out the door. Nash and I both glared at him.

"You chipped my tooth," Nash bitched.

"Fuck you. At least I didn't break your rib."

"No, seriously, look." Nash raised his upper lip and sure enough, half of his front tooth was missing.

"You look so Bubba right now," Evan said through a snort of laughter.

"More like Lloyd from *Dumb and Dumber*," I murmured. The next thing I knew, we were all three laughing.

# CHAPTER TWENTY

## "Feel the Pain"

*Olivia*

After running around like a chicken with my head cut off all day, I was more than ready for tonight. Even though Indigo Road was joining us, it was still my party. Frank made that very clear when he refused to help.

"Sweetheart, I'm manager of a rock band, not a party planner," I mimicked, as I raced like a mad woman up to my room to grab a quick shower. It was a hundred degrees out, so tonight's outfit consisted of a cute pair of jean shorts, a Meltdown t-shirt, which I'd stolen from Chaz, and a pair of rhinestone flip-flops. Hank texted right as I was about to blow dry my hair. Apparently, hotel management needed to have a quick word with me. *So much for good hair*, I thought as I blew the front dry and swept the rest up on top of my head in a messy bun. On the way out the door, I slid on my flip-flops and grabbed both my room key and my phone.

The hotel manager was waiting for me outside the pool entrance. I expected our chat to be about the party, but instead it was about a complaint concerning some unspecified disturbance in one of the hotel rooms occupied by Meltdown. I pressed him for specifics, but he claimed he'd received the news from one of his employees and was simply passing it along to me. In other words, he didn't actually know what had transpired. When I asked Hank and Sampson if they knew anything about it, they both said no. So, even though I didn't have the first clue as to what or who he was referring to, I apologized for the disturbance, agreed to accept charges for all damages, and promised to get my crew under control. The moment he mentioned the word disturbance, I thought of Chaz and the mess he'd made of his hotel room. That got me thinking about how I hadn't seen nor heard from Mr. Jones all day, which then made me worry. As much as I wanted to check up on him, my job came first. A job, mind you, that I was honestly beginning to hate.

"It's probably nothing," Hank said, once the manager was gone. I shrugged it off, but I had a niggling feeling it was definitely something. Worry was soon replaced with anticipation as everyone prepared for the band members and their crews to arrive.

In a wise move, Marcy and Frank agreed that Hank would take charge of both security teams for the party. Hank placed Marcel and Andrew, a member of Indigo's security team, at the entrance to the pool area. Their job was to check IDs and manage wristbands. He then placed the rest of security around the perimeter. Frank and I were in charge of damage control. Not even ten minutes in, and Frank had his ass parked on a pool lounger with a glass of wine in his hand. I told Hank this would happen, but even though I called it, it still annoyed the hell out of me. Frank was a real go-getter back when I worked for him. Now, he was just plain lazy. That, and I was pretty sure Marcy had him watching me and Hank, which made him a lazy snitch.

By six thirty, a total of four roadies had shown up. I shot off a quick text to Chaz, asking where he was, before sidling up to Frank's chair to inquire about Indigo Road's pending arrival. He told me soon and asked if I would be so kind as to refill his wine glass. I wanted to tell him to fill his own damn wine glass, but since tonight wasn't the night to make waves, I swallowed down my nasty reply and took his glass to the bar for a refill. I'd just handed the glass back to him, when I saw Evan exit the hotel, take three steps, and fall flat on his ass.

"Oh, God," I whispered.

Hank stepped up beside me and muttered, "He's drunk." My heart sank as we watched Evan pick himself up off of the sidewalk and stumble his way towards us. *Yikes!* He wasn't just drunk, he was hammered. "I'll get him," Hank said. While he was busy corralling an intoxicated Evan onto a pool lounge, several more roadies showed up. Grant and Mallory walked in shortly after that. On their coattails were Nash and Rowan.

I took one look at Nash's black eye and grotesquely swollen lip, and freaked. "What happened?"

Rowan rolled her eyes and Nash let out a puff of air that kind of sounded like laughter, but could have just as easily been a gasp of pain. "Your boyfriend happened, that's what," Nash glibly answered. Grant shot him a look. "What? I didn't say anything bad. I just answered her question," he huffily responded. Oh my God, these guys were nuts.

I gave Rowan and Mallory a what-the-hell look and Mallory mouthed, "I'll tell you later." Rowan just shook her head. I was about to ask about Chaz, when I saw him exit the hotel. As it was nearly dark outside, I couldn't see his face. That is, until he stepped under the pool lights.

"What in the world..." I whispered. His left eye was completely swollen shut. I turned to Nash and hissed, "What did you do?" but didn't bother to wait for his response.

"I'm fine," Chaz said upon my arrival.

"No, you're not," I snapped at him. "Have you seen a Dr. yet?"

"I'm fine," he repeated.

"Chaz-" I started to argue, but swallowed my words when he pierced me with his one good eye.

"I'm fine, Olivia. Now, Nash, on the other hand..." We both looked over at Nash.

"Fuck you, gimpy!" Nash responded from halfway around the pool.

"At least I have all of my teeth, Cletis!" Chaz shouted back, and smiled when the crowd surrounding Grant and Nash erupted in laughter. Clearly, I'd missed something. On our slow trek to where the others were sitting, I drilled Chaz about his injuries. He mumbled something about sore ribs and a messed up eye, before commenting, "Nice shirt, by the way."

"Thanks. I got it from this really hot guy."

"Yeah, how hot?" he asked.

"Smokin hot," I responded in a low, sexy voice. We slowed to a stop and just stared at each other.

"Leave with me," he said. God, how I wanted to, but I couldn't.

"You know I can't do that." Even with a busted eye, the man was the sexiest thing I'd ever seen.

He smiled, and I nearly lost my breath. "But you want to."

"I really, really want to."

"What's wrong, Grandpa, did you forget your walker?" Nash called out.

"Fuck off snaggletooth," Chaz called back. His eyes, however, remained on me. After a very intense stare down, he looked away and the moment was broken. I asked if I could get him a drink. "Don't drink," he muttered. This made me realize how much I didn't know about him. Right as we reached our destination, Hank shouted my name. I turned to see what he wanted and spotted the crowd of people heading down the sidewalk in our direction. Sander was in the lead and Gio was right behind him. With them were some less than desirable looking women.

*Dammit, I knew they were going to pull something.*

"Be right back," I said, and marched my ass back around the pool to head them off at the pass. As I passed by Frank's chair, I gave it a good solid kick. "We said band members and crews only, Frank."

"They aren't members of the band or crew," he drawled, pointing at Mallory and Rowan.

"That's Grant Hardy's wife and Nash Bostwick's fiancée, Frank, not some bimbos off the street." With a growl of frustration, I made my way over to address the group. "Hi, guys. I'm really sorry, but this party is for Meltdown, Indigo Road, and their crew members only."

"Frank said it was cool if we added a few extras," Gio responded. I could feel Sander's eyes on me. *Stupid, stupid Frank!* He never could say no to Sander, which is why Sander acted like such an entitled asshole.

"Well, Frank lied," I stated in an extremely diplomatic tone, when what I felt like doing, was knocking some sense into Frank.

"Come on, Olivia, be reasonable," Sander urged, as if we were friends...as if we were anything.

"I'm really sorry, guys, but we only have enough food and drinks for the band members and their crews. If we break the rules for you, we'll have to break them for everyone. I've already said no to the Melties, so I'm going to have to say no to you as well. I really am sorry." I was so not sorry. I was livid with Frank for putting me in this position.

"No, you're not," Gio snarled. I lasered him with a glare.

"Hush, G," Sander ordered.

"Yes, do hush, G," I repeated. I may have sounded calm, but I was anything but. For years I'd been sitting on a landmine, yet, out of respect for the man I'd once loved and the band I'd once worked for, I'd kept my silence. I gave Sander a do-you-really-want-to-mess-with-me look, and was surprised when he backed down.

"Party in my suite in an hour!" he called out to the crowd. "In the meantime, drinks are on me at the downstairs bar." He gave his date a pat on the ass. "Go on, I'll be up there soon," he told her. With a few grumbles and moans, the crowd parted ways. Ignoring Gio's glare, I stepped back to let Sander and the rest of Indigo Road into the party.

After putting out a few more fires, I finally managed to make it back to Meltdown's side of the pool, only to discover Chaz gone. Granted, I'd been missing for quite a while, but still... couldn't he have waited to say goodbye?

"He took Evan back to his suite," Mallory explained, and added quickly, "but he said to give you this." She passed me the key card to his suite. Feeling marginally better, I thanked her, and slid the key card into my pocket.

"Look out!" someone yelled. Mallory and I turned in just enough time to get completely doused by a gigantic splash of pool water.

"What the fuck?" Grant shouted.

"Shit!" Mallory screamed.

"Gio, you fucking dick!" Nash shouted.

"Sorry!" Gio called out from the edge of the pool. "I just wanted to cool off and didn't see you there." He addressed Nash's comment, but his eyes were on me. My first thought was, *Sander put him up to this*, but when I scanned the side of the pool for Sander, he wasn't there. That didn't mean he wasn't in on it. It just meant he was smarter than Gio about it. When I told Sander to leave me alone, that extended to Gio as well. They could blow off steam all they wanted just as long as they left me out of it.

"Oooh, look, you're all wet now," Gio taunted. Without so much as a word, I turned and walked away. On my way to the bathroom, I remembered my phone. *Shit, it's probably ruined*, I thought as I fished it out from my back pocket, only to discover it wasn't there. *Oh, no, no, no, this isn't happening.* Deep breath. *Don't panic*, I told myself as I retraced my steps back to where Grant and Mallory were toweling off. My entire life was on my phone.

"I think we're going to head out," Grant announced when he saw me. My head was spinning. My phone was not only missing, but if Grant and Mallory took off then Nash and Rowan wouldn't be far behind them. Once they were gone, the party was basically over, which meant that, once again, I'd wasted money that could have been allocated to something else. Marcy warned me. God, I was so getting shit canned for this.

"Please, don't leave," I all but begged. "At least, grab some food before you go. Have any of you by chance seen my phone?" I asked.

About that time Sean called out, "Is anyone missing a phone?"

"I am!" I screamed. He jogged over and handed it to me. Then he jogged off to put out another security fire. "Thanks, Sean! I called out after him. He waved, and I turned my focus back to Grant. "Please stay," I pleaded.

"The party was a great idea, but we're beat. We've got a busy day tomorrow and I want to spend as much time with Mallory as possible before she has to leave. Sorry, O.," he patted me on the back. "I promise to make it up to you at the next one." What could I say to this? *No? If you leave Marcy will fire me?* In the end, I said nothing. I let Mallory give me a hug and I watched them walk away.

Thirty minutes later, Nash and Rowan took off. This left me with a very drunk Frank, a few straggling Meltdown roadies, and most of Indigo Road's crew. In order to avoid another confrontation with Gio, or for that matter, Sander, I began cleaning up stray cups and plates at the opposite end of the pool. At some point, I noticed Frank had left, but it wasn't until I saw the back of Gio that I began to relax. I didn't see Sander until I was almost on top of him. He was sitting off to the side, out of the beaten path, in one of the pool chairs...waiting for me.

"Can we talk?" he asked. Go figure. The one time I needed Hank or Chaz to bust in and save the day and they were nowhere to be found. As if sensing my hesitation, he added a heartfelt, "Please?"

"It depends. Are you going to shut down Gio?" I asked.

He was quick to answer. "Gio doesn't know anything."

I arched my brow. "Gio doesn't know about the baby, but he knows why I left."

His eyes flickered with surprise. "That's not what he told me." Stupid Gio.

"Yeah, well, he's lying." Sander frowned. I blinked. Neither of us said a word. Gio and Frank were two peas in one big manipulative pod. It was past time Sander realized that he was the object of their manipulations. He was the first to drop his eyes.

"Shit. I'm sorry. I didn't know. Jesus, Olivia. I was so fucked up back then. Please, sit." He held up his hands in a gesture of peace as I sat down next to him. "Granted, that's no excuse, but it's true. By the time I got clean, you were gone. Frank said you needed a break and that you'd be back."

I snorted. "Yeah, well, Frank says a lot of things, doesn't he?" It was a rhetorical question, so it surprised me when he chose to answer.

"Frank has changed since you were with us. I realize this, but regardless, he's the reason I'm here. He's the reason I got clean. I owe him." I didn't bother to respond because there really was no point. Sander, Frank, Gio...none of them were my concern anymore. I made a move to stand. "What was he like?" he quietly asked.

"Who?"

"Our son." My heart literally spasmed in my chest. This is why I'd been avoiding him. I didn't want to talk about our son. I knew it was selfish, that I was selfish, but I viewed my pregnancy, our child, the entire horrific experience as mine. Not his. Mine. "Just this once, and I promise I'll never bug you about it again," he cut in, as if reading my mind. Tears stung the backs of my eyes. It took me a moment to swallow them down.

"He had dark hair like you." I cleared my throat, before continuing, "My mom said that other than his hair color, he looked just like me when I was born."

A sad smile appeared on his face. "That's good," he whispered. "You are crazy beautiful, Olivia. You always were." *Then why?* I wanted to scream, but then I realized I didn't want to know why. I didn't want to hear why, because I didn't care. Other than the drug use, nothing had changed. He was still nailing Gio, still protecting Frank, and still making excuses for both. He was exactly the same person now as he was then. I was the one who'd changed. Why he did what he did no longer mattered. "Are you happy?" he asked. It had been a long time since someone had asked me that question. I immediately thought of Chaz - my surly, dominant, grouch of a man – and smiled. He chuckled. "Don't answer that. I can see it in your smile." He leaned forward and dropped his elbows to his knees. Then he pierced me with a vintage Sander stare. "I've missed that smile. I've missed you, Livie." My heart clenched at the sound of my old nickname.

"Sander, don't," I whispered. The crickets chirped around us as we sat there staring at each other. Finally, he stood.

"Well, it seems I have an after-party to attend to. I'm glad you're happy, Olivia. Gio won't give you any more trouble. You have my word." I quietly thanked him. "Take care of yourself," he said, and then he walked away.

The overwhelming urge to cry was interrupted by Hank's sudden appearance.

"How much did you hear?" I asked.

"Just the goodbye part. Are you okay? I had to all but carry Frank back to his room. That guy is a dick."

"I'm good. I have a few more things to take care of and then I'm heading up."

"I'll help. That way I can walk you to your room." His offer was sweet, but I wasn't planning on going to my room. Well, maybe I could stop there first. That way I could grab a change of clothes for the morning.

It was approaching one by the time Hank and I finally left the pool area. Sean caught up with us in the lobby and we all three stepped onto the elevator together. On the way up to my floor, we discussed whether or not to throw another party, and decided to wait to get everyone else's thoughts before making any decisions.

"I'll make sure she gets to her room," Hank told Sean as we stepped off of the elevator.

"Night, guys," Sean said.

"Night, Sean. Thanks for tonight," I called out as he went one way and we went the other. Outside my door, I said, "Thanks for helping with clean up and for walking me to my door." Hank had a look on his face, an intensity in his eyes I'd never seen before. It hit me what was about to happen right as he swept in for the kiss. I slapped my hand over my mouth and grunted when his face awkwardly bumped my hand. This caused me to pull back and bang my head against the door.

"Shit, are you okay?" he asked. No, I wasn't okay. This was Hank. My friend. The guy I'd defended to Chaz. My face must have betrayed my feelings, because he suddenly stepped back.

His mouth twisted with disgust, but I also saw pain.

"Hank-"

"I'm sorry. That was stupid of me."

"No, it's just that...I'm not the answer. This...isn't the answer. You're hurting right now. You need to talk to Marcy. You both need to figure things out."

"You're right. Fuck, Olivia, I'm sorry. I know you're right. That was a dick move. I know you've got feelings for Chaz-"

I cut him off. "And it's because of those feelings that this can't happen. You're a great guy and a good friend, but that's all it is, okay?"

"Can we forget this ever happened?" he asked.

"It's already forgotten," I assured him. He gave me a quick hug and waited for me to open my door before saying goodnight.

It took me all of three minutes to gather my things and another two to make it up to Chaz's suite. The entire way I contemplated what to tell him. The last thing I wanted was to cause problems, or should I say more problems, between him and Hank. Hank wasn't really into me, he was just confused. I quietly let myself into Chaz's suite. When I reached his room, I was surprised to see him sitting at the hotel desk. His back was to me and he wasn't wearing a shirt. After the night I'd had, I couldn't wait to get my hands on him, to feel him inside me. He might not be able to erase what happened, but he sure as hell could make it better. As I got closer, I could see he was on the computer. A few steps more and the screen came into view. The screen with a picture of a naked man lying on a bed. A feeling of dread washed over me. On closer look, it wasn't a man, but a boy. A naked boy who looked as if he'd had the shit beat out of him. Then it hit me...nearly knocked me off my feet...completely shredded me.

The boy in the picture was Chaz.

# CHAPTER TWENTY-ONE

## "Heroes"

*Chaz*

"Oh, my God, Chaz? Is that you?" Olivia asked from behind me. I closed my eyes and dropped my head. The shock in her voice made me want to hurl. *Fuck!* I took a deep breath and slowly let it out. How I'd failed to hear her enter the suite, much less my room, was beyond me. My first instinct was to rip my computer from the wall and smash the shit out of it. Humiliation and shame, two of my nearest and dearest friends, festered like a steaming pile of shit in my gut as I slammed the laptop closed. At this point, it didn't matter where the picture had come from or who'd sent it. All that mattered was that Olivia, the only person whose opinions and thoughts mattered, had just seen it. Olivia, the one person on this hellhole of a planet that I would walk the fuck away from before tainting with my shitty past, now had a visual of me at my absolute worst burned into her frontal lobe.

"Open it back up and answer my question," she demanded. *Motherfuckingshit!* I didn't want to answer her question. I wanted to pretend it never happened. Charles Dunn was dead. I'd buried that part of my life the night Bill had shown up and taken me away from it all. "*He* did that to you, didn't he?" Her voice shook with emotion, or maybe it was disgust, but I was too much of a pussy to look at her and find out. Instead, I stared at the top of my computer and scrambled for something to say. I was torn by my urge to run, but also my need to stay. What I didn't want was to answer her damn question.

"How was the party?" I calmly asked, when deep inside I was anything but calm. My side ached and my pulse hammered like crazy behind my swollen eyelid, and the urge to run was growing stronger by the second.

"I knew it," she hissed. "Your no good, shit of a stepfather didn't just burn you, he tortured you, didn't he?" It was only a matter of time before she connected the dots, figured out my sick fuck secrets, and ran. "Let me see the picture," she ordered.

I jerked my head around. When our eyes connected, I gave her a simple, but very direct, "No."

She leaned over the desk, pursed her pretty little mouth at me, and in a scary, yet calm voice said, "Let me see it, Chaz." I could tell by the expression on her face that she wasn't going to give up.

"Fine!" I flipped open the computer, pushed back from the desk, and stood. "You want to see it? Here it is. You'll find that if you scroll through, there are several more images. When you're finished getting your cheap thrills, make sure you close the door on your way out," I added, before walking out of the bedroom. I thought about leaving the suite altogether, but opted for the living room sofa instead.

After my earlier conversation with Bill and my fight with Nash, I wasn't in the mood to party. As much as I wanted to bail, I knew it would be a dick move not to show up to support Olivia, so I decided to make a brief appearance. The moment an excuse to leave arose; I took it. That's when I gave Mallory my spare room key to give to Olivia. Back in my suite, I fired up my laptop with the thought that I'd see if I could find a record of my mother's death. Before I had the chance to search, I noticed two more emails addressed to Charles Dunn. I clicked open the first one.

"Motherfucker," I whispered as I stared at another picture. Whoever was sending these had upped their game. This one was taken later than the others, after the beatings had gotten out of control.

Somewhere between my fourteenth and fifteenth birthday, something changed. The beatings went from sporadic to almost every night. Don would wait until I was asleep and then visit to smack me around. At this point, I'd learned to sleep in a long-sleeve t-shirt and pajama pants with one eye open and one foot on the ground. Don didn't like obstacles. He didn't want anything getting in his way. One night in particular, I was startled awake with a hand over my mouth and a heavy weight on my lower back. It took me a moment to realize he was on top of me with both knees straddling either side of my back. I tried to buck him off, but he was stronger...stronger and a whole hell of a lot meaner.

"I told you not to lock your door," his gruff voice whispered in my ear. The smell of booze was gag-worthy. I managed to nod my head, to let him know I got it, and that it wouldn't happen again. "I see I'm going to have to teach you a little lesson." In his inebriated state, the word sounded more like "leshon." The low tone of his voice and the way in which he slurred his words, scared the living shit out of me. A part of me knew that if I didn't fight, there would be no coming back from what he was planning to do to me.

During this time, I hit a major growth spurt. I shot from five feet, four inches to five-eight in a matter of months. Little did

Don know, but around that time, I'd also started lifting weights. I was known as the quiet kid. The kid who refused to take off his shirt in gym class - not a nerd, but also not a jock. No one knew me because I refused to let anyone in. My one saving grace was music. I would have given anything to join the band, but didn't dare for fear of calling attention to myself. I felt beaten down and helpless. I thought if I was stronger, I would be able to fight back and maybe even stop him. So, I decided to do something about it. After school was a popular time in the weight room, so I opted for early morning before school. I wasn't anywhere close to Don's strength, but I was no longer a lightweight either. That, and the element of surprise, were what saved me that night.

As Don grasped both of my wrists in one hand and the waistband of my pajama pants and underwear in the other, I screamed. On the off chance my mother would take pity on me, I shouted for her to help me. "Shut it," he hissed as he lifted up, and with a vicious jerk, yanked my pajama bottoms down. Right as I felt the air hit my bare ass, I freaked. I wasn't sure what he had planned, but I sure as hell wasn't going to stick around to find out. As hard and as fast as I could, I reared up. At the same time, I twisted my torso sideways. Don catapulted off of me and I heard him land with a thud on the floor. Like a bat out of hell, I took off out the door. In my pajamas and bare feet, I ran three miles to my best friend Marco's house. Marco's parents took one look at me and quickly ushered me inside. I never said a word, but they knew. Even though I tried to hide the evidence, they'd seen the bruises and burn marks. If it had been any other kid but me, they would have called the police, but as my abuser was the police, their hands were tied. I spent the next week sleeping on their sofa and would have stayed longer if Don hadn't started harassing Marco's dad. Surprisingly, when I returned home, nothing happened. After a week free from Don's nightly visits, I began to let down my guard. I shouldn't have.

The picture staring back at me was evidence of what happened after that week at Marco's house. My stomach revolted as I reflected back on that time in my life. This was me at my absolute lowest. The fact that Don had photographed me, naked, beaten, and passed out, and all without my even knowing about it, was too fucked up for words. The busted lip and gash above my eye were remnants of my decision to fight back. These were mild compared to the scars you couldn't see.

*I HOPE IT HURT* was written in bold and all caps below the picture.

I closed the email and opened the second one. This was what I was looking at when Olivia walked in.

"Chaz, please talk to me," she said from the bedroom doorway.

"How was the party?" I asked for a second time. She sucked her bottom lip into her mouth, and I could practically see the wheels spinning.

"If I tell you, will you give me something in return?" she hesitantly replied. I thought about it for a second, before nodding my head. I'd give her something, alright. Somehow, I was pretty sure that's not what she meant. I made a hurry up motion with my hands. "Fine," she huffed, and in one long sentence, said, "The party sucked. Frank got hammered, Gio was an asshole, and Sander cornered me. Your turn." Frank was a douche, however, the part about Gio and Sander bothered me.

"What did Gio and Sander do?" I asked.

"Nope, that's part two. Your turn," she slowly reiterated.

"My uncle called today. He told me my mother died." Olivia's eyes bugged.

"What?" she screeched. "When?"

"Uh-uh, that's part two. Now tell me about Gio and Sander." I could tell she was about to blow.

She managed to swallow it back long enough to say, "Gio and

Sander showed up with a bunch of people and Gio got pissed off when I refused them entry. Like a two-year-old, he jumped into the pool for the sole purpose of splashing me; only he managed to drench our entire corner of the pool. Of course, he was quick to apologize when Grant and Nash called him out on it. After everyone took off, I thought I was home free, but then suddenly Sander was there, wanting to know about the baby. I told him and he left. Now, tell me about your mom." I had to admit, I was impressed. What she was lacking in detail, she'd made up for in speed. I wanted to ask for more, but fair was fair.

"My uncle didn't give me any details. He simply said she was gone."

"That's it?"

"I don't know. I mean, the whole conversation was weird. I used to be close to my uncle. When I joined the band, we stopped talking as much, but today on the phone he acted like a stranger. Something was off. *He* was off. This got me thinking, and now I want proof of her death."

"Your mother's brother?" she asked.

"No, my stepfather's." Her eyes narrowed.

"From what you've said, I take it they weren't close?"

"Fuck no. Don was a dick to everyone, including his own family."

"Do you know where your mom was living when she died?"

"I assume she was still in Indianapolis."

"If you call the Indiana Vital Statistics Office, they should have record of her death," she instructed.

"Well, aren't you just a fount of information. And you know this how?"

She smiled, and I swear I felt it all the way down to my cock. "Is that one of my questions?"

"No, and since you answered a question with a question, you now owe me two. Tell me more about Sander." Her smile instantly vanished and I wanted to kick myself.

"There's nothing to tell. He wanted to take a trip down memory lane." She pushed my feet out of the way and plopped her pretty little ass onto the ottoman in front of me, before continuing, "And I didn't. But then, I felt bad. I mean, he was his child, too. So I changed my mind and told him as much as I could without completely breaking down and crying like a huge titty." The thought of her crying to him pissed me off.

"Cry to me, not him," I said. She blinked. Then she smiled.

"Aww, you like me," she teased. I fought back a smile, and realized I'd been doing a lot of that lately. I also fought the urge to pull her into my lap, strip her clothes off, and fuck her... very slowly. "You've been doing a lot less of that lately," she commented.

"Less of what?" I asked, thinking that she was referring to my boner, and wondering how she'd come to that conclusion.

"Finger drumming," she clarified. The second she mentioned it my eyes dropped to my spastic fingers.

"And your question is?" I asked. She responded with a cheeky grin, which didn't help the status of my boner in the least bit.

"The picture?" she asked.

*Fuck.* Talk about instant dick deflation.

"Okay, how about we do it this way. I ask and you answer. First question: do you know who's sending the pictures?"

"If I did, we wouldn't be having this conversation," I glibly replied. Her face scrunched in frustration and I wanted to kiss her.

"Did you know they were being taken?"

"If I did, we wouldn't be having this conversation," I repeated.

She leaned forward and I instinctively jerked back. "That's why you got the tattoos, isn't it?" That one was easy to answer.

"The day I turned eighteen, I got my first tattoo. I didn't stop until I'd covered every last mark." Her expression turned all soft and mushy. I wasn't sure what it meant, but somehow, I knew it wasn't pity. I don't know what made me do it. Maybe it was the weight of carrying it for so long. Maybe it was simply because it was her. Hell, maybe my desire for someone in this godforsaken world to understand me finally overrode my sense of self-preservation. Whatever it was didn't really matter. All that mattered was this moment and my need to make Olivia understand. So I told her. I told her how my stepfather burned and beat me. I told her about the night he tried to rip my pajama bottoms off and I ran three miles to my friend's house, only to have to return home a week later. I explained how I thought he'd learned a lesson, how smug I'd been. How I thought he'd felt shame for his actions. Finally, I told her what happened two weeks later, the night he snuck into my room, cuffed my wrists to the headboard, tied my feet to the footboard, cut off my pajamas with a hunting knife, and proceeded to rape me repeatedly. I didn't stop there. I told her how, finally having enough, my mother called my uncle Bill. When Uncle Bill showed up, Don was sitting in his recliner, drinking a beer, and acting as if nothing had happened. Bill took one look at me: tied spread-eagle to my bed, beaten, burned, bloody, barely conscious from what all Don had done to me, and lost his mind. That night, he nearly beat his own brother to death. That night, he rescued me from the hell I'd been living in. When I finished telling Olivia the long, sordid tale of my fucked-up childhood, she launched herself into my lap and burst into tears.

"Hey," I said as I stroked my hand over her hair and down her back. "I'm good. My uncle took me to live with my cousin Earle. He had a farm. When I wasn't in school, he paid me to help him work the land. He even bought me a drum kit, since I had to leave my old one behind."

"He hurt you," she cried. Then she pulled back, and gasped, "Why didn't your uncle take you in?"

199

I wiped the tears from her eyes, before I explained how my Aunt Darlene was a major bitch. Darlene hated Don, which in turn, trickled down to Mom and me. I was perfectly fine not living with them.

"Do you think Bill's sending the pictures?"

"I don't know. Bill was there that night. He saw what Don did. Hell, he got me medical help."

"Well, it can't be your mom, since she's dead. Oooh, maybe it's Darlene?" she whispered in a conspiratorial tone.

"Darlene is a narcissistic twat, babe. She can barely write, much less send emails." A cute little snort slipped from her mouth, followed by a giggle.

"Twat is a really good word," she admitted after a few more giggles.

"You would make a shitty detective," I teased.

"Shut up," she said through another gush of laughter. A second later, her laughter faded back to serious. "I hate your stepdad," she whispered. "How did he die?"

"Someone shot him."

Her brows jumped into her hairline. "Seriously?"

"Yep. I was nineteen when it happened. Earle called and told me Don had stopped off at a bar for a drink after work. On the way to his car, he got jumped. They shot him and walked away with his wallet, gun, and badge."

"Wow. Did they ever find out who did it?"

"Not that I know of." As she settled back into my arms, I knew I'd made the right decision to tell her.

"What happened to your mom?"

"Who the fuck cares?" I asked, and smiled when she smacked me on the arm. She twisted her body sideways and opened her mouth, probably to give me shit, but before she let me have it, I sealed my lips to hers. A few minutes later, we came up for air, and she let me have it anyway.

"You know, if anything, you should thank your mom for saving you from Don."

"Save me, my ass. She let him beat the shit out of me, tie me down, and mark me. She let him..." She slapped her hand over my mouth to shut me up.

"She did do all of that, which is awful, and I seriously hate her for it, but...when it counted the most, she stepped up and saved you. Think about it. Don probably beat her down, too."

Pulling her hand from my mouth, I said, "He never laid a hand on her. I'm not saying he didn't verbally beat her down, but I made sure he saved the worst for me." She got that soft look on her face again.

"What are you going to do about the emails?" she asked. I told her about the pictures I'd received in the mail and she went all detective on me again with conspiracy theories. I had to admit, she might be onto something with her fingerprint idea. What if the sender left prints? It was a long shot, but not out of the realm of possibility. "I think you should tell someone," she finally advised.

"Nope," I said, shaking my head. Telling her about my past was enough for now.

As Olivia pressed her forehead to mine, I braced for the argument. "God, Chaz, you're my hero," she whispered. I jerked my head back and frowned at her.

"Trust me, I'm no one's hero."

"Yes, you are. You're mine. After I lost the baby, I started drinking. When that didn't make me feel better, I turned to pills. When that didn't work, I drank *and* took pills. I was weak... and so pathetic. You had something horrific happen to you and what did you do? You got strong and healthy. In my eyes, that's heroic. Not just heroic, but sexy...sooooo sexy." I was shocked speechless. From the time my uncle rescued me; I'd been fighting. I'd fought not to be seen as a victim. I'd fought to gain control of my anger and shame. I'd fought for my place in this world and my place in the band. No matter how hard I fought, it was never enough. As I stared into Olivia's eyes, I saw acceptance, and for the first time in twenty-nine years, I felt like maybe it was enough, that maybe *I* was enough.

I touched my lips to hers. After giving her a long, slow kiss, I slid one arm around her waist, the other under her legs, and ignoring the pain in my ribs, I lifted her up from the sofa.

"What should my hero name be?" I asked as I carried her into the bedroom.

"How about Chazerooni?" she asked.

"Yeah, nope, that doesn't work for me," I told her, and smiled when she busted into laughter. It wasn't long before her laughter turned to moans and I showed her exactly what a superhero could do.

# CHAPTER TWENTY-TWO

## "Finest Worksong"

*Olivia*

The next morning, I jerked awake to the sound of my phone ringing.

"Who in the hell is calling you this early?" Chaz muttered against the back of my neck. *That's a very good question,* I thought, as I snagged my phone from the nightstand and attempted to focus in on the screen.

"Shit, it's Marcy."

"She seriously needs to get a life," he grumpily responded.

I shushed him, and answered, "Hello?"

Without so much as a greeting, Marcy launched in. "I just spoke with Frank and he's most unhappy with you." My stomach dropped. Frank was such a shit.

"If Frank is unhappy with anyone, it should be himself," I calmly retorted. The line went completely silent, and I wanted to kick myself for giving such a candid reply.

"Yes, well, I'm glad you find this a joking matter. I, however, do not. Frank claims you treated his team unfairly last night and is threatening to pull out of the tour."

"What?" I gasped. Chaz's head shot up and a look of concern appeared on his face. I placed my finger over my lips. If Marcy knew we were together, she would freak.

Chaz mouthed the word, "Speaker." I pressed the speaker button and set the phone between us on the bed.

"I'm confused," I told her. "We all three agreed on band members and their crews only, did we not?" My gut twisted when she didn't respond.

"Yes, well, it's important we learn how to properly gauge these things. Frank didn't think it was a big deal. You should have deferred to him, Olivia." Her tight-lipped response irritated me.

"Are you kidding me?" I hissed, and snapped my eyes to Chaz when he touched my arm.

"Keep your cool," he mouthed, and I nodded my head in acknowledgment. He was right. Being an ass would only further alienate me.

"I've never been more serious. In fact, Frank claims that very few people attended last night's soiree and felt the entire thing was a waste of both time and money. Not only that, but the members of Indigo Road thought you acted in an unprofessional manner." My jaw dropped, right along with my heart. Chaz stiffened beside me and I shook my head at him. The last thing I needed was him weighing in on the matter. "At this point, it would be catastrophic for Indigo Road to pull out of this tour," she finished. I tried to keep my cool, but this was too much.

"Do you want to know what Frank did last night, Marcy? He sat his ass on a pool chair and got drunk, while I handled everything. I'm talking ev-er-y-thing," I slowly enunciated. "I was there when we set the parameters. Did you call to tell me they'd changed? No. Did Frank tell me they'd changed? No. I was doing what you hired me to do, nothing more and nothing less."

Sensing my anger, she backpedaled. "I appreciate that, Olivia. I really do, but you still should have deferred to Frank, and because you didn't, we're now in a jam." Her words stung. What stung even more was the fact that she was dressing me down in front of Chaz.

"From now on, I'll be sure to defer to Frank," I caustically replied.

"There won't be a next time. I'm pulling the parties. If the bands and crew want to hang out together, they can make their own arrangements." I clamped my mouth shut and ground my back molars together. This was bullshit. Last night would have been fun if Indigo Road hadn't been there. There went all of my hours of planning and budget reallocations down the drain.

"So, what you're really telling me is that you trust Frank's word over mine," I posed as a statement rather than a question. Frank wasn't the only one who'd changed. Marcy had changed, too. The Marcy of old would have told Frank to shove it up his ass.

"Welcome to my world, Olivia. What? Do you think this job is easy?" She let out a hollow sounding laugh. "You have no idea what I've had to do to get where I am." I bugged my eyes at Chaz and tried not to laugh when he stuck his tongue in his cheek and waved his fist back and forth in a mock blowjob motion.

"You hired me to step in, yet you're tying my hands at every turn. Why is that?" I asked her.

She let out a long, tired sounding sigh, before replying, "Just smooth things over with Frank and Indigo Road today. We're depending on them for this tour. I have to run. I'll check in later." She hung up before I could respond, and I flopped back onto the bed with a groan.

Chaz pulled me close. "She hates me," I murmured into his chest.

"How long has she been treating you like shit?" he asked. I could tell he was angry by his chilly tone of voice. I wasn't sure what to say. I wasn't looking to get Marcy in trouble, but I couldn't lose this job either.

"Since the morning of the conference when she called Hank and I out." His jaw tensed when I said Hank's name, which reminded me that I needed to tell him about last night. Now was probably not the right time.

"I'll deal with Marcy," he clipped. Whereas I was thrilled he had my back, I was pretty sure I didn't want Marcy to receive Chaz's form of retribution.

"That's sweet, but I've got it," I told him. My belly fluttered when he pierced me with his *do not fuck with me stare.*

"I'll deal with her," he slowly repeated.

"Okay," I whispered, and he kissed me. After that, he made me forget all about Marcy.

♪♪♪

After what happened outside my room last night, I wasn't surprised to discover Hank had opted for airport duty with Marcel over riding in the bus with the band. This morning the girls were on their way back to Austin, and from the looks of it, Grant and Nash were seriously bummed. They'd barely said two words when they stepped onto the bus and both steered immediately for the bunks. Chaz and Evan went straight for the video game console, while I tried to focus on work. What I really did, was reflect on last night's conversation with Chaz. I wasn't kidding when I told him he was my hero. My scars were merely flesh wounds compared to his. When he shared what his stepfather had done, I wanted to scream. My tongue was still sore from where I'd bitten down on it in order to keep from crying. It was a good thing his stepdad was dead, or else I would hunt the man down and kill him myself.

The first three hours of the trip rolled by quickly. I worked for a bit. Then I talked to my parents and brothers. Whenever possible, I stole glances of Chaz. Today he was wearing holey jeans and a black t-shirt with a beer logo on it. I'd never heard of the beer, but as it had the word "stein" added to the end of it, I assumed it was German. The dark ink covering his arms and hiding his painful past had taken on a whole new meaning for me. The realization that stoic, detached, grumpy, Chaz had let me in, did funny things to my head, not to mention my heart. He didn't say it with words. He didn't have to, because he showed me each time he touched me, the way he looked at me, protected me, spoke to me – he didn't have to tell me he loved me because I felt it.

After a lunch of deli sandwiches and chips, my late night started to catch up with me. When no one was looking, I slipped into one of the spare bunks for a quick nap. Sometime later, I awakened to something solid and warm wrapped around me.

"You awake?" Chaz rasped. I felt his, sexy, sleepy voice right where it counted.

"You shouldn't be in here," I chastised, and felt his smile on the back of my neck

"When I'm with you, I feel settled. My fingers, the need to move, to jump out of my own skin, settles," he confessed, and my heart flip-flopped in my chest. He was answering my question from last night, and I knew how huge this moment was. "You make me forget," he whispered. My body spasmed with lust when I felt his lips on the side of my neck. "I didn't want to tell you," he continued in a tone I'd never heard him use before.

I sucked in a deep breath, and mentally urged him to keep sharing. "I thought you'd look at me different, that you'd act different. I was wrong." My eyes stung when he kissed the back of my head, and whispered, "Thank you for giving me that." Everything I'd been holding in, holding back, came pouring out, and my tattered heart skipped, jumped, and tumbled straight into love with Chaz Jones.

"I love you," I blurted, and felt his body tense behind me. Oh God, what was I thinking? This was Chaz...dark, dangerous, closed up tighter than Fort Knox, Chaz.

"What did you say?" he asked.

"Nothing," I quickly replied.

"Say it again," he ordered. When I didn't respond, he flipped me onto my back. "Open your eyes." My eyes snapped open. He was hovering over me, his dark blue stare piercing through me, into the deepest parts of my heart. They were electric, lit up with something I didn't understand, but wanted to. "Again," he repeated.

"I love you," I said with a little less gusto. His forehead dropped to mine. Then he pulled back and kissed me, and it was long, wet, and so damn hot. I gasped for air as my heart soared and my body ignited. His hand shot up my shirt at the same time my fingers dropped to the top button of his jeans. His thumb and forefinger found purchase on my nipple as I flicked open the button, lowered the zipper, and wrapped my hand around his hard cock. He swallowed down my gasp of pleasure as I inhaled his moan. While one hand worked my nipple, the other slid beneath my skirt and inside my panties, zeroing in on the spot.

"Jesus," he hissed as I began to pump him hard and fast. As he whipped up my shirt, jerked down my bra, and latched his mouth onto one of my nipples, I arched up to give him easier access. His hips lifted, and I somehow managed to get his jeans and briefs down to his mid thighs. "Panties," he murmured, and quickly rose up into a modified plank position, so I could slide them off. His hips lowered, and he was there, between my legs, hard and ready. At the same moment he took my mouth, he slid inside and filled me up. God, he was big, bigger than I'd ever had, so big he hit the spot without even trying. I loved him...loved this. He was in me, on me...a part of me. "Fuck, you're so beautiful," he rasped right as it hit me. It was huge, overwhelming, so beautiful it brought tears to my eyes. His thighs squeezed my sides as he planted his knees into the mattress at my hips, and gave it to me. All of it. His respect, his trust, his love...I felt Chaz Jones to the depths of my soul.

"Oh my God," I whispered as he collapsed on top of me.

"Is that a good or bad cry to the heavens?" he asked, and I couldn't help but laugh. He slowly eased out, and we both froze. His smile morphed into a look of panic. "Fuck, I didn't use a condom." We'd never had the protection talk. He'd always just taken care of it. I gave myself a mental slap. *Stupid, Olivia.*

"I'm on the pill. I have been ever since..." The end of my sentence hung between us.

He dropped to my side and jerked his pants up. Then he flipped around to where he was facing me, and shared, "I've been tested twice in five months and haven't been with anyone but you in that time period." My eyes widened in surprise, yes, because he hadn't been with anyone in all that time, but also because he was sharing. "Are we cool?" he asked. I nodded my head, and he smiled. "You still tired?" I thought about it and decided I could stand another hour or so of sleep. I nodded my head again. He gave me a full-blown smile, and for a moment I forgot how to breathe. "I'm going to kick Evan's ass in COD. I'll see you in a few." His mouth dropped to mine for a quick kiss before he brushed back the curtain and was gone. A few seconds later, the curtain opened and a hand appeared, a hand that was holding my panties. My panties, which had fallen onto the floor for everyone to see. Laughter erupted from the other side of the curtain as I yanked them from Chaz's hand.

So much for discretion.

♪♪♪

We arrived in St. Louis around six that evening. As a crowd was congregating at the front of the hotel, we were directed around back to the loading dock, where our security detail was waiting to receive us. Standing next to Hank were two men I'd never seen before.

"Who are they?" I asked as we pulled in.

Nash was closest to me, so he answered, "The beefy white guy is Bobby and the tatted black dude is Tut. They both work for LASH." So, these were the guys from LASH. Both men were tall, muscular, and scary looking. Bobby was shorter than Tut by a few inches or so, but no less intimidating. Nash leaned in, I thought to tell me some big secret about one of the LASH guys, but instead he whispered, "Lavender lace." It took me a minute to realize he was speaking of my panties. I gave him my best eat shit glare, and he laughed. The cat was majorly out of the bag. Let's just hope Marcy didn't catch on to it.

Security escorted us into the hotel. While I quickly checked us in, the guys signed a few autographs. In the elevator, Hank introduced me to Bobby and Tut, told us they had information, and to meet back in Grant's suite in fifteen minutes.

I started to get off on my floor, which was two floors below everyone else's, when Chaz declared, "You're with me." Even if I was, I wasn't, at least not as far as the guys knew.

"This is my floor," I said, while trying to convey my true meaning with my eyes. He slapped one hand on the close door button, while hooking his other arm around my waist. I swiveled around and blasted him with an arctic glare. "That was my floor," I snapped.

"Not anymore," he clipped. When I turned back around, the entire elevator of men was smiling, including Bobby and Tut. My foot twitched with the urge to kick Chaz where it counted. What didn't he understand about keeping this on the down low? Once we hit his suite, I let him have it. To which he responded, "What's so wrong with wanting you with me?" What could I say to that?

Fifteen minutes later, we reconvened in Grant's suite, where Bobby and Tut proceeded to explain what the police had discovered.

"What do you mean Larry was involved. How?" Grant more or less growled.

"The cables on both sides of the rigging were practically sawed through. They didn't break. They weren't faulty. Someone wanted that rigging to come down. They got two recognizable prints belonging to a Mr. Larry Barber. That's the same Larry Barber who manages your roadies," Bobby explained. We stood there, staring at him with shock and horror on our faces. "The police pulled Larry in yesterday afternoon, along with the other roadies, for questioning. Larry told them he always does a brief rigging check before each show as part of the standard protocol. That would have been the end of it, but then two of Indigo's people placed Larry near the rigging during Indigo's practice that afternoon. Larry was released, but after chatting with the officers who questioned him, we believe he's holding back."

"Larry wouldn't do that," Hank instantly responded.

"I agree," Marcel added.

"Larry has led our road crew from the beginning. He's loyal to a fault," Grant explained.

Tut's brows shot up. I tried not to stare, but the guy was super scary in a hot, macho man kind of way. His skin was light mocha in color and his head was shaved, as in bald. He was covered in what looked like tribal tattoos. "Are you telling us to let it go?" he asked in a deep and very masculine sounding voice. Chaz's eyes narrowed when he caught me staring at Tut and I quickly looked away.

"What do you propose we do?" Nash inquired, ignoring Grant's dirty look.

"Let us question him," Tut answered. "Between the two of us, we'll have him talking in no time." This did not sound good.

"What if there's nothing to get?" I asked, now seriously worried about Larry's well-being.

"Then there's nothing to get," Tut responded with a shrug. I wanted to ask more questions, but I wasn't sure I wanted to hear the answers, so I nodded my head and let it go.

The plan was in motion. While Hank and Marcel took the guys over to the venue to check on their instruments, Bobby and Tut were going to have a get to know you chat with Larry. While this was happening, I was going back to Chaz's suite to move my things.

A few hours later, Chaz appeared at my door, his brows drawn together in a frown.

"If Marcy finds out, she'll fire me," I blurted, before he could say anything.

"Fuck Marcy. She can't touch you," he responded.

"She's my boss, Chaz."

"And I'm her boss, Olivia. She'll have to go through me to get to you. That's not going to happen. Now, grab your things and let's go." I thought about fighting him, but could see that something else was wrong, so I gave in and went to get my things.

"Is it Larry?" I asked, once we reached his suite.

"No."

I dropped my things in the bedroom and followed him back into the living area. He was standing in front of the window, but his eyes were on me. Something was clearly wrong. "What is it, Chaz?"

"I called the vital statistics office. Apparently, there's no record of my mother's death." Relief washed through me. I thought he was going to tell me I no longer had a job, or even worse, that he was going to end things between us.

"Could they have been mistaken?" Even though I doubted this was the case, it still could happen.

"Who the fuck knows? But after the conversation I had with my uncle, I feel the need to find out. When's our next break?"

I understood his need to confirm his mother's death, but I wasn't sure about the rest, so I asked, "What exactly are you hoping to find?"

"I'm not sure. If Mom's still alive, then maybe she can tell me about the pictures." He flopped onto the sofa and I settled in next to him.

"Why would your uncle lie about her death? I asked.

"That's what I'd like to know."

"Do you think she'd really do that to you?" I couldn't imagine my mother ever doing something so horrible. Then again, I couldn't imagine my father hurting me, either.

"It crossed my mind, but my mom was like my aunt in that she barely knew how to use her phone, much less send an email. That, and she was already into pills by the time I left. I doubt she got sober. Still...someone got those pictures from Don. If I can figure out who..." The desperation in his tone made my heart ache. I got it. Someone out there knew his deepest, darkest secrets, and that someone could expose him.

"Maybe you should talk to someone, like the guys from LASH?"

"Yeah, not gonna happen. When's our next break?" he asked

again.

"We're here for the next two nights and then we're on to Chicago for three nights. There's a three-day break between Chicago and Ohio. You could go then, but Chaz, there's no way you can do this alone. You know that, right?"

"Then come with me." He said this as if it was no big deal, as if I could just waltz away for three days without repercussions.

"I can't just leave. Not now, and especially with things the way they are with Marcy."

"How 'bout this, I'll make it a day trip. That way we'll still get a few days alone together." Butterflies raced through my stomach and flittered around my heart.

"You'd do that?" I asked in a lovesick, breathy voice.

"You don't get it, do you? I'd do anything for you," he replied.

I seriously, from the depths of my soul, loved this man.

---

# CHAPTER TWENTY-THREE

## "Inside Job"

*Chaz*

The last person who told me they loved me was my mother. That was pre-Don, back when my thoughts centered around mud pies, backyard tag, catching frogs, and searching for fireflies. Olivia's confession of love opened a place inside of me I'd forgotten existed. A place where I was free to feel, could speak my mind, and be myself – a place of acceptance. It's not like I didn't have people who cared about me. Uncle Bill and Earle had been good to me, but when Olivia said those words, it reminded me of the time before we were coated with the stink of Don's shit, back when life was good. Those three words, coming from her sweet lips, brought back memories of golden days. More than that, they made me want, wish, and hope for something better... something more.

Bright and early the next morning, I left Olivia asleep in my bed while I went to work out. My routine before Olivia was: wake up early, work out in the hotel weight room with the security team, and eat breakfast. I'd fallen out of my routine and missed the simplicity of it, so yesterday at practice; I made plans to meet up with Marcel and Sean. I thought it would be easy. I was wrong. Things had changed. I'd changed. Leaving Olivia naked and warm in my bed, the knowledge that I could be buried in her instead of getting my ass kicked in the weight room, screwed with my head enough so that it took a fifteen-minute treadmill run and a ten-minute cycle before I was warmed up and into the groove. After a series of dead lifts, leg presses, and squats, I was feeling pretty good. In the middle of my second set of push-ups and flies, Gio walked in. He took one look at me and smiled, as if we were friends. His smile faltered when he realized I wasn't interested. If he was smart, he'd keep his distance. He wasn't smart, though. He was a fucking dumbass.

"Nothing like a good workout to get the blood pumping," he stated in a conversational tone. I didn't respond. After a minute or so, he tried again. "What's the news on the rigging? One of my guys mentioned something about your roadie captain." Again, I gave him nothing. Sean and Marcel took my lead and we all three pretended he wasn't there. We moved on to throw downs and ab crunches. Gio, being the narcissistic attention whore that he was, didn't like this. "Do you have a problem with me?" His tone had morphed from conversational to confrontational. Now, we were getting somewhere.

Slowly, I lifted my gaze to his, and in a flat tone, answered, "Right now, yes, but if you stop fucking with Olivia, we'll be just fine." His brows hit his hairline as his eyes blew up with surprise.

"Me?" he gasped. "If anyone's fucking anyone, it's Olivia and Sander. You should have seen them at the party the other night. They were all over each other."

"Out," I ordered, nodding my head at Sean and Marcel. As they evacuated the room, I stared over at Gio's security guy.

"You sure you want him to hear what I have to say?"

"Go ahead," Gio said, motioning for his guy to leave.

Once we were alone, I shared what was on my mind. "I know everything; your secret, why Olivia left, and what you're doing. If you don't want everyone else to know, you'll back the fuck off."

"I have no idea what you're talking about," he nervously stammered.

"Yes, you do. It's clear to me that you and Sander want to stay hidden in the closet. I have no problem with that. What you do with your dicks is your business. Only, you're fucking with my girl, and I don't like that. Sander and Olivia are cool. You need to be cool, too. This means, you need to call off Frank, stop threatening to quit the tour, and keep your fucking distance."

After several hisses and groans, he finally sputtered, "Who said anything about quitting the tour?"

"As long as it doesn't happen, who gives a fuck who said it?" I snapped.

"Are you threatening me?" he screeched. The guy really was an idiot.

"No, I'm telling you. Leave Olivia alone. Consider yourself warned," I said, and walked out of the room.

Olivia was gone when I returned to my suite, which was probably for the best, because I was wound up. After a long, hot shower, I shot her a quick text. She responded that she had a meeting with the caterer and would catch up with me later.

By the time the bus left for practice, I'd managed to lock my shit down. At least, I no longer wanted to rip Gio's head off. Practice went surprisingly well, considering that we were working with instruments from Grant's Austin studio. Normally, it took me a few days to warm up a new kit, but by the time practice was over, I was feeling pretty good. During our final song, I saw Olivia standing off to the side...watching me. The skirt she was wearing reminded me of yesterday on the bus, and my cock instantly perked up.

"I think we're good," Grant announced. I waved Olivia over as everyone took off.

"How long before dinner?" Evan asked her.

"You have an hour," she told him. Her eyes hit me, and she smiled. "Hey drummer boy, what's shakin'?" she sweetly asked. My cock was now painfully trying to escape from the confines of my jeans. If I didn't get some relief I would have a permanent zipper mark.

I scanned her from top to toe, before responding, "I like your skirt."

"Yeah? I like your drums," she shot back. I stood up and her eyes dropped to my cock bulge.

"Sit," I told her.

"Really?" she asked, her voice conveying her excitement. This was my sacred space, a space I shared with no one. This was huge, monumental, fucking unprecedented. As if worried I might rescind my offer, Olivia quickly scrambled around me and plopped her pretty ass cheeks on my throne. Just the thought of her bare ass on my throne made my cock swell even more. I handed her my sticks. She took them, and with a huge smile on her face, said, "Show me."

"Scoot up," I told her. Her breath hitched as I slid in behind her, and I couldn't help but smile. I then showed her how to hold the sticks. While she took them for a spin, I tried to keep my mind out of the gutter, but she was here, in my sacred space, looking like a rock princess and smelling like gardenias. "I want to fuck you," I whispered against the back of her head. Her body tensed.

"We can't. Not with so many people around," she protested in a husky, low tone. I skimmed my palms up her bare thighs.

"They can't see us."

"They can, too," she breathily argued.

"Not from the waist down," I murmured, and waited for her to slowly spread her legs before continuing my ascent to the tops of her thighs.

In a whispered, "Chaz," her head dropped back onto my shoulder.

As I cupped my hand over her pussy, I could feel the moist heat seeping out from beneath her panties. "Do you want me to touch you, Olivia?"

Her "Yes" vibrated through me.

With a twist of my wrist, I shoved her panties aside and slid a finger back and forth across her wet slit. At the same time I dipped my finger inside, I murmured, "Are you going to suck me off after?"

"Yes." Her voice hitched again as I slid a second finger in, and she slowly began to ride my hand. I could tell she was getting close when she sped up her pace and her breaths came out in little pants of air. The moment I zeroed in on her clit, her fingers dug into my thighs and the back of her head burrowed into my shoulder as her orgasm rocketed through her. When she came down from her orgasmic high, she laughed. "I can't believe that just happened," she said with a shaky breath.

"Good?" I asked.

Her head swiveled around and her light blue eyes landed on me. "Do you even have to ask?" Her smile slightly faded. "Ummm, part two seems slightly more complicated."

"Up," I said, tapping her thighs. She stood and waited for me to push back and adjust the chair height. Since her eyes were already on the target, I decided to give her a little preview - button open, zipper down, cock in hand...her eyes never left their mark. In fact, they looked a little glazed, as if deep in a cock trance. "You still with me?" I asked, and held back a groan as she slowly dropped to her knees in front of me. At this point, she didn't have to suck me off. The eager look on her face was reward enough, but then she took me inside her mouth. Having her down on her knees, in my sacred space, with her lips wrapped around my cock, was so fucking hot...a fantasy come true. When I was with Olivia, nothing mattered – not the bullshit with the band, the emails, or my fucked-up past. None of it mattered as long as I had her by my side.

That night, we killed it. After two days off, we were rested and fired up to bring it. The crowd was pumped, we were pumped, and we more than delivered.

On our way off of the stage, we passed Indigo Road.

"Good show," Sander said. I could tell from the way he was acting that Gio hadn't mentioned our earlier confrontation. As long as they kept their distance, I didn't care.

We hit the dressing room ten minutes before the VIP party was due to begin. On my way to the bathroom to change shirts, I checked to see if I'd missed a text or call from Olivia, and noticed a missed text from an unknown number. Without thinking I hit on it. It took me a minute to register exactly what I was looking at. It was a picture of Olivia with her back pressed against the door. In front of her stood Hank. His hands were on her arms and their lips were almost touching. Hank and Olivia...kissing. *Are you fucking kidding me?* Forgetting all about my shirt, I shot out of the bathroom.

"What's wrong?" Evan asked as I passed him on the way to the door. Right as I reached it, the door swung open and in came a swarm of people.

"Great show, Chaz!" several Melties called out as I passed by. I didn't respond. I couldn't. All I saw was the picture of Olivia and Hank...touching...kissing, and who the fuck knows what else.

I found Marcel in the hall and asked him where Hank was. He pointed down a long hallway, and I took off. A few minutes later, I found Hank. Of course, he was with Olivia.

"Well, isn't this cozy?" I snarled. Olivia's brow furrowed in concern and I wanted to scream.

"Chaz? What's wrong?" she asked, as if she didn't already fucking know.

"Hmmm, let me see. You tell me there's nothing going on between the two of you. We argue about it, but you finally convince me you're just friends. I finally believe you, only to discover that I'm a chump and you're a fucking liar!" I shouted.

"What in the hell are you talking about?" Hank shouted back at me. I flipped to the text and handed him my phone. "Shit," he hissed, before saying, "It's not what it looks like." Olivia stood there with a deer in the headlights expression on her face, and my chest constricted. *Motherfucker, she's guilty. They both are,* I thought as I took in the scene.

"Yeah, tell me, how is it?" I sharply responded.

Before Hank could answer, Olivia said, "I was going to tell you, but there was never a right time." Hank's eyes shot to her, clearly in surprise, and I shook my head. Sander...Hank...me - how many times did this have to happen before I finally got it?

"Don't bother," I told her, and I meant it. Fuck. Them. Both.

"Hey, man, don't get mad at her. This was all me," Hank said.

"Really, 'cause the picture sure looks like both of you. You just couldn't leave her alone, could you? I have to hand it to you; it looks like all of your manipulations finally paid off. Tell me, have you tasted her yet?" Ignoring Olivia's gasp, I dug deep, down into the depths of my self-loathing, into the endless pit of pain, the pain that Olivia and her magic snatch had somehow managed to annihilate. "Have you sunk into her yet, because I'm here to tell you, she's good, maybe even the best." Her sob cut, to the point I almost couldn't finish. "A word of advice. Don't let her blow you, because once she wraps those golden lips around your cock, you'll do anything for her," my eyes flicked from

Hank to Olivia, who was now openly crying, and finished, "but make sure you don't give her your heart, because she'll fucking destroy it."

"You're one cold sonofabitch," Hank snarled. "You can do better than this," he told Olivia, and I charged him. Marcel and Sean walked in as I swung the first punch. It landed on the side of Hank's jaw with a loud smack. Olivia screamed. Before I could land another blow, they were on me and pulling me back.

"What the fuck?" Marcel shouted.

"I deserved that, but it's the only one you're getting," Hank warned. I dove at him again, but Sean and Marcel had too tight of a hold on me. "You're a stupid motherfucker," Hank growled. "For reasons I will never know, she loves your sorry ass." I was too messed up in the head to listen. Every part of me hurt, but especially my heart.

"Fuck you." I glanced at her, and said, "Fuck you both. I'm good," I growled, shrugging off their hands. On the way out the door, I told Marcel to take me back to the hotel.

"Chaz!" Olivia called out, but I was done.

We were done.

# CHAPTER TWENTY-FOUR

## "Times Like These"

*Olivia*

"What have I done?" I whispered as I watched Chaz, Marcel, and Sean walk out of the room. I was so stupid. All I had to do was tell Chaz the truth, and what did I do? I sat on it and made excuses in my head because I didn't want to rock the boat. Well, the boat had just capsized with me in it. Why didn't I tell him? The truth always, always, always comes out. I, of all people, knew this.

"If you ask me, he just did you a favor. Motherfucker, that hurt," Hank growled, while rubbing his hand over his jaw.

I whirled on him, and said, "I want to know who sent him that text, and I want to know why."

Earlier, after my scorching hot drum lesson with Chaz, I rushed back to the dressing room to make sure everything was in order for dinner. My plan was to do a quick clean up while the guys played their first set, so I could make it to the stage for set two. On the way to the stage, I ran into a group of Melties who'd had a little too much to drink. When asked what they were doing, they explained how they were trying to break into Grant Hardy's dressing room. When I attempted to steer them back toward the stage, they got mouthy, which meant I had to call security. This resulted in me missing the remainder of the show. If that wasn't bad enough, Hank, who conveniently came to my rescue, decided he wanted to apologize for the other night...in great detail, which he was in the middle of doing when Chaz walked in and blasted us both.

I knew that Chaz had a mean temper. I'd seen it directed at other people, but never at me, and never like this. I may have hurt him, but in return, he shredded me.

"I've got to go."

"Not a good idea," Hank replied. "Security can't leave right now, so you'll have to wait until someone can break away to take you."

"I need to go," I repeated.

"Don't you dare leave this building without a security escort," he snapped, and my eyes immediately filled. Great, now I had Hank mad at me.

"I hurt him, Hank. I was trying to protect you, the band, myself...and for what?"

"Olivia—"

"No, really? Yes, he was ugly to me, but I messed up. You don't know Chaz like I do, none of you do. I love him, genuinely from the bottom of my heart, love him. Now, I have to *go*."

"Olivia—" he tried again.

At the door, I turned and gave him a few words of advice. "You need to stop. Stop antagonizing Chaz. Stop with the dick measuring games. Someone is trying to hurt us. Not just you and me, but all of us. This has to stop. *We* need to stop it."

As I walked out the door, I heard him say, "Don't you dare leave the building, Olivia," but I was no longer thinking of

Hank. My mind was on how to make things right with Chaz. The dressing room was filled with fans, which was good, because then no one would be watching me. After making sure everything was running smoothly, I grabbed my purse from the locker and slipped out of the room. My phone rang right as I hit the front doors of the arena. When I saw Hank's name, I sent the call to voicemail. It rang again as I was getting into the cab. This time, I turned it off altogether. During the cab ride back to the hotel, I worked on what to say to Chaz. Somehow, I didn't think saying, "I didn't tell you Hank tried to kiss me because I was worried you would kill him," would fly. When the cab pulled in front of the hotel and I still didn't have a plan in place, I decided to wing it.

Outside of Chaz's door, I contemplated whether or not to knock. After a few minutes of pacing, I opted for the element of surprise. What was the saying, "in for a penny, in for a pound?" Well, I was in for much more than that. I was in for my heart. So, I dug inside my purse, found the key card to his suite, and inserted it into the slot. Chaz wasn't hard to find. He was sitting in one of the living room chairs. On the coffee table in front of him was a bottle of whiskey. His fingers were wrapped around a half empty glass and his eyes were watching me. The blank expression on his face made me tread carefully. When I saw my bag sitting at the foot of his chair, my heart plummeted. He was kicking me out. Pulse pounding, dry mouthed fear sliced through me as I dropped my eyes to the glass of whiskey in his hand. The realization that I'd driven him to drink was more than I could bear.

"Let me explain," I said.

"No explanation needed. Here's your shit, now get out." His stone-cold tone, combined with his glacial stare, made my heart squeeze.

"Don't do this," I whispered.

"Do what, Olivia? Kiss other women? Lie to you? *This*," he stressed, "isn't on me. It's all on you." He was right, but he was also wrong.

I tried again. "Please, just hear me out. Then I promise I'll leave." His glass hit the table with a loud thud as he leaned forward and dropped his elbows to his knees. For a split-second, I thought I was getting somewhere, but his eyes drifted back to mine with that same frigid stare, and I knew I was losing him.

"You don't get it, do you? The time to share has come and gone. I don't care what you have to say, because I wouldn't believe it anyway. You've made it perfectly clear I can't trust you. So, other than the fact that I don't want or need another lying bitch fucking with my life, there's nothing left to say."

"I'm not lying," I cut in.

His eyes flashed in anger as he grabbed the glass, hurled it against the wall, and roared, "Get. The Fuck. Out!" Surprisingly, the glass didn't shatter. It bounced twice and rolled right to where I was standing. In a wave of overwhelming emotion, it hit me. I tried to stop it, but couldn't, because it was bigger than me. His words hurt. The thought of losing him over something so stupid, something I could have prevented, was too much, and I burst into tears. He made a move, not in my direction, but toward the door, and I completely panicked. Before he walked out of the suite and locked me out of his life forever, I rushed forward, slid in front of him, and blocked his escape.

"If you won't go, then I will," he said through clenched teeth.

I rose up onto my tiptoes, fisted his shirt, and sobbed, "Don't do this. You're right; it is on me. I should have told you. The night of the party, Hank walked me to my room. At the door, he tried to kiss me."

He shook his head. "It's too late, Olivia."

"The picture must have been taken seconds before I stopped him," I continued, ignoring his last comment. "I stopped him,

Chaz, I swear. His lips never touched mine. I put my hand over my mouth before that could happen. His lips hit my hand and I bumped my head on the wall, but they never touched mine. I know it was stupid. I should have told you. I didn't kiss him. I wouldn't do that to you, I swear." My breath hitched when his expression marginally softened, so I kept at him, "Hank apologized, said he was messed up about Marcy, and that he knew I was with you. I was worried you would kill him. I was going to tell you, but then I saw the picture on your computer, and we started talking; I forgot because it wasn't important to me." I paused to take in a deep breath.

"Are you done yet?" he asked in that same icy-cold voice, and my heart sank.

Angrily swiping at my tears, I said, "Don't go. Please... forgive me." When he didn't respond, I knew I'd lost, that it was time to give up. "I'm done," I quietly replied, as I dropped back onto my heels and let go of his shirt. With my heart in my throat, I turned to leave.

"Olivia," he called out. I paused with my back to him. Afraid to turn around. Afraid of losing him. Just plain...afraid. "Jesus, you drive me absolutely insane, woman. I don't know how to do this shit. One minute I'm riding high and the next I'm scraping rock bottom. I want to kill Sander because he had you first, and I want to kill Hank for trying to take you from me. I want you all the time, to the point where I sometimes think I'm losing my mind." His confession was more than I'd ever hoped for, more than I probably deserved. As I turned to confront him, to tell him that he wasn't the only one losing his mind, he was there...right in front of me. Suddenly, his arms were around me and we were moving. I'd barely had time to take a breath before I felt the wall at my back. He leaned into me and dropped his face to my neck.

"I'm scared to let you go," I whispered.

"Then don't," he whispered back, as he titled his head and

slowly touched his mouth to mine. Right as our lips connected, someone pounded on the door.

"Fuck," he growled. Then he pushed back from the wall and yanked open the door.

"Is Olivia here?" I heard Hank ask. *Someone, please shoot me!* I screamed in my head.

"I'm here!" I called out.

Hank stepped in and I watched his shoulders visibly sag with relief when he spotted me standing there. I felt bad. I'd blatantly disobeyed his orders. "What in the hell were you thinking?" he asked. "Someone is fucking with us and you decide to just take off on your own, without telling anyone? What if something had happened to you?"

"I'm fine, Hank." I held up my arms to show him I was still in one piece.

"What am I missing?" Chaz asked, skeptically eyeing the two of us.

"Nothing," I abruptly answered, and shot Hank a *shut the hell up* look.

"Nothing my ass," Hank countered. "She left the venue early, walked right out of the building, without telling anyone she was leaving, and caught a cab back to the hotel." Chaz let out a sigh of frustration. I, however, didn't say a word. Hank was right. It was irresponsible. At the time, all I could think about was getting to Chaz and making things right. Still, Hank didn't have to tattle on me.

"Well, as you can see, she's fine," Chaz responded.

After a long, angst-filled minute, Hank turned to me, and said, "Don't do that again."

"Duly noted," I swiftly replied.

"Are we done here?" Chaz asked.

"No, we're not," Hank snapped, his eyes still on me. "You're right, I need to get my shit together. Things haven't been good between Marcy and me, for a while now, and it's well past time I dealt with it." His eyes moved to Chaz. "There was never a kiss. Olivia stopped me before I made a fool of myself." He let out a dry laugh. "A lot of good that did me, huh? Look, I'm sorry. I've been a dick, especially to you. I don't expect your forgiveness, but you shouldn't take it out on her." Chaz responded with a nod of acknowledgment, but I could see he wasn't completely sold on Hank's apology.

"What are we going to do about the text?" I asked.

"I think you two have better things to discuss right now. The text can hold until tomorrow," Hank replied, and without another word, he walked out of the suite.

"What a night," I sighed as I collapsed onto the sofa. When Chaz opted for the chair instead of the seat next to me, my stomach dropped in disappointment. "Please, don't be mad," I pleaded for the millionth time. A frustrated sigh shot from his mouth as he lowered his elbows to his knees and dropped his stare to the floor. *He's done with me*, I thought, and ice-cold fingers of fear slithered through me. *Do something!* I screamed in my head. Without thinking, I popped up from the sofa. His head rose, his dark blue eyes on me, warily watching as I neared where he was sitting. I stopped in front of him - almost touching him, but not quite - with my heart in my throat, wishing, wanting, praying for him just to reach out and touch me. He didn't, and the thought that maybe he hadn't forgiven me, that maybe he wasn't going to, made me want to cry all over again.

"I'm sorry," I whispered. After a long pause, he tagged my legs and pulled me onto his lap. My heart danced like crazy inside my chest.

"I said some shit things to you tonight," he softly murmured in my ear. "I wasn't lying when I told you I was a dick, but tonight I let it get out of control."

"You did," I agreed.

"I meant what I said."

"Which part?" I asked.

"About you destroying my heart." With my hand to his chest, I pushed back and glared at him.

"Though, I meant it when I said you were the best." In a gentle motion, he swept his finger across my bottom lip. "And you do have golden lips."

"Thanks, I think, though that's not quite what you said," I dryly responded, and smiled when his body shook with quiet laughter. His laughter faded to something I couldn't read, and I was relieved when he decided to share.

"You're killin' me here, Hot Mess. I'm not kidding. You've got me by the nuts, and it scares the living fuck out of me." Deep in the depths of his blue eyes, I saw fear, but I also saw love.

"I didn't mean to hurt you. It was stupid and I'm sorry, because I really, really love you. I—" His mouth swooped down and cut off the remainder of my sentence. I opened for him and sighed when he swept in with a tender kiss.

That night, he took me slow and easy, making sure to touch and taste every part of me. For the first time since we'd been together, he gave me free rein to do the same. I knew I wasn't fully back in yet, but it was a start in the right direction, and I vowed to never hurt him like that again. He'd gifted me with his heart and I needed to protect it. Long after he fell asleep, I lay there thinking. The more I thought, the angrier I got. That picture was taken with the intent to do damage. It almost worked, too. My mind wandered to Chaz's emails and I wondered if they were somehow connected. Chaz didn't want to talk to LASH, but hopefully I could convince him otherwise...

I awakened the next morning to an empty bed. Chaz's spot was cold, which meant he'd been up for a while. On my way to the bathroom, I lifted his t-shirt from the bedroom chair and slipped it over my head. As I passed by the bed, I snagged a fresh pair of panties from my bag, slid them on, and made my way to the living area, only to discover that Chaz had left me coffee, but no note - not that I expected him to leave one or anything, because that would be way too domesticated of him. I poured a cup of coffee and plopped down onto the dining room chair with a loud sigh. I was worried about the pictures. If you asked me, the whole thing was super creepy. I got why Chaz didn't want to share. I wouldn't have either, but what if it was more than he was making it out to be? I was running over scenarios in my head when he rolled in wearing running shorts and a tank top. Under the tank, his muscles glistened with sweat. Normally, this would turn me off, but this was Chaz, and sweaty Chaz was seriously hot. Visions of wall sex, or maybe even dining room table sex danced through my head as I watched him lean against the kitchen counter and suck down a bottle of water. His lips turned up into a smile when he noticed me staring at him.

"Sorry, sweetheart, you'll have to wait until later to jump me. LASH wants to meet with us in Grant's suite in thirty minutes." His cocky tone was cute, but irritating. I let him know this with a dirty look, which he responded to with a laugh. When I explained how I needed to run to my room for a quick shower and change of clothes, he sauntered over to where I was sitting, pulled me onto my feet, and planted a wet one right smack on my lips. Then he strolled off to the bedroom whistling what sounded like John Cougar's, "Hurt So Good."

Forty-five minutes later, Marcel answered the door to Grant's suite.

"You're late" he said as he ushered me inside.

"Sorry. I couldn't get my hair to behave," I lied, when in fact,

I was late because I'd discovered my period had started and I had to run downstairs for last minute provisions.

"How hard is it to pull it back into a ponytail?" he remarked.

"Shut it, smart ass," I responded with a laugh.

As we rounded the corner to the dining area all eyes turned to me.

"You're late," Grant stated.

"She had hair trouble," Marcel replied.

"Rowan takes like three seconds to pull her hair into a ponytail," Nash commented.

"Oh, for Christ sake. I started my period, people. Give me a break!" I shouted, and the entire room froze as I circled the table and plopped down onto the chair next to Chaz. "Where are Bobby and Tut, and are you ever going to get that tooth fixed?" I directed at Nash as I ignored their horrified stares.

Nash glared at Chaz. "Thanks to dickhead, here. I have to see a specialist."

"The hillbilly look suits you," Chaz remarked in a smart-ass tone.

"Bobby and Tut will be here in about ten minutes or so," Grant cut in before Nash could respond. "Marcy wanted a few minutes of our time, so I'm conferencing her in." My stomach pitched at the mention of Marcy's name. Sensing my unease, Chaz reached over and grabbed my hand. While we waited for Marcy to answer, he twined our fingers together and gave them reassuring squeeze.

Marcy finally answered, and Grant dove in. "Hi, Marcy, we're waiting on Bobby and Tut to arrive, so I thought it would be a good time to call."

"Thanks, Grant, I promise to make this as short and painless as possible. As you all know, my father is dying and my mother can't take care of herself. I'm stressed to the gills because I want to be there with you, but I have to be here. I'm not able to effectively do both, therefore, I think it's best if I step away." My pulse leapt into my throat.

"You don't need to step away. How can we make it easier on you?" Grant asked.

"You really can't. I'm stuck between a rock and a hard place. Believe me when I say I've agonized over this, but at the end of the day, I have to do what's right for everyone, and right now, that's for me to take a step back. So I'm tendering my resignation, effective immediately. I can help Olivia, or whomever with the transition, but I'm just not able to handle the job and my family at this time." Chaz's eyes sliced to mine and widened in surprise. In fact, everyone seemed surprised... but Hank...Hank looked completely poleaxed.

"There's no need to resign. Concentrate on your parents and don't worry about us," Grant told her. He glanced over at me as he said, "Olivia has us handled on this end, at least through the end of the tour. Once the tour is over, we'll reevaluate." I nodded in agreement and he mouthed, "Thank you."

"Thanks, guys. I've really enjoyed working with you and I apologize for acting like such a shrew these past weeks." It was clear she could not be persuaded to stay on.

"Family first, Marcy," Nash said, and everyone chimed in with similar sentiments. Then Grant disconnected the call. Hank didn't utter a sound.

"You okay?" Grant asked. At first, I thought he was asking Hank, but then Chaz squeezed my hand, and I realized he was talking to me.

"Who me? I'm good. A little stressed, but good," I told him.

"We'll make sure the transition runs smoothly, right, guys?"

"Right," Evan replied.

"Yep," Nash chimed in.

Chaz just smiled.

"While we're all together, Hank wanted to talk about the

upcoming three-day break. It's almost here and he needs to know your plans," Grant said. All eyes moved to Hank, who looked as if he was still recovering from Marcy's call. I couldn't help but feel bad for the guy. It was obvious she hadn't told him. If you asked me, this was another strike against her.

Hank pushed off the wall and moved to the front of the table, where he talked about security measures for the upcoming break. After explaining how no one was going anywhere without a security escort, he asked for everyone's plans.

"Nash and I are going home," Grant said.

"I'll cover the two of you," Hank told them.

"I'm going home as well," Evan added.

"I'll take Evan," Sampson said with a huge grin on his face. "I have a lady friend who lives close by. I think I'll pay her a little visit."

"I need someone to drive me to Indiana," Chaz said. All eyes shot to him.

"What's in Indiana?" Grant asked. Chaz's gaze slid to me, and I gave him a nod of encouragement.

"My mom," he told them.

"Are you going with him?" Hank asked me.

"I would, but now that Marcy's stepped down, I could use the spare time to familiarize myself with her files and such." Chaz gave my hand a comforting squeeze.

"I'll be back in time for the bus," Chaz told Hank.

"I'll hang here with Olivia," Sean offered. Hank's brow furrowed in thought.

"No, I'm flipping this around. Sorry, Sampson, you'll have to visit your lady friend later. I want you with Chaz. Marcel, other than me, you have the most knowledge about the business. You're with Olivia. Sean, that leaves you with Evan."

Sampson gave Chaz a hopeful look. "Does your mom cook? 'Cause right about now I could use a home-cooked meal and a big ass slice of homemade pie."

Chaz's hand spasmed in mine, before he answered, "I think she's dead." It felt as if the air had been sucked from the room.

Evan jerked his eyes from his phone and frowned. "Whoa, did we miss something?" Surprisingly, Chaz answered him.

"My mom and I weren't close, so we didn't talk often. Something came up, and I needed to talk to her, but found that her phone service had been disconnected. When I called my uncle to get her new number, he told me she'd died."

"Fuck, that sucks. Sorry, man," Nash responded. I gave Chaz's hand a squeeze of encouragement.

"Yeah, well, since my uncle said he didn't really have any information about it, I called the vital statistics office to see if they had a record of her death and they didn't. I'm not sure what to believe, so I want to check shit out for myself," he finished with a shrug.

"You could always ask Bobby to look into it," Evan proposed.

"I could, but I'm not. At least, not yet," Chaz answered. Bobby and Tut walked through the door, and the conversation turned to what they'd found.

Once they were seated, Bobby launched in. "We wanted to give you a quick briefing on what's transpired over the past few days. Larry hasn't given us much. As of right now, we know there's someone pulling his strings, but he's holding tight in his refusal to implicate anyone. As of right now, we need to look for a paper trail."

"Which means?" Grant asked.

"We try and find an exchange of money, any emails, or other forms of communication that help establish that someone other than Larry was involved.

"Do it," Grant said.

"Done." He turned to Chaz, and asked, "Now what's this I hear about a text message?" Chaz explained about the text he'd received. "Show me," Bobby said. He slid his phone over to Bobby. After staring at it for a moment, Bobby's eyes shifted to Hank.

"I didn't kiss her," Hank defensively responded. Bobby shook his head. Then he punched a bunch of buttons and explained how he'd forwarded the text to his phone in order for him to properly dissect the message. Once this was done, the meeting was adjourned.

"So, Aunt Thelma has landed," Chaz said on the way back to our rooms. It took me a minute to decipher his reference.

"I think you mean, Aunt Flo," I remarked. "And yes, I'm very happy she's here."

"Is that something we need to worry about?" His question caught me off guard.

"I told you, I'm on the pill. I'm not out to trap you with little Chazs, if that's what you're asking," I stiffly replied. When I realized how bitchy that sounded, I buffered it with humor. "What? Don't you want children?" I teased as we stepped onto the elevator.

His eyes locked on mine, and in a deep, sexy-as-sin voice, he said, "With you, I want it all."

# CHAPTER TWENTY-FIVE

## "Road Trippin'"

*Chaz*

The morning Sampson and I were due to leave for Indiana, Bobby and Tut showed up with news about Larry. Grant, Nash, and Evan had flights to catch, so we all met in Grant's suite with little time to spare. When Bobby explained that Larry was not only guilty, but also working for Blane Hamilton, the room went silent.

Then Grant exploded. "Are you shitting me? Christ! He's like a fucking fungus!" He wasn't exaggerating. Blane Hamilton was a menace.

"Told you we should have pressed charges," I muttered under my breath.

"How is Blane involved?" Nash asked, right as Hank walked into the room. After catching Hank up, Bobby answered Nash's question.

"According to Larry, Blane came to him shortly after he was fired. Blane knew Larry's wife had been diagnosed with breast cancer and that Larry was drowning in medical bills, so he offered him a way out. Blane's plan was to make Marcy look incompetent. When she failed, he would sweep in and save the day."

"Blane is a sneaky rat fuck," I stated.

"So, because of Blane's manipulations, Larry's now going to jail?" Nash asked.

"Fuck!" Grant exclaimed.

"Once we explained what we had on him, Larry cracked wide open," Tut answered.

"I'm confused. Marcy's not even in the picture," Olivia commented.

"Larry said he pointed that out to Blane, but Blane didn't care. You're Marcy's proxy, therefore, if you fuck up, Marcy will still take the fall," Tut explained.

"Larry took money from Blane with the intent to do harm. Sick wife or not, he deserves what he's getting," Hank angrily retorted.

"If Blane was trying to make Olivia, or Marcy look bad, then why fuck with the rigging?" Evan questioned.

"Good question. Larry said Blane just wanted to scare everyone, that he only partially loosened the rigging, and there's no way it could have fallen all the way," Bobby responded.

Nash's eyes flashed with anger. "He could have killed us."

"Please tell me Blane's going down for this," I remarked.

"Blane was picked up by the police late last night. He spent the night in jail and is currently waiting for a bail hearing," Bobby told us.

Nash turned to Grant. "Blane should be considered a flight risk. Is there any way we can make sure he doesn't get approved for bail?"

Grant addressed Olivia. "I need for you to call and fill our legal team in on what's happened. They'll know what to do."

"I'm on it," she replied. As I watched her make notes in her notebook, I thought about how good things had been between us lately. The night in St. Louis when the shit blew up with Hank, I was beyond chafed. I was ready to kick her ass to the curb and call it quits, but thankfully, Olivia kept at me. Since then, we'd spent every night together. There was no better feeling than falling asleep with Olivia pressed to my side. A couple of times since then I'd awakened in the middle of the night, soaked in sweat after being chased by nightmares. Both times, Olivia gave me what I needed. In return, I'd given her all of me. No more secrets. Just me.

Bobby's next statement pulled me from my thoughts. "The only thing Larry refused to cop to was the text to Chaz."

Grant's brow shot up. "And you believed him?"

"Larry held out for all of three seconds before breaking. He was in it for the money. When the rigging fell, he told Blane he was out, but Blane had other ideas. He was freaked, but still holding onto the hope that Blane would rescue him. By the time we rolled in with evidence, he'd smartened up and realized that Blane was hanging him out to dry. The moment we offered him a deal in exchange for his cooperation, he snapped it up. At that point, his future behind bars was on the line, so yes, I believe him when he said he had nothing to do with the text. Think about it. Why would he admit to the rest but lie about that?" Bobby answered.

"Did you try tracing the number?" I asked.

"We did, but whoever sent it used a prepaid phone and unfortunately has it turned off. If the phone gets turned on, we might be able to trace who is on the other end by using a spy app to monitor their messages, but until that happens we've got dick," Tut said.

"So you think there's more than one person fucking with us. Is that what you're trying to say?" Grant snapped, his eyes locking on mine. At the same time, Olivia glanced my way, and I knew what she was thinking. She wanted me to tell them about the pictures. If I did that, the rest would come out. I didn't respond to Grant's question. I didn't look over at Olivia. She could push all she wanted, but it wasn't hers to share. It was mine, and I wasn't ready.

"What aren't you saying?" Nash asked, his eyes darting back and forth between the two of us.

"Nothing," Olivia quickly answered. "Just...the thought of someone creeping around, taking pictures of us, bothers me."

Bobby nodded his head in agreement. "I can't say I blame you, but you are in a high-profile business. It's not unheard of for someone to slip past security and make it onto a celebrity's floor. Do I think this is the case? No, but for right now, it's all we've got." Olivia bugged her eyes at me, but I wasn't budging. "We're going to wrap a few things up here, but wanted to let you know that, unless you need anything else from us, we're scheduled to leave for Charlotte on Sunday."

"I think we're good. I hate to see Larry go down, but I can't say I won't be happy to finally have Blane out of the picture for good," Grant told him. After we said goodbye to Bobby and Tut, Hank told us to wait for our security detail to come and get us before leaving.

Olivia and I stepped onto the elevator, and I pulled her in for a kiss. "When I get back tonight, I want you in my bed," I told her. She tilted her head up and I could see something working behind her eyes.

"I wish you'd told them about the pictures," she finally admitted.

"I know."

She dropped her forehead to my chest. "What if whoever sent them does something bad, like tries to hurt you or something?"

I gathered her hair in my fist and tugged on it until I got her eyes. "If things get more serious, I will say something."

"You promise?" she asked.

"Will you be in my bed when I get back?" I countered. She answered with a smile, which earned her another kiss.

♪ ♪ ♪

The drive took us three hours and twenty-two minutes. Three hours and twenty-two minutes of listening to Sampson sing, fart, belch, and babble about nonsensical shit. He tried several times to stick his nose into my business, but I shut him down. We weren't girlfriends out for a springtime drive. He didn't need my life story, and I sure as fuck didn't want his, but he didn't get the hint and decided to give it to me anyway.

Once in Indianapolis, we drove straight to the vital stats office and hit our first dead end. I can't say I was surprised to discover there was no record of my mother's death, but I was disappointed.

Next, Sampson drove me to the house I grew up in - the exact same house I swore I'd never return to.

"You okay?" he asked as he pulled up to the curb and parked.

Without thinking, I replied, "I swore I'd never come back here."

"Bad memories?"

"You have no idea," I muttered, as I opened the passenger door and stepped from the car.

"What are we looking for?" he asked as we made our way up the front drive.

"I'll let you know when I see it," I told him and pressed the doorbell. A few seconds passed before we heard someone coming. The door finally opened.

"Yes? Can I help you?" a woman at least a decade older than my mother asked. Surprise got my tongue and I stumbled for what to say. Somewhere, in the back of my mind, I thought my mom would answer the door. Sampson elbowed me.

"Uhhh, yeah, I'm looking for Francine Dunn," I half-stammered. Her brow crinkled.

"Who?" she asked.

"Francine Dunn. She owns this house, or she used to," I replied. With a flick of her wrist, she dislodged her horn-rimmed glasses from the top of her ice-blue beehive, slid them onto her face, and scanned me up and down.

"And you are?"

"Her son, Chaz," I answered, and followed it up with, "we're not here to bother you. I just want to know where my mother is, that's all."

"Well, let's see. Your parents sold me the house a little over four years ago, though, off the top of my head, I can't say I remember where they moved to."

"Parents?" I asked, thinking I'd misheard her.

"Yes, your father was such the charmer, and your poor mother. You know, I get a little confused every now and then..." Her voice trailed to silence and her brow furrowed. "You don't know where your own parents are?" I tried to think of what to say, but came up blank.

"They've been estranged for a while now, but Chaz would like to make amends, which is why we're here," Sampson cut in. I gave him a look of gratitude.

Blue hair clapped her hands like a little girl. "Oh, I bet they would love that."

"Do you happen to have a copy of the paperwork from the sale?" I asked.

"Oh, look at me, I'm being so rude!" she gasped. "Come in and let me fish it out for you. Would you like some tea while I look?"

"No thanks," we both replied, and followed her inside the house.

"What am I missing?" Sampson whispered, while we waited in the living room, which thankfully didn't remotely resemble the living room from my childhood.

"I don't have a dad," I flatly responded.

"So?" he asked, clearly not getting it.

"How did my charmer of a dad sell the house if I don't have one?" I asked.

"Ohhhhh, shiiiiiiit," he drawled, when clarity hit.

"And you're in security?" I questioned.

"Fuck...youuuuuuu have a really nice house," he said, shifting his words when blue hair suddenly reappeared.

"Thank you. Here you go. I'm Mavis, by the way," she said, handing me the contract. I took it from her, quickly flipped to the back page, and scanned to the bottom, where the name Francine Dunn was written.

No dad, and unfortunately, no contact information.

"Well?" Sampson asked. I shook my head and handed her back the contract. Then we thanked her, and got the hell out of there. We'd hit dead end number two.

Back in the car, Sampson turned to me, and said, "You've got to give me something."

"I don't know. I keep circling back to the conversation with my uncle. As of right now, he's the only one who knows anything."

"Where does your uncle live?" Sampson asked as we headed to the car.

"In Bedford, which is another three plus hours away from here."

"I say we pay old..." his eyes flicked to me.

"Bill," I told him.

"I say we pay old Bill a little visit."

Three hours later, we arrived in Bedford. By that point we were beyond sick of each other, or at least I was with him. The man never shut up. Not only that, but he sang whether or not he knew the lyrics to the song, bitched nonstop about my finger drumming, calling it a form of Tourette Syndrome, and even picked his nose a couple of times on the sly.

We pulled in front my uncle's house and I laid it out for him as plain as day. "My aunt is a raging bitch and both she and my uncle are bigots."

"So what are you really trying to say?" he asked. I stared at him as if he was the biggest idiot on the face of the planet. Then I opened the car door, and extracted myself from his presence before saying something I'd later regret. He caught up with me right as I rang the doorbell, and whispered, "This should be fun." After what seemed like years, a little old woman answered the door.

"Can I help you?" she asked.

"Uhhh, yeah, I'm looking for Bill and Darlene Dunn."

"I'm sorry, but Bill and Darlene no longer live here." Sampson shot me a look as if to say here we go again.

"Do you happen to know their new address?" I asked.

"Why, yes I do. Are you familiar with the area?"

"I am."

"Well, they bought the old Malvern house." My jaw hit the ground with a thud. Literally, the Malvern house was worth at least a million dollars. My uncle was a civil servant for Christ's sake. How in the hell did he afford the Malvern house?

"How long have you lived here?" Sampson asked. Okay, so maybe he wasn't stupid after all.

"Gosh, a little over three years now," she responded.

"Did they win the fucking lottery or something?" The second I asked it, her face froze in this *oh shit, these men could be bad* kind of expression. Then her eyes darted back and forth between the two of us. "Who did you say you were again?" she asked.

"We didn't," I angrily bit out as I turned and started back for the car.

"Where're we off to now?" Sampson asked as he caught up to me.

"We're going to visit my uncle in his mansion."

Five minutes later, we pulled in front of my uncle's new pad.

"Holy shiiiiiit, this place is dope," Sampson drawled. He was not wrong. The house was impressive - as in the cover of *Architectural Digest* impressive. When Earle and I would visit my uncle and aunt, we would drive past this place. How in the hell were my uncle and aunt living here?

"Brace," I said, as I rang the doorbell. After a few more tries, we gave up. We'd officially hit dead end number three.

An hour into the drive back to Chicago, Sampson and I were discussing the ways in which my uncle could have obtained a house like that on his salary, when my phone rang. "It's Olivia," I said, before answering. "Hey, babe. We're on our way back now."

"Chaz?" Her voice sounded off, and I immediately knew something was wrong.

"Talk to me."

"Someone sent me an email. I think it's from the same person that's been sending the pictures to you." The sound of her voice made my gut twist.

"Shit! What does it say?" I asked.

"Ummm...I think you need to see it for yourself." Her hesitant response told me it was bad.

"Are you in my suite?"

"Yes." Damnit! Here I was, in the middle of Bumfuck Egypt, while someone was fucking with my girl.

"Lock yourself in. Sampson will call Marcel. He can keep

you company until we get back. Don't open the door for anyone but Marcel. I'll call you back in a little while," I told her, and hung up.

Sampson's eyes cut to me. "You'd best start talking, white boy."

After giving the dash a few hard punches, I told him everything.

# CHAPTER TWENTY-SIX

## "Bang and Blame"

*Olivia*

Half an hour after Chaz's departure, Marcy called to discuss the transition. She was polite, but distant, which was fine with me, because I was no longer interested in being her friend. The call took approximately forty-five minutes, in which time we developed a plan of action. In the next day or so, I would send her a list of questions, which she would respond to in detail. In the meantime, she would email any pertinent information needed for me to effectively finish out the tour. By the time we hung up, Chaz and Sampson had been on the road a little over an hour and I was beginning to regret my decision not to join them.

The rest of the day dragged. Marcy's files were straight-up, no-nonsense, easy to read, and took me no more than an hour to look at. Over my fourth cup of coffee, I made my list for her. As the tour was almost over, the list wasn't very long. After that, I called to confirmed Meltdown's reservations in Philadelphia, and triple-checked that both the venue and the caterers were ready to receive the band. I moved my things from my room to Chaz's suite before taking a long, hot shower. Marcel stopped by to check up on me on his way to work out and again on his way to see on how the roadies were faring without Larry. Chaz texted while I was on the phone with my mom to let me know he was going to be delayed getting back.

Marcel stopped by around six and we ordered room service. During dinner, he shared a little about himself. I learned that he was the youngest of six, that he, Sampson, and Hank had known each other since high school, and that one day he wanted kids, but had yet to find the right person to settle down with.

He took off shortly after dinner, but only after making me promise to call if I needed anything. Before getting ready for bed, I checked emails. One particular email stuck out - probably because the subject line was written in all caps. It read, YOU'RE JUST ANOTHER NUMBER. I hovered the cursor over it for a second before clicking it open. My chest constricted as a picture popped onto the screen.

"Holy shit," I whispered as I scrolled through picture after picture of Chaz, each with a different woman, and all focused on the same thing: Chaz having sex. I didn't know whether to be disgusted or impressed. One thing was for sure, Chaz liked variety and he wasn't fond of beds. *Yikes!* I paused on the last picture. In the photo, Chaz was leaning with his back against the bus. Chelle was on her knees in front of him. I recognized her from all of the media hype. Her mouth was on him...as in on him, on him and his hands were in her hair. His head was tilted down and his eyes were intently focused on what she was doing.

Directly below the picture was a note.

*You think you're special. But you're not.*

I didn't know what to do with this. I mean, I wasn't stupid. Rock stars were notorious dogs, some more so than others, as proven by these pictures, but still...these weren't taken randomly.

In order to get these shots, for someone to get this close...my lungs seized as my next thought hit me.

"It's someone we know," I whispered, and immediately started to panic. *Breathe,* I told myself as I scrambled for what to do. I could call Chaz, call Marcel, or take another shower to collect myself and try to scrub off the grime I'd just been spattered with. What I didn't need to do, but really, really wanted to, was lose my shit.

In the end, I decided to call Chaz. After all, it was his sexual reputation on the line. Chaz wanted to know what the email said, but I just couldn't explain how someone had sent fifteen different pictures of him doing the nasty. He told me to call Marcel. I wasn't sure this was a good idea. As it turned out, I didn't have to worry, because the minute I hung up with Chaz, Marcel called.

Within minutes, Marcel arrived. Gone was my easygoing dinner companion and in his place, was a stone-faced, do-not-fuck-with-me, security man. He took one look at me, and said, "Let me see it." Chaz and I hadn't talked about what to do. What if I showed Marcel and Chaz got mad at me? "Show me the picture, Olivia," he commanded in a scary-as-hell voice.

"Pictures," I corrected, "and I can't. Not without Chaz's permission." His jaw clenched with irritation, right before he reached inside his back pocket, yanked out his phone, scrolled to a number, and hit send.

Sampson's voice rang through the room. "Yo."

"Put Chaz on," Marcel told him.

We heard shuffling and then Chaz ask, "Yeah?"

"Your woman won't show me the email without your permission," Marcel told him.

"Tell her I said to show you," he replied.

"Done," Marcel responded, and disconnected the call. "Show me," he ordered.

"Fine!" I snapped, and quickly moved to retrieve the computer from the bedroom.

While Marcel took the photographic trip through Chaz's very active sex life, I paced the floor. After several minutes, his eyes lifted to mine.

"We all have a past," he said in a gentle sage-like voice, as if telling me something I didn't already know. "You, of all people, know the lifestyle. Grant and Nash were wild as shit before Mallory and Rowan tamed their asses. This right here," he pointed to the computer screen, "is someone trying to fuck with you. That's all."

"It's not the pictures that bother me." His brow rose in a gesture of disbelief, and I waved my hand in the air. "You know what I mean. Yes, it bothers me that I'm sleeping with the village bicycle, but look at them. In order for someone to take those, they had to be close, right? As in, *follow Chaz around and not get noticed because they're part of the inner circle* close."

"The village bicycle?" he asked, his lips twitching with humor.

I let out a frustrated growl. "You're not listening, Marcel." His expression sobered.

"I hear you and I'm not discounting your theory, but think about it. Chaz is surrounded by people twenty-four-seven. Paparazzi are around all the time. They are both persistent and very sneaky. As you can see from those pictures, he wasn't exactly concerned about discretion. In fact, you're the first woman I've ever seen him spin his wheels over." His words were sweet, but there was a lot he didn't know. A lot I couldn't tell him. In the end, I opted to shut my mouth and wait for Chaz to arrive.

After our talk, Marcel and I settled in front of the television, where we proceeded to watch back-to-back episodes of a show about animals in the wild. It was gory, but at the same time, fascinating. I called it a night around one and stumbled to bed. It was a quarter after three when I heard voices in the living area. Chaz was back. For a moment, I considered staying put, but then I thought about Chaz having to face Marcel and Sampson without support, and hopped to.

Chaz was sitting at the table. His head snapped up from the computer screen as I walked into the room. The tick in his jaw and frenetic finger drumming told me what he thought of the pictures.

"You need to tell them," I quietly urged.

"Bobby and Tut are on their way up," he said. I watched him push back from the table, but didn't make a move in his direction. It was one thing to know and another to see. I could have gone my whole life without seeing Chaz with those women, but now that I had, it was impossible to unsee. I wasn't mad. I wasn't even disappointed. I was simply disturbed. Chaz stood and made a move toward me. "Knock when they get here," he told Marcel. Then he tagged my hand, pulled me into the bedroom, and kicked the door shut behind us. I'm not sure what I expected, but it wasn't for him to drop his forehead to mine and whisper, "I'm so fucking sorry." This, right here, is what I loved about this man. He was jagged and raw on the outside, yet smooth and tender on the inside.

"Someone wants to hurt us, Chaz." He pulled back and his eyes blazed with fury.

"I know, and I'm going to take care of it. This is the second time someone's tried to split us up. They want my attention? They've got it. Right now, I need to know that you're okay...that we're okay."

"We're okay," I replied without hesitation, and could see in his eyes that he was struggling with something.

"I wish you hadn't seen that," he shared, and my heart went out to him.

"Chaz—"

"Those pictures, the women...meant nothing. Hell, I don't even remember most of them." I placed my hand on his mouth to shut him up.

"We're *okay*," I slowly repeated.

"They're here!" Marcel shouted from the other side of the door. Chaz dropped his lips to mine, and after a slow, sweet, kiss, he grabbed my hand and walked me out to the living room, where he proceeded to tell Bobby, Tut, Sampson, and Marcel his deepest and darkest secrets. Once he answered all of their questions, he showed them the photos. Bobby confiscated the envelopes and pictures. He said he would dust them for fingerprints when they got back to Charlotte, but it was highly unlikely we would get a hit. Chaz and Sampson explained what they'd discovered in Indiana. Bobby wasn't convinced the two weren't related, but was definitely going to look into it. When he mentioned the possibility of it being two different people, my blood ran cold.

"I want to make something clear," Chaz said, before everyone took off. "This isn't a Meltdown situation. It's personal, which means that the band isn't footing the bill. I am. No one outside of this room hears anything without—"

Bobby cut him off. "As soon as you engage us, we are bound by a duty of confidentiality whether there is ink on a contract yet or not."

"You know we won't talk, but keep in mind, you're a part of a group. What hurts you; hurts everyone, and everyone deserves to know there's a threat. Also, Hank is the head of our team—" Marcel started to add before Chaz cut him off.

"We'll have a sit down, but only on my terms, and not until everyone's back. I'm not doing this shit more than once," Chaz stressed, and they both nodded.

"Just so you know, we have to be back in Charlotte on Sunday.

We're both tied up on other jobs next week. That doesn't mean we won't still be focused on you, we'll just be handling it from our Charlotte office. That being said, we can't afford to waste eleven hours on the road tomorrow when we could be working, so we're going to stay put here and fly out on Sunday," Bobby explained.

"Do you need us to stay?" Chaz asked.

"Is that an option?" Bobby asked. Chaz and Marcel discussed how to make it an option. Once the plan was in place, the meeting was adjourned.

While everyone shuffled to the door, I asked, "What if it's someone we know?"

Bobby was quick to reply. "Oh, it's definitely someone you know."

That's exactly what I was afraid of.

# CHAPTER TWENTY-SEVEN

## "Run-Around"

*Chaz*

I woke before Olivia, which was good because it gave me a minute to think. None of this made any sense. Bobby thought there might be a connection between the emails, but I didn't see what one had to do with the other.

"You okay?" Olivia asked in a sexy, sleepy voice. She was lying on her stomach with her head turned in my direction and her eyes focused on me.

Earlier this morning, after Bobby, Tut, and the guys had taken off, Olivia didn't have much to say. The fucker who sent the email didn't split us up, but there was now a distance between us that wasn't there before. Olivia denied it, but I could tell she was affected. Hell, how could she not be? If someone had sent me an email of her getting off with fifteen different guys, I would have lost my damn head. So, I gave her some space, didn't push for sex - even though I wanted to, and let her call the shots. What did she do? She crawled into bed, rolled away from me, and fell asleep. I'd given into her play, but now it was my turn.

"As a matter of fact, no. I'm not okay, and after the cold shoulder you've been giving me, it's pretty damn clear you aren't either." She gave me a wide-eyed stare, but didn't deny it. "Fuuuuuuuuck," I loudly moaned, and flopped onto my back.

"Chaz—"

"So this is it? You kept your cool when I told you I'd been sodomized, you forgave me for being a dick, but you end it over something I did before I even met you? Fucking unbelievable."

"Oh my God, could you be any more of a drama queen? I mean, seriously! Excuse me if I needed a minute to catch my breath. After seeing pictures of my boyfriend reenacting the fucking Kama Sutra with every Tina, Dawn, and Harriet in a sixty-mile radius, I think I should be allowed a minute, don't you?" She ended her ridiculous rant with a loud huff, and I couldn't help but laugh.

"Tina, Dawn, and Harriet?" I asked, and laughed even harder when she slapped me.

"It's not funny."

"It's fucking hilarious," I replied through more laughter. When she made a move to get up, I twisted sideways, grabbed her by the hips, pulled her back onto the bed, and pinned her under me. At this point, I was no longer laughing. It was time to get shit straight between us. "I told you I was sorry and I meant it. Sending those pictures to you was a crap thing to do. I won't lie, if the tables were turned and I got pictures like that of you, I would need a minute too, but your minute is now up. So let me tell you what's about to happen. First, you're going to lose the shirt and panties. Second, I'm going down on you, until you beg me to stop. Then, and only then, am I going to slide in deep and fuck those pictures from your head. Are you good with that?"

"I'm good," she breathily replied. As promised, I got down to business.

A few hours later, Bobby and Tut called. Shortly after, Sampson, Olivia and I met them in my suite for an update.

After Olivia brought out some coffee, Bobby began. "We left this morning with a lot of questions. So I went back to my hotel room and did some digging. I started with your uncle and discovered that a little over four years ago, he came into some money. At first, I thought inheritance, but when I couldn't find any documentation to validate this, I dug a little deeper. Does the name Ernie Deal ring a bell?"

"Never heard of him," I replied.

"About the third time his name popped up, I did a search. It turns out that Ernie was your stepdad's financial advisor. He handled all of his money. When your stepdad was killed, your mom continued to use him." I had no idea where he was going with this, but I could tell it wasn't good.

"You act as if Don had money."

"He did," Bobby replied.

I laughed, because it was clear he had no idea who he was talking about, so I decided to inform him. "Don Dunn was the stingiest motherfucker on the face of the planet. I'm not shitting you, the guy barely gave us enough money to buy groceries each week."

"He may have been stingy, but at the time of his death he was worth over two million dollars," Bobby apprised. Sampson let out a whistle. I just sat there in stunned silence. "Stay with me, here," he urged. "So, Don has money, Don dies, and Francine inherits. Four years ago, give or take a few months, Don's brother, Bill, comes into some money. Again, we're talking in the ballpark of two million dollars."

All eyes shot to Olivia as she sucked in a breath. In a loud exhaled gush of air, she declared, "Oh my God. Bill killed Francine and stole the money."

"Someone needs to watch a little less television," Sampson

dryly commented.

Bobby cut off her scathing reply with, "More like Francine signed the money over to Bill."

"She what?" Olivia and I exclaimed in unison.

"I found bank statements that reflect that in December of 2012, Francine transferred a little over two million dollars to Bill's investment account. Now, here's where it gets tricky. A few months after this, Francine sold her house. After that, I got nothing. It's as if she disappeared."

"So Bill could have killed her?" Olivia asked.

"At this point, we're not ruling anything out," Bobby answered. Her eyes darted to Sampson and she gave him a *told you so* smirk. "All of this is fairly easy to trace. Anyone with moderately good hacking skills could find it," Bobby further explained. "Now, I'm not going to lie. This smells rotten to me, so I dug a little deeper into the files on Bill's hard drive."

"And? What'd you find?" Marcel asked.

"Nothing that would incriminate him. He had a couple of pictures of Chaz, but they were taken much later than the ones sent in the emails. That doesn't mean he's not the sender. It simply means he's smart enough not to have saved them on his computer.

"Did you find anything on my mom?" I asked.

"Good question. Here's what we've got: your mother transferred the money over to your uncle. A few months later, she sells her house and disappears. A year or so later, your uncle and aunt sell their house and move into the new place. Shortly after that, your uncle retires. What we don't have is: your mother's current location and the identity of the person sending the emails."

"I think it's Bill," Olivia stated. Crazy thoughts spun through my head. Fucking Don. All those years we went without and he was sitting on a gold mine. What a fucking dick.

"None of this makes sense. After the hell Don put my mother through, she was finally rid of him. Not only that, but she was sitting on a shit pile of money...his money...money he withheld from us. Why would she just give it away? As for Bill, he got what he wanted, so why fuck with me now?"

"Tut and I were discussing this earlier and feel it's in your best interest if we pay your uncle a visit."

"And do what?"

"You know how my specialty is computers? Well, Tut's is people. In order to get a read on Bill, Tut needs a face-to face with him. We'll have two things going for us; experience and the element of surprise. Not only will your uncle not be expecting our visit, but he has no way of knowing what or how much we know," Bobby explained. This sounded good, but they were forgetting something, my uncle was a cop through and through.

"He's not going to tell you anything," I firmly stated.

"What happens if he outright refuses to speak with you?" Sampson asked. Tut smiled.

"Then we bluff," he answered.

Before Bobby and Tut took off for Bedford, Bobby pulled me aside and asked me to study the pictures from the email sent to Olivia. He wanted me to look for three things: recognition, time frame, and pattern. When I explained my assignment to Olivia, she curled her lip in disgust and opted for a hot shower over helping me put names and dates to my sexual exploits. I couldn't say I blamed her.

An hour later, I called Bobby and told him what I'd pieced together. Of the fifteen women, I remembered three. The first dated all the way back to my very first tour with the band. There was this chick with a kick-ass viper tattoo on her neck. She kept telling me to "kiss her snake." I remember shoving my hand over her mouth, so I could finish boning her and get the fuck out of there. You could see part of the tattoo and my hand on her mouth in the picture. I told him I was pretty sure her name was Natalia. The second was from the night Grant fell off the stage. Nash and I tag teamed these two chicks in the parking lot right before we had to leave for the hospital. If you looked closely at the picture, you could see part of Nash's leg. The third, as everyone knows, was Chelle, and the rest were just faces with no names.

"You know how messed up this is, don't you?"

"Which part?" Bobby asked.

"All of it. My uncle was a good guy. He got me out of that house when no one else would. He has no reason to steal, kill, or send fucked-up emails to me. It just doesn't make sense."

"Look, this is how it works. We get a lead, and we chase it down until it's dead. As of right now, we know your mother sent your uncle the money. What we don't know, is what made her do it, or where she is, so we're going to ask him. Now, while we're chasing that thread, we need you to think. Have you pissed anyone off lately?" Bobby's question made me laugh. "Okay, let me rephrase that. Have you pissed anyone off to the degree they'd want to hurt you, damage your reputation, or break up your relationship with Olivia?"

"The only name that comes to mind is Chelle, and she's currently behind bars," I answered.

"That doesn't mean she doesn't have eyes on you. You'd be shocked at the shit people get away with while they're incarcerated," Tut interjected.

"Could Chelle, or someone she knows, have taken those pictures?" Bobby asked. "Think about the time frame. Was Chelle around when you joined the band?" I immediately thought of Paula.

"Chelle was with Grant when I arrived on the scene. I can't exactly picture her creeping around and take photos of me boning chicks for shits and grins, but that doesn't mean she didn't have one of her posse do it for her."

"Do you know of someone specific who could have helped her?"

"Yes, but I don't think it's her."

"You never know. Give me her name and I'll check her out," Bobby offered.

"Paula Benson," I told him.

"Think about it this way. Did you help put Chelle away?" Tut asked.

"You know I did," I snapped.

"Was she pissed about it?" When I didn't bother to answer, he answered for me. "Then it's not out of the realm of possibility that she would want to exact retribution."

"Okay, for the sake of argument, let's say it's Chelle. Unless she had a time machine and could blast her ass back to the past, there's no way she had access to those pictures from my childhood. Hell, I didn't even know they existed until I saw them with my own eyes."

"Which supports my theory of it being two different people," Bobby confirmed.

I exhaled a loud, "Fuuuuuck."

"And this is why we're paying your uncle a visit. We'll call when we're on our way back," he said, and hung up.

"Any news?" Olivia asked from the doorway.

"No, but I'll tell you this. I'm sure as hell glad I'm not a PI."

Olivia and I were camped on the sofa, watching a show on Animal Planet about the world's deadliest insects, when the phone rang.

"It's Bobby," I announced. I pressed the speaker on my phone, placed it on the coffee table in front of us, and answered, "Hello?"

"We just left your uncle's place, and I've got to say, it's quite the place," Bobby responded.

"Your aunt is a bitch," Tut chimed in.

"Tell me something I don't know," I muttered. "Did you learn anything?"

"He refused us entry until we helped to jog his memory," Bobby answered.

"So he confessed?" Olivia asked in a hopeful tone of voice.

"Hardly. He was one cool cat," Tut commented.

"He had an answer for everything. He told us he received a call about your mother's death, but had no idea why there was no record, and to check with the coroner's office. He confirmed that your mother sent him the money, and said she did so because it was meant for him," Bobby added.

"How so?" I asked.

"According to Bill, their dad was a financial wizard. Their mom died when they were young and the dad never remarried, so it was just the three of them. When he died unexpectedly, the role of executor went to Don, as he was the oldest. The money was to be split between the two boys. At that time, Bill was too young to handle the responsibility of so much money, so Don and Bill agreed that Don would take the money and continue to invest it. At some point down the line, they would divvy it up, but then Don died, and by default, everything went to Francine," Bobby explained.

"When confronted, Bill denied any coercion. He said that Francine was acting of her own free will when she signed that money over. That's when Darlene started ranting about how you're trying to get Bill in trouble because you want the money, how she knew this day would come, and that you were always a selfish brat. She bitched that we were going to hell for doing your dirty work, and if you cared, you would have kept in touch. She was scared, which told me exactly what I was looking for," Tut said.

"Bill was lying," I finished for him.

"About which thing?" Olivia asked.

"We're not sure, but Darlene's rambling sure did make ol' Bill nervous, because suddenly he remembered an appointment they had to attend, and we were being ushered to the door," Bobby answered.

"Did you mention Mom selling the house?" I asked.

"Bill said that he and Darlene helped your mom move into an apartment complex on the south side of town. I looked it up when we got into the car and guess what? It no longer exists."

"So they could have seen the pictures," I stated.

"If they helped her move, then it's likely they came across the pictures," Bobby agreed.

"And did what? Took them and is now sending them to Chaz? Why?" Olivia asked.

"That's the million-dollar question," Tut answered.

"So what now?" I asked.

"As soon as we get back to the office, I'll dust the envelopes for prints. In the meantime, I'll dig deeper on Bill. I'm also going to check on Paula, Darlene, and Don. As soon as we get a spare minute, we'll pay Chelle a visit. We've got an early flight out tomorrow, but I'll be in touch in the next few days," Bobby said.

As I disconnected the call, I locked my eyes on Olivia and told her what I'd been thinking throughout the entire conversation. "I have a bad feeling about this."

"You're not the only one," she muttered.

# CHAPTER TWENTY-EIGHT

## "The Spirit of Radio"

### Olivia

The flight to Pennsylvania was smooth, but also a little tense. Chaz scowled at anyone who so much as even glanced our way. On edge didn't even remotely describe his state of mind. He was strung tighter than I'd ever seen him. Of course, he wouldn't admit it, but I was pretty sure his mood boiled down to one thing; he was worried about telling the rest of the gang about the emails. When we touched down in Philly, the stewardess gave Marcel and Sampson the opportunity to escort us off the plane before allowing the rest of the flight to disembark. Airport security met us at the gate, where we were immediately loaded onto an express cart and driven to our waiting vehicle. Once Sampson had our bags, we were off. Other than Chaz's grumpy mood, the trip had been painless and easy. That is, until we hit the hotel.

"You're staying in my suite," Chaz declared in front of Marcel, Sampson, and the hotel manager. The manager's eyes nervously shifted between us as he waited for further direction.

"Not a good idea," I said under my breath. At the same time, I calmly smiled and nodded for the manager to continue checking us in.

"She's in my suite," Chaz informed the manager.

"I'm not," I replied through gritted teeth. The manager paused with an expectant look on his face, and all I could think about was tomorrow's magazine headlines. "Excuse us," I said, and quickly jerked Chaz off to the side.

"I want you with me," he declared in his *I'm the master and you're my slave* tone of voice.

"I am with you and I will be with you tonight, but the whole world doesn't have to know this," I harshly whispered. My stomach pitched as his body visibly tightened.

"I knew this would blow back on us," he angrily bit out.

"Chaz—"

"Do whatever you want," he snapped, and stormed away.

The manager was warily eyeing me when I stepped back up to the desk. "Go ahead and cancel my room," I told him.

As the four of us rode the elevator up to our floor, no one said a word.

Marcel let us into the suite and Chaz immediately took off for the bedroom, where he slammed the door with a loud bang. Marcel's gaze swept from the door to me, and I sighed. "The gang is due in this afternoon. What do you want me to tell them?" he asked.

"Let's plan on meeting here. Text me a few minutes before, so I can prepare Grumpy Pants," I told him.

"Olivia," he called out as I turned for the bedroom. I glanced over my shoulder, and in the same sage-like voice from the night before, he said, "It's all going to be okay. You'll see."

A few minutes later, I entered the bedroom and found Chaz lying on the bed. I thought about confronting him, but nothing spells 'Do not disturb' louder than two pillows over the head, so I opted for the living area, where I attempted to focus on work.

Marcel texted around three that afternoon. The guys were in and the meeting was set. Now, I had to inform Chaz.

"Are you awake?" I called out from across the room. When the headless lump failed to respond, I crept closer. "Chaaaaaaz," I softly cooed. Again, he gave me nothing, not even a flinch. I tried a third time, this time while hovering over his prone form. "Chaaaaaaz," I sang out, and shrieked when his hand shot out and latched onto my arm. The next thing I knew, I was under him and he was hovering over me.

"Everyone will be here in about ten minutes," I informed him, and sucked in a breath when his face dropped to my neck and I felt his lips on me. "Did you hear me?" I half-whispered, half-moaned.

"They can wait," he gruffly responded, followed by something that sounded like, "I'm gonna fuck or suck you." Both sounded good to me, however, I knew what he was doing, and as much as I wanted it, now wasn't the time.

"I know this is hard for you—" I started to say. His head snapped up, his eyes locked on mine as he slid his hand into my yoga pants. His fingers hit the spot and I forgot the rest of my sentence. It didn't take long for him to get me there. The second my orgasm hit, he yanked my pants the rest of the way off, flipped open his fly, lined himself up to my entrance and powered in. Holy shit. The feel of him...hard, pulsing, huge... inside me, never got old. With his eyes glued to mine, he pulled out and slammed back in. Then he did it again, and again, and again. Chaz wasn't making love to me. He was straight up fucking me, using me to chase away his demons, and I let him. I let him because not only did I love it, but I loved him, and that's what you do for someone you love...you give them exactly what they need. We peaked at the same time, and it was both intense and raw.

"Now, I'm ready," he announced, once we'd had a moment to catch our breath. For some reason, I found this funny. So funny, that I burst into laughter. Pretty soon, he was laughing with me. God, how I loved my moody man.

The suite door opened at the same time we resurfaced from the bedroom. Marcel was the first in, followed by Evan, Nash, Grant, Hank, Sean, and Sampson. Once everyone was seated, I broke the ice by asking about everyone's break.

It took a moment before Nash replied, "Rowan and I have moved the wedding to September, and we've decided on Vegas instead of Austin."

When the comments and congratulations calmed down, Grant said, "I'm not supposed to tell, but Mallory's pregnant. She's spotting, the doctor is worried, and I'm freaked. He's put her on bed rest for the time being. Ava is taking care of her, but the second this tour is over, I'm heading back to Austin."

"Shit, is she okay? Tell her to call Rowan," Nash commented.

"Uhhh, I'm pretty sure Rowan knows," Grant replied. Nash frowned. Grant smiled, and I was struck with how close we'd all become.

"Did they say how long she would have to be on bed rest?" I asked.

"Not really. The doctor mentioned something about the first trimester," Grant answered.

"I'm sorry, man. It sucks that you can't be with her. Just so you know... ummm, Mandy and I kind of made up," Evan announced. All eyes swept to him.

"Who?" Nash asked.

"My *wife*," Evan replied. He didn't have to add dumbass onto the end of his response because it was clearly implied by his tone.

Chaz scowled. "Seriously?" he asked.

"Seriously," Evan retorted.

"Why are you acting like someone just ran over your puppy?" Nash asked Chaz.

"Because she's been trying to get him to quit the band and move back home," Chaz told him.

"I'm not saying that's going to happen," Evan hesitantly admitted.

"But you're not saying it's not," Grant stated. Evan just stared at him. *Yikes!* This was not going as planned.

"Chaz has something to tell you," I blurted. Sampson let out an *oh, shit* whistle, which earned him a shut-it glare. Chaz's jaw ticked in anger and I gave him an encouraging smile.

A long moment passed before he spoke. From the very first letter to the final sexcapade email, he told it all, and by all, I mean *all*. When he was done talking, no one said a word.

"Why didn't you tell us?" Grant asked. I could tell by his tone that he was not a happy camper.

"Because it wasn't yours to know," Chaz testily clipped, and then added, "If I had my way, you'd never know."

"No wonder you're suck a dick," Nash muttered loud enough for everyone in the room to hear.

"That was uncalled for," I scolded.

"Fuck you, Bucky," Chaz replied. I could tell by his twitching lips that he was humored more than angered by Nash's crude comment.

Nash bared his two front teeth to the room, and loudly crowed, "These babies are bonded and sealed. You can take a sledgehammer to them and they won't break, motherfucker!"

"Challenge accepted," Chaz told him, and they both laughed. I just shook my head at them both. *Stupid boys.*

"That night in Grant's office, after my call with Mandy, that's when you got the first letter, isn't it?" Evan asked.

"Yeah," Chaz gruffly responded.

"You could have told me."

Picking up on Evan's hurt tone, Chaz admitted something both heartbreaking and insightful. "No man, I don't care who he is, wants to admit his weaknesses, especially to the people who matter. Not because he doesn't trust them, but because he wants them to think more, rather than less, of him."

"Fuck that. If anything, I think more of you now than ever," Grant interjected.

"Same here," Nash responded.

Evan pushed back from his chair, walked over to where Chaz was standing, and pulled him into a macho man hug. My heart melted into a giant puddle.

Grant loudly clapped his hands together. Once he had everyone's attention, he announced, "Okay, so here's what's going to happen. Chaz, you're going to tell us if anymore emails come in. In the meantime, LASH has you handled. The rest of us need to focus. I know we all have shit going down in our personal lives, but we owe it to ourselves, our fans, and Indigo Road to finish out this tour with a bang instead of a whimper. We have two days here, three in Boston, and we're done. Five days and we are done!" he shouted. "Are we good?"

"We're good," everyone in the room replied.

That night, Chaz and I took a long, hot soak in the Jacuzzi tub. We made sure to get each other nice and clean, among other things. We also managed to talk about us and our future. Chaz started the conversation by asking about my post-tour plans.

"To be honest, I haven't really thought about it. I guess I'll go home," I answered with a half shrug. I'd been so caught up in today, that I'd forgotten to think about tomorrow, which was new for me, as I was a notorious planner.

"I've never been to California," Chaz murmured in my ear.

"It's beautiful, but also crazy expensive. You'll have to come for a visit. What are your post- tour plans?" I asked.

Answering my question with a question, he asked, "Do you like New York?"

I turned my head, so he could see my eyes when I rolled them at him. "Who doesn't like New York?" I dryly responded, and laughed when he dug his fingers into my side.

"Okay, smartass. Do you think you'd be up for spending time there with me? I'd like to show you the city...my city," he amended. My heart danced inside my chest. Just the thought of spending more time with him made me happy.

"I think that—" He cut me off with a scorching-hot kiss.

"Don't think, just say yes," he whispered against my lips. I nodded my head, and he kissed me again...and again...and again.

The next morning, we hit the ground running. The guys had an interview with a radio station before an extended afternoon practice. Normally, these interviews were fun. The guys got to mix it up and play games with the radio hosts. *Normally*, they were fun...

But not today.

"What the hell are they doing here?" Chaz murmured under his breath as we entered the building. I glanced up from my phone long enough to see Frank. He was standing next to Sander, who appeared to be deep in conversation with Gio. My stomach twisted at the sight of them. Somehow, by the grace of God, we'd managed to keep the bands separated since the night of the party. Well, it looked as if our luck had run out.

"Hang on," I said, and quickly pulled the schedule Marcy had sent, up on my phone. Nowhere on the schedule did it say anything about sharing interview space with Indigo Road. Not only were we not prepared for this, but I was pretty sure we were being set up. I just didn't know how or why. "I'm pretty sure they're not supposed to be here," I quietly responded.

"Shit," was all he could get out before the crowd converged on us and the band was swept into an autograph signing frenzy. Sean was kind enough to see me safely inside the building, where I was immediately confronted by Frank.

"What are you doing here?" he asked in a low, barely controlled voice.

"I could ask you the same thing. Marcy didn't say anything about sharing this space," I replied in a harsh whisper.

"Yeah, well, apparently Marcy didn't tell you a lot of things," he snapped. I was about to ask what he meant, when the station producer appeared.

"I'm sorry, but it appears we've had a bit of a mix up," I told him.

"Not at all. We're thrilled to have both bands with us today. The hosts are beside themselves. In fact, they're working on a new set of questions that will incorporate both bands, as we speak. Ahhh, here the boys are now. Welcome to WPSN 99.7. We're absolutely thrilled to have you," he called out.

Grant stepped up beside me, and under his breath, asked, "What the hell is going on?"

I turned, and with a smile on my face, I pretended to adjust his shirt. At the same time, I answered under my breath, "I'm not sure. It wasn't anywhere in Marcy's notes. I have a bad feeling about this."

"This shit has got to stop," he whispered, before he followed the moving crowd into the studio's green room. I slowly trailed behind him.

Chaz caught up with me inside the green room. The first thing out of his mouth was, "What did Frank say?"

"This wasn't planned," was all I managed to get out, before

both bands were escorted inside the studio. Hank and Alex, Indigo's head of security, stepped inside with them. When Frank and I attempted to follow, we were informed that the studio was at full capacity. My ass it was. I managed to catch Chaz's eye as he found a seat between Nash and Evan. "Behave," I mouthed. He responded with a sexy wink that made my pulse race. Only Chaz could make me think dirty thoughts at a time like this.

The first half hour went surprisingly well. The hosts asked questions and allowed each of the band members to answer. The guys were somewhat stiff with each other, but otherwise, seemed to be enjoying it. In fact, it was going so well that Marcel, Sean, and Sampson drifted off to check out the rest of the studio. Frank was nowhere to be seen, which was fine with me.

About halfway through the interview, two things happened; Frank appeared beside me and the hosts changed the game to "How well do you know your bands."

"What did you mean by that comment?" I asked.

His eyes flickered from the studio window to me. "Hmmm? What comment?"

"The one about Marcy not telling me a lot of things," I ground out. We both paused for a moment to listen to what was happening inside the studio. The first question was directed at Grant. The caller wanted to know how he came up with his songs. Grant got three words out, when Sander jumped in and hijacked the question.

"What is he doing?" I hissed.

"Surviving," Frank retorted. My eyes snapped to his.

"Explain," I demanded. His eyes flashed with anger.

Grant was kind enough to let Sander answer the question, but I could tell he was seething inside. The next question was directed at Gio, but before Gio could answer, Chaz butted in and answered for him. Now, both Grant and Gio were fuming. This was not going well...at all.

"Look at your numbers, Olivia. Meltdown is kicking our asses all over the place. I knew this tour was a fucking bad idea, but Marcy convinced me it would be worth it. I had no choice but to believe her. She promised both bands would benefit. Well, she was wrong. Imagine my surprise that first day when I saw you standing there and not Marcy. The fucking bitch set this whole thing up."

While I attempted to process his words, I also tried to keep tabs on the interview questions.

The next one was directed at Chaz.

"Rumor has it you have a new love interest. Can you tell us a little about her?" the caller asked. *Oh, God,* I thought. Chaz's eyes locked on mine and I shook my head. *Don't do it.*

"She gets around," Gio muttered loud enough for everyone to hear. Chaz's head swiveled in Gio's direction and my breath seized inside my chest.

"What did you say?" Chaz asked in a scary as hell voice.

"G, stop," Sander warned.

"Don't do it," I whispered.

At the same time, Frank exclaimed, "Fuck!"

"Haven't you heard? Chaz prefers women who get around," Gio loudly announced. No one said a word. The dangerous look on Chaz's face said it all.

"Shut it down," I hissed.

"Yeah, well unlike you, I prefer pussy to cock, you fucking poser," Chaz responded.

"Shit!" Frank exclaimed, and lunged for the door. When he realized it was locked, he began banging on it. Frank's banging was so loud that I couldn't hear what was being said inside. When Sander's head dropped and Gio shot across the table at Chaz, I knew it was over. Chaz must have let the cat out of the bag, and to boot, he'd done it on live air. Marcel, Sean, and Sampson, along with the rest of Indigo Road's security team, came running.

While pandemonium was taking place inside the studio, Frank whirled on me, and shouted, "This is a set up! Marcy planned this, didn't she? And all because I owe the bitch a little money. I was going to pay her back! All I needed was this tour. That was it!" Like a hammer to the gut, his words slammed into me.

"What are you talking about?" I asked.

"Don't play innocent with me, you little bitch!" he shouted.

"Hey! That's enough," Marcel cut in.

"What? You think you got this job because you deserved it? She knew about you and Sander," he snarled. "She hired you to gain leverage on me." I shook my head at him. He was wrong. Marcy wouldn't do that.

"You're wrong. She didn't know," I whispered.

Frank leaned in, and shrieked, "I fucking told her!"

"What the hell?" Grant asked. Chaz suddenly appeared in front of me with Sander following after him. The minute Chaz pulled me into his arms, I burst into tears.

"We're done," Sander exclaimed, as soon as he reached Frank. "Get your shit and get the fuck out." He turned to us, and said, "I had no idea any of this was happening. I don't blame you if you want to call off the rest of the tour."

"You can't do that!" Frank screamed. Sander nodded his head at his security, and they escorted an out of control Frank from the building.

"I say we call it off," Gio spat.

Sander angrily turned on him. "Then you can go. I told you to shut your fucking mouth, but you just couldn't, could you?"

Gio stared at Chaz. "He threatened me," he whined.

"I don't care what he did! You've just cost us this tour!" Sander shouted.

"Let him go. I'll double up and play your set," Chaz told

Sander.

"Fuck you, Chaz!" Gio hissed. He turned to Sander and in a very calculating voice, said, "You can't fire me. I'm under contract."

Poor Sander looked beaten down. "Fine, but after this tour, we're done. Either you're out or I am," he told Gio. His eyes moved to Grant as he said, "We're all under contract here. It will take some finagling to get out of the tour at this point, but anything is possible."

Grant's lip curled in disgust. Ignoring Sander, he addressed his fellow bandmates. "We have five days left. I say we end it on a high note, but I need you with me."

"I'm in," Nash replied.

"Me, too," Evan responded.

"I'll stay IF Olivia stays, and only if Gio keeps his fucking mouth shut and agrees right here and now to stay the fuck away from us," Chaz threatened. I wasn't sure I wanted to stay. Not anymore. As if sensing my hesitation, Chaz's hands slid from my back to the base of my neck. I tilted my head to look at him, and he slid them up, to where they cupped either side of my face. "If you go, I go," he whispered. I could tell he wanted to go. They all did, but Sander was right. We were all under contract. People were depending on us. If we all pulled out now, fans would be disappointed and millions of dollars would be lost.

"I'll stay," I told him.

"Are you sure?" I nodded my head yes, and was rewarded with a very public kiss.

Yep, the cat was definitely out of the bag.

# CHAPTER TWENTY-NINE

## "Open Road"

*Chaz*

"What the hell just happened, here?" Grant asked. I heard the question, but my focus was on Olivia.

Once Frank was escorted out of the building, Sander was forced to step up. He and Olivia were currently handling damage control with the studio producer and radio show hosts. I was worried about her. This entire tour had been one disaster after another, and all of it had just crashed on top of Olivia's head, thanks to Marcy.

"Marcy fucking happened, that's what," I finally answered.

"No, I mean the shit you spewed about Gio," he corrected.

Still focused on Olivia, I answered, "It's not shit. He and Sander have a thing. Olivia caught them in the act. That's why she quit."

Grant coughed. "Gio and Sander?"

"Daaaaaaamn," Nash drawled.

When the producer held his hand out, and Sander and Olivia

both shook it, I knew it was handled. As Olivia broke for us, I turned to the three of them, and said, "It's handled."

"I'll tell you about it in the car," Olivia muttered under her breath as she approached where we were standing. After more apologies were made - mostly from Grant and Evan - and pictures were taken with the hosts and the producer, we took off.

Once we were secured inside the vehicle, Olivia gave us the lowdown on what had transpired.

"Chaz's comment wasn't caught on air. They could tell, by the way you guys kept cutting each other off, that there was tension between the two bands. The second time Gio mentioned Chaz liking loose women, they cut to a PSA," she told us.

My muttered, "Damn," got me several dirty looks. I scowled back at them. "What? You can't say you blame me for wanting to knock that fucker down a few pegs."

"We don't need a lawsuit right now, Chaz," Grant grumbled.

"What's this shit about Marcy blackmailing Frank?" Nash asked. I felt Olivia's body tense next to me. While Olivia explained what all Frank had said, I pulled her close and kissed the side of her head.

"Right now, this is purely conjecture. For all we know, Frank could be lying," Evan pointed out.

Hank spoke up for the first time since the Marcy bomb had been dropped. "I'll get the truth from Marcy."

"I appreciate that, man, but this is bigger than simply hearing her out. I'm not sure how deep it goes or what she's done, but if she's done anything illegal or violation of her obligations to the band, we will need to play it by the book. As soon as we get back to the hotel, I'll put a call in to our legal team," Grant told him.

"I don't know about you guys, but I'm tired of all the bullshit. At what point is it not worth it anymore?" Evan asked. No one bothered to respond, but I could tell we were all thinking the exact same thing.

Practice that afternoon sucked. As in, we played like shit, weren't into it, didn't give two fucks about it, sucked. We all felt it. We all knew it. No one was willing to put a voice to it, but we'd hit the end of our rope. Last night's talk with Olivia and Evan's earlier comment, got me thinking. What if I stepped back for a while? I had more money than I could ever spend in one lifetime. What if Olivia and I took off after the tour and went someplace exotic? Hell, we could stay home for all I cared. I'd even relocate to California. All she had to do was ask.

*Two days later*

"I like busses," Olivia murmured against my chest.

"Is it the bus you really like, or is it my cock in you while riding on the bus?" I asked. Laughter spilled from her lips as I flipped to my side and took her with me.

Philly had been a complete bust. It felt like we were just going through the motions both nights. The crowd didn't know it, but we sure as hell did. It felt like the magic, the energy that unified us while we were on stage, was gone. The thing with Marcy and Frank only added insult to injury. Marcy had spoken with the attorneys. While there was nothing we could sue her over, we clearly had reasonable cause to terminate her contract. That was little comfort, as she was already mostly out the door anyway. As it turned out, she was one manipulative bitch. What was it with Meltdown and our managers? First Blane and now Marcy.

Hank had come to us yesterday morning with the real scoop on Marcy. Little did anyone know, but Frank and Marcy were having an affair at the same time that Olivia quit her job with Indigo Road. The affair ended amicably. So when Frank went to Marcy and told her he'd "borrowed" money from the band, and they were being threatened with an audit, Marcy helped him out, but only with the understanding that he would pay her back within a certain time frame. When he failed to do so, she blackmailed him into doing a summer tour with Meltdown. According to Hank, she had two reasons for doing this. One, to get Meltdown better exposure, and two, to keep her thumb on Frank. When her father fell ill, and she realized her plan was in jeopardy, she came up with Plan B: Olivia Marshall. As it turned out, Frank had manipulated Sander, Gio, and Olivia. He didn't necessarily want Olivia to quit, but he wanted her away from Sander, so he set it up for her to find them together. When she quit, he not only paid her to keep her mouth shut, but he had Sander sign the contract under false pretenses. To make matters worse, he never told Sander about it. Marcy hired Olivia to remind Frank what was at stake if he didn't do what she asked. She didn't allot for the Hank-Olivia connection, and she sure as hell didn't see the thing between Olivia and me happening. At the end of the day, it backfired on both managers. Indigo Road was pressing charges against Frank for embezzlement and Marcy was out for good. As for me, I was still waiting to hear back from Bobby and Tut.

"Should we get back out there?" Olivia asked. I was about to answer her when my phone rang.

I snagged it from my jean pocket. "It's Bobby," I told her, as I lifted the phone to my ear, and said, "It's about time you called."

"Yeah, well, tracking your fucked-up shit ain't exactly a walk in the park," Bobby clipped.

"I bet not," I replied, as I pressed the speaker button and set the phone on the bed between us. "What do you have for me?"

"We found your mother." Olivia sucked in a breath.

"Shit. Is she alive?" My voice cracked with emotion. I didn't expect to feel anything, so why did my chest suddenly feel like a fifty-pound weight was resting on it?

"Yes, she's alive, but before you get your hopes up, let me explain. In early 2012, there was a police report filed involving your mother. Apparently, she was found wandering through a neighborhood a good mile or so from her home. She knew her name, but had no recollection as to how she got there. You were listed as her next of kin. When they couldn't reach you, they called the other name on her list."

"Bill?" I asked.

"You got it. Bill picked her up from the police station. This was about six months prior to the time she transferred the money and sold her house."

"Where is she?" Olivia asked.

"She's in a long-term care facility in Ohio. She's been diagnosed with dementia. She has no idea who or where she is, Chaz." Olivia's hand latched onto mine.

"And Bill?" I asked through clenched teeth.

"Even if he coerced her into giving him the money and selling the house, there's no proof. Her signature is on everything, including the intake forms for the facility," Bobby answered. The more he told us, the angrier I got.

"Was Bill's name also on the forms?"

After a long pause, he answered, "It was."

"Fuck! He took everything from her, put her away, and lied to me about it. He told me she was dead. Why in hell would he do that?"

"You'd be amazed at the lengths people will go through for money. Tut also was able to obtain copies of both Don and your mother's wills, among some items, we located in a storage locker where Bill moved what's left of her personal property. Don's half of his father's fortune was supposed to go to your mother and then to you. Your mother giving it over to Bill prevented that from happening."

"And that motherfucker and his whore of a wife got it all. Son of a bitch!" I shouted. "What about the pictures? Please tell me you found them somewhere in Bill's shit."

"No pictures," Bobby replied.

"Fuck! Did you check Darlene?"

"I checked everything I could gain access to. I'm sorry, man. I wish I could give you a different outcome. Have you received any more emails?"

"No, not since the last one."

"Is it possible that Bill could be sending the pictures from a different computer?" Olivia asked.

"Anything's possible," Bobby replied, but we both could hear the doubt in his voice. Suddenly, it was too much. I needed air.

"Hey, Bobby, let me call you back in five."

"That's cool. Take your time. In fact, you might want to have everyone present for this next part. In the meantime, I'll send you the address and phone number of the facility...just in case."

"Thanks," I muttered, and hung up. Of all the places for my mother to end up, I never thought it would be a long-term care facility. "I can't believe my uncle would do this," I whispered.

Olivia comfortingly stroked her hand up and down my back. "I'm sorry, Chaz."

"She doesn't even know who she is. Do you know how many times I wished for something horrible to happen to her? Christ, too many times to count." Olivia scooted closer.

As she rested her head on my shoulder, she quietly answered, "You didn't cause this, Chaz. It just happened." We sat together in silent contemplation, with Olivia rubbing my back, and me dwelling on what could have been. The realization that Bobby had more to tell us made my gut ache. I wasn't sure how much more I could take.

"Fuck it. Let's do this," I finally said.

Ten minutes later, we were all sitting at the table in the bus, minus Hank and Sampson, who were behind us in the SUV. I wasn't waiting any longer. Someone could fill them in later. First, I told them what Bobby and Tut found out about my mom. Then I told them there was more.

Bobby answered on the third ring. "We're all here," I told him.

Instead of wasting time on pleasantries, he jumped right in. "Tut and I paid Chelle a visit. Our overall goal was to find something that linked her to the emails being sent to Chaz. Well, we succeeded." All eyes shot to the phone.

"It was Chelle?" I asked, in a somewhat shocked tone. I was so sure Bill was the guilty party.

He laughed. "Yeah, the "it" you're referring to insisted that she slept with the entire band."

"I didn't sleep with her," Evan commented. Nash stared at his feet and Grant looked off to the side. Okay, so three out of four had slept with her.

"I don't get it," Grant murmured.

Bobby continued, "While she was rambling on about what studs you were in bed, she mentioned that she also slept with your security team." All eyes moved to Sean and Marcel.

"I don't do crazy bitches, and that bitch is craaaaazaaaaay," Marcel declared. Sean simply shook his head.

"When asked if she took photos of the band, she said she'd taken millions of photos, had eyes everywhere, and was always watching you. She then broke off to ask how Grant was doing and wondered when he was coming for a visit."

"Did you search her online activity? Maybe she has a

computer stashed somewhere with the photos on it?" Olivia suggested.

"She doesn't have access to a computer and her files have already been combed through. That doesn't mean someone isn't doing her dirty work for her, but I've got to tell you, the girl is seriously fucking whacked."

"In other words, you don't think it's her," I stated.

"My gut tells me she may be somehow involved, but she's not the one sending the emails," Bobby replied. *Shit.* It felt like we'd just hit another dead end. "There is one thing. I looked into Don. A few years before he married your mom, he was either friends with or involved with someone by the name of Aileen Hampstead. Does the name ring a bell?"

"Don had friends?" I sarcastically replied.

"I've got a hunch about this, so if it's cool with you, I'm going to see if I can track her down." I told him to knock himself out and disconnected the call. No one said a word, because really, what could they say? We still didn't know who'd sent the emails, but at least I now knew where my mother was.

♪♪♪

After we checked into the hotel, Olivia and I holed up in my suite where we ordered steaks and baked potatoes for dinner. We talked about places we'd been to and things we'd seen. Olivia had never been to Europe and I'd never seen California. After dinner, we watched a movie, or should I say, Olivia watched a movie. I mostly watched her. It wasn't lost on me that we had three days left in the tour. Three days together. I needed more. I wanted a lifetime with her. Never, in a trillion years, did I think I would end up here.

The next morning, I woke early and hit the hotel gym with Sampson. He was worried. Hank was hung up over the whole Marcy thing, but wasn't talking about it – not even to Marcel, which was unheard of. I didn't know what to tell him, especially since I was still ticked at Hank for trying to get into Olivia's pants.

Olivia was walking out the door when I returned from my workout. Before she could get away, I pressed her against the door and gave her some hella good tongue action. Once I had her panting for it, I released her.

"See you at practice," I called over my shoulder, as I made my way to the shower, and smiled when I heard her huff.

Practice went surprisingly well. The gloom seemed to have dissipated. Our sound, rhythm, and tone were spot-on. We were ready to rock Boston.

And we did.

That night, I couldn't get out of the after-party fast enough. We barely made it to my suite, before I had Olivia bare and begging for it. Not able to get enough, I took her over and over again. She was in my blood, filling my heart...a part of me. I was panicked that I was running out of time, so I told her. I didn't finesse it. I just blurted, "Fuck, I love you."

Her head swiveled in my direction, and with huge eyes, she asked, "What did you just say?"

"You have a great rack?" I teased.

"No."

"Your pussy smells like gardenias?"

"No," she laughed, and slapped my arm.

"I want you to move in with me?" Her mouth dropped open. Before she did something crazy, like pee the bed, I gave her what she asked for. "I fucking love you."

"I knew it!" she cheered, pumping her fist in the air. "Now, go back to what you said before you declared your undying love for me," she commanded.

"The one about your smelly pussy?" I asked, and broke into laughter when she pounced on me. When I had her pinned down, I repeated, "Move in with me."

She smiled, and in a bored tone of voice, murmured, "I'll think about it." I kissed her saucy mouth. Then I fucked the yes right out of her.

Our final night of the tour was bittersweet. We were on. We were at the end of the tunnel and ready to break free, but we were also a little bummed. Tomorrow it would all be over. Grant was going home to his pregnant wife, Nash was getting married, Evan was making a go of his marriage, and Olivia and I were moving in together. The emails had stopped and my mom was alive. Life was finally looking up.

On the way to the stage, I pulled Olivia in for a kiss. "Love you," I whispered against her lips.

"Kill it out there," she whispered back.

The place was packed. The crowd was electrified. Grant was right to make us stay, because we killed it. Boston didn't know what fucking hit them.

After three encores, we were hustled off of the stage, down the hallway, and into our dressing room, where we had approximately ten minutes before the doors opened and the party began.

"Have you seen Olivia?" I called out as I made my way to the bathroom to change out of my sweat-soaked clothes.

"Not since before the show," Evan answered.

After a quick change, I checked my phone for missed messages. *If Sander has cornered her again, I'm going to fucking kill him*, I thought as I hit on a missed text message. A picture popped onto my screen. It wasn't just any picture. It was the one I'd taken in bed with Olivia after our first night together.

"What the fuck?" I whispered. Then I read the message, and

nearly lost my mind.

*You took everything from me. Now, it's my turn to return the favor.*

"Chaz! Get the fuck out here!" someone shouted. Swallowing down the vomit that was creeping up my throat, I hauled ass out of the bathroom. I hit the dressing room and came to a screeching halt. Everyone was there except Hank, Sean, Marcel, and Olivia, most importantly. Sampson started talking.

"Bobby just called. He tried to reach you while you were on the stage. He looked into Aileen Hampstead." I had no idea what he was talking about. My head was spinning.

"Olivia's missing," I blurted.

He continued as if he hadn't heard me. "Aileen Hampstead lived with Don Dunn for five years. She had a son named Anthony - Anthony S. Hampstead. Don left Aileen for your mother."

"What the fuck does this have to do with anything?" I shouted. "Olivia is missing!"

"The S stands for Sean!" he shouted back at me. "When Anthony enlisted in the army, he took his middle name as his first and his biological father's last name. Aileen Hampstead's son is Sean Latimore." It was if time had suddenly stopped. Sean Latimore...Our Sean...had Olivia.

"Fuck!" Grant shouted. Other shouts rang out, but all I could think about was Olivia.

"They've been trying to get through his firewall all day, but didn't get in until you were already on stage. The pictures were all there. It's him. Hank and Marcel have been searching for him since we got the call from Bobby."

As his words crashed into me, I held up my phone, and said, "He has Olivia."

# CHAPTER THIRTY

## "State of Love and Trust"

*Olivia*

This was it; the last show of the tour. I was so proud of the guys for sticking it out. After the twisted Marcy-Frank story came to light, none of us were thrilled about staying, but we all agreed that it was the right thing to do. Tomorrow, Chaz and I were renting a car and driving to New York. He was going to show me 'his' city, and in return, I would show him mine. After that, the sky was the limit. As long as Chaz was with me, I didn't care where I landed.

"Here they come!" someone shouted. My heart hammered in my chest as the energy surrounding me suddenly intensified. Murmurs turned to shrieks and shouts as the members of Meltdown poured from the hallway and headed for the stage. Grant, Evan, and Nash high-fived me as they passed by, but my sexy-hot man did one better. He pulled me in for a kiss.

"Love you," he murmured against my lips.

"Kill it out there," I murmured back, and laughed when he

slapped me on the ass and bolted onto the stage.

Meltdown began their first set with two songs from the new album. The crowd was extremely receptive, but when Nash opened the third song with the chords from their hit, "Avalanche," they went berserk. In the middle of dancing with a few Melties, I felt my phone buzz in my back pocket. When I saw that it was a text from Sean, I moved off to the side to read it.

*I'm at the back door with the delivery guy. He won't let me sign for the delivery. He says it has to be you.*

Glancing at the clock on my phone, I wondered, *Who's delivering something this late?* Shit. I didn't want to miss the set. If I hurried, I would only miss a song, maybe two at the most.

"Be right back," I told Hank as I passed him by. He nodded his head, and I took off down the hallway for the loading dock.

Halfway down the hall, I spotted Sean waiting next to the delivery door.

"Is he out there?" I asked, nodding at the door.

"I tried to sign for you," he responded.

"No worries," I told him. As I made a move to open the door, I felt something touch my ribcage. Blinding pain hammered through my body. I tried to scream, but it came out as more of a grunt. The next thing I knew, I was falling. I hit the ground hard...and then nothing.

I woke to the feeling of someone's hand on my forehead, as if they were checking for a temperature.

"Where am I?" I asked, though it sounded more like, "WhamI."

"I didn't want to do this," a strange voice answered from somewhere in the room. It took a moment for my brain to come back online. My head was pounding and my face felt numb, as if the dentist had gotten slaphappy with the Novocaine. I blinked several times to clear my head and realized why I couldn't see anything; I was lying on my side, facing a wall. It took some effort, but I finally managed to roll myself onto my back. As I lay there panting from the exertion, I could sense movement around me, but I couldn't make my head turn. An overwhelming sense of panic filled me.

"WhamI?" I shouted, again.

"I should have sent more pictures. Why didn't I send more pictures?" the voice chanted. It sounded familiar, but I couldn't place it. A minute or so passed before I was able to wedge my elbow far enough under my body to slowly push myself up to a seated position. With my back pressed firmly to the wall, I could focus on where I was...or better yet, who was with me. Recognition hit and I sucked in a chest full of air.

In front of me, pacing back and forth like a madman, was none other than Sean. And that's when it hit me, smacked into me, bowled me over...

"You?" I gasped.

He stopped pacing long enough to reply, "I didn't want to hurt you, Olivia, but you've given me no choice. I mean seriously, who gets pictures of their boyfriend fucking other women and stays with him?" When he picked the pacing back up, I noticed an object in his hand. At first, I thought it was a gun, but as he continued to rant about Chaz and the millions of women he'd nailed, and how I'd failed to heed his warning, I realized it was a stun gun, or maybe it was a Taser. Either way, that shit seriously hurt.

"Did you...electrocute me?" I asked.

He scowled. "None of this would have happened if he just would have stayed away."

"Who?" I asked, still shocked that he'd actually stunned me.

"Charles!" he shouted. "Or should I call him, Chaz?" He made a sour face as he spat the word out, before abruptly changing the subject. "Did you know that I got him this job?" My eyes must have reflected my surprise, because he laughed. It wasn't a normal laugh, either. It was the laugh of someone who'd come completely unhinged. "Don't look so surprised. It was all part of my master plan. I would *make* him, and then I would *break* him, just like he did to me and my family." I had no idea what he was talking about, which also must have registered on my face, because he suddenly decided to share. "I'm going to give you a little history lesson, so listen up. Don was my dad first. *Mine!*" he hissed, pointing to his chest. "Imagine coming home from school one day to discover that your father had left you and your mother...for another family." He snapped his fingers. "In the blink of an eye, your entire world turned to shit. At first, I was hurt. Then, I got mad, but my mother...she was shattered. I was eleven, fucking years old."

While taking his trip down memory lane, Sean continued to pace back and forth in front of me. I pretended to listen, when what I really did, was try to figure out where in the hell I was. It looked like an old dressing room, which made me think that we were still at the venue.

"By the time I was fourteen, my mother had sunk so deep into depression that she couldn't get out of bed." He stopped pacing and lasered in on me. I froze. "Imagine spending your teenage years working four jobs just to pay the bills and then having to come home night after night to feed, bathe, and wipe your own mother's ass!" He shouted the last part. His words, and the pain behind them, sliced deep, but if anyone deserved the blame, it was Don, not Chaz.

"I get you're upset, but don't you think you're blaming the wrong person?" I calmly tried to reason with him.

"Don't worry, I made sure Don got what he deserved," he flippantly replied. An abnormal light danced behind his black-as-night eyes as he leaned in, and in a hushed voice said, "You know what I did after I killed him? I broke into his house. That's when I found the pictures. I'll tell you one thing; karma is a wicked bitch. Chaz deserved what he got. After all, fair is fair." He rambled a bit more about karma, before switching gears to Larry and the rigging. "Larry was a dumbfuck. I knew he was doing Blane's bidding, but seriously, what was the point? If he wanted to kill someone, he was going to have to do better than stealing sandwiches and playing with cables."

"You sawed through the rigging cables, didn't you?" I stated more as a fact than a question.

Suddenly, he stiffened. His head swiveled toward the door as if he heard something. My pulse leapt at the thought that someone was out there. I knew it was a risk, but what other choice did I have?

"Help meeeeeeeeee!" I shouted at the top of my lungs. In a flash, he was on me. "Help! He's—" Before I could get the rest out, he slapped his hand over my mouth. The back of my head connected with the wall and stars danced across my vision.

"Shut. Your. Fucking. Mouth," he menacingly growled. My eyes welled with tears. I didn't know what he was planning, but I knew one thing; it wasn't good. "Are you done?" he asked. I nodded my head and he pulled his hand away. "Don't piss me off again," he warned. As I scanned the room, I thought about what to do. Should I try to run? My legs and arms still felt heavy from being stunned. I wasn't positive I could stand up, much less run. When I blacked out, I lost all concept of time, therefore, I had no clue as to how long I'd been missing.

"I didn't want to hurt you," he muttered.

"Yeah? Well, you seemed to get over that, didn't you?" I angrily snapped. Insane eyes locked on mine, and I immediately regretted my outburst.

"Bitch, you have no idea what I've been through."

"What? You think you're the only one who's ever suffered? I had a baby, Sean. It died in my womb. Chaz was molested by a man who was supposed to have loved and protected him. I hate to break it to you, but you're not the only one who's ever felt heartache."

"You weren't there, Olivia! He stole my life! While I was starving, suffering, alone...he was living the life that was meant for me!" He pounded his chest for emphasis. Clearly, he wanted me to feel sorry for him, but all I felt was rage.

"He was being raped! He would have traded places with you a million times over! His mother didn't protect him. No one did!" I shrieked at the top of my lungs, which earned me a smack across the mouth. This time I tasted blood.

"I told you to shut the fuck up," he hissed. A minute or so passed before he removed his hand from my mouth and began to pace back and forth in front of me again.

"Why are you doing this?" I asked.

"Because you gave me no choice. Hank has been like a brother to me. Did you know we met in Germany? He was supposed to start his own company. When I caught up with him and discovered he was head of security for some pansy-ass rock band that no one had ever heard of, I looked down on him. I thought he'd sold out, but then God spoke to me. It was like divine, fucking providence. He told me to join hands with Hank, that I would find my answers there. So I joined Hank's team. At the same time, I continued to follow Charles's career. One night, I happened on Dale and some Melties getting high, and the answer just landed in my lap. If Dale wanted to fly so badly, why not give him a little push?"

*Noooooooooo!* I screamed in my head. "Please tell me you didn't kill Dale?" I barely managed to get the question out through the tears that were threatening to spill. When his mouth turned up in a triumphant smile, they dissolved into stone-cold anger.

"It was so easy," he bragged. "All I had to do was sneak in

when they weren't looking and switch out the pills. Poof! Dale was dead. Then all I had to do was put a bug in Hank's ear about a drummer I'd seen while I was visiting my granny in New York. The next thing I knew, Charles was hired." His brow furrowed. "Don't think it was easy. Pretending to like someone you fucking despise is hard work. I made it my mission in life to succeed. I embedded in deep with the team and became one of the guys. When Grant kicked Chelle out and she turned to Chaz, I made sure to get in on that action. She was a crazy snatch, but damn! The bitch was a master at sucking cock. I got why Chaz went a little nuts when she betrayed him. You know, I even had a slight moment of remorse when she used the poison I'd given her on Rowan and Mallory, but they survived. All's well that ends well." The more he rambled, the angrier I became. Talk about a master manipulator. Sean had manipulated us all, and we never saw it coming.

My breath hitched when he paced over to where I was sitting and squatted down in front of me. I tried not to flinch when he touched my hair. "Tell me, Olivia, do you like sucking cock? I bet you do. Otherwise, Charles wouldn't give your sweet ass the time of day. If you show me how he likes it, I might let you live. What do you say?" When I flinched back against the wall, he laughed. And then it happened. I didn't even know my phone was still in my back pocket, until it vibrated against the wall behind me. Our eyes connected, and we both froze.

For a moment, time stood still.

Then everything happened at once. I reached for my phone at the same time Sean lunged for my arm. Right as he wrenched the phone out of my hand, the door flew open. I heard a deafening noise, and he was on me, pressing me to the wall...suffocating me.

Suddenly, the weight was gone and I could breathe. When something wet rolled off of my arm, I glanced down and saw the blood - red, warm...everywhere, and then it hit me.

And I screamed.

"Are you sure you're okay?" Chaz asked for the thousandth time.

After we finished being examined by paramedics and what seemed to be an endless series of interviews with the detectives, Marcel drove us back to the hotel. During which time, Chaz told me about the text Sean sent to him, and how Hank and Marcel heard shouting coming from the room. Chaz and Marcel had managed to get most of Sean's blood off of me, but it was still caked in my hair. When Chaz stepped into the shower with me and gently began to wash my hair, I completely lost it. A man had died in front of me tonight. Even worse, he'd died on me. I understood why Hank and Marcel shot him. He was hovering over me. He had something in his hands that looked like a gun. I got it, but I couldn't help but grieve. Sean was sick, but would he have really hurt me? We'd never know the answer to that question...and that is why I cried.

♪♪♪

Later that evening, with Bobby and Tut on speakerphone, we were all huddled together in Chaz's suite.

Before I explained what happened, Bobby helped to fill in some missing pieces; starting with Sean's background. He told us that Don had stepped into Sean's life when Sean was five years old. When Sean was eleven, Don walked out on them. His mother was diagnosed as clinically depressed when Sean was nine, which might have contributed to Don leaving. He enlisted in the army at eighteen and sent most of his money home. When he was twenty-two and home on leave, his mother killed herself. Apparently, he'd come home after a night out with friends to discover she'd hung herself. Two days later, Don was murdered.

I took over from there and recounted Sean's confession about killing Don. I relayed that Sean broke into Chaz's mother's house and found the pictures. I broke down again when I got to the part about him killing Dale and explained how he manipulated Chaz's hiring. I cried again when I told them about him giving Chelle the poison. Chaz took it surprisingly well. He held my hand the entire time. The only time he lost his cool was when I mentioned Sean's crude blowjob comment. Of all of us, Hank took it the hardest. Not only had Marcy betrayed him, but so had Sean.

"I can't do this anymore," Hank quietly admitted, once the full story had come out.

"Do what?" Grant asked.

"Be the head of your security team."

"Hank—" Grant said.

"No, I'm serious. I've been stewing over this for a while now. I'm no good in here." He pointed to his head. "Or here." He moved his hand to his heart. "If I stay, I will only compromise the band and my team."

"You just need time," Marcel wisely stated.

Grant held up his hands. "Look, it's clear we all need a break right now. Why don't we just push pause for a moment?"

"How long is a moment?" Nash asked.

"I don't know, six months? A year? The past three years have been some of the best and the worst for us all. Maybe it's time to step back and actually enjoy living our lives for once," Grant responded.

"We can't just stop playing," Nash argued.

Grant smiled. "Olivia's our new manager. I'm sure she could hook us up with some small venues," he suggested. My eyes bugged and Chaz laughed.

"I don't know," Evan added. "At this point, I need to focus on my marriage."

Grant shrugged. "So we take six months off. It's not as if we'll never see or talk to each other again."

"I'm good with taking a break," Chaz chimed in.

"Same here," Nash agreed.

"I'm still out," Hank stated.

"Sure you are," Nash teased.

"Yeah, we'll see," Grant replied.

"Has anyone ever been to Brazil?" Sampson asked, and the room broke into laughter.

# EPILOGUE

## "In The End"

*Chaz*

The morning after Sean was killed, everyone met for breakfast in Grant's suite. When it was time to say goodbye, no one really knew what to say. I felt conflicted. I was ready to go, but at the same time, weirded out by the fact that this could be the last time we were all together. The past three months had changed us all, but especially me. I no longer felt like an outsider looking in. I *was* in. Grant acted as if the split would be temporary, but I wasn't so sure. Everyone was moving on with their lives. I had no doubt we'd gig again; I just didn't see it ever being the same. After slaps on the backs and promises to stay in touch, each of us went our separate ways.

A few years back, I purchased a three-bedroom townhome in Greenwich Village. I hadn't really done anything with it yet, but the location was perfect. Olivia stepped one foot into the place and squealed like a little girl. Then she started yammering about space and decorating and shit. I told her to have at it. As long as

I had a place for my kit, a television, and my gaming system, I didn't care what she did with the place.

That first week, we spent our days in bed and our nights exploring the city. I took the time I needed to work through the past three months and Olivia gave it to me.

At the beginning of our second week, I contacted Bobby at LASH. With his guidance, I placed a call to my mother's lawyer. Surprisingly, it took very little coercion before he came clean about the part my uncle played in getting my mother to sign over her half of Don's money. With the help of the attorney and the documentation Tut had found, we approached Bill. He saw the handwriting on the wall, and agreed to make a deal.

Now, we were on our way to Ohio to see my mom.

"You okay?" Olivia asked, as we pulled into the visitor parking lot. She'd been doing a lot of that over the past two weeks; taking my temperature, worrying about me and my feelings. She didn't need to worry. I was good, the best I'd been in a long while, and it was all because of her - my Hot Mess... my Dirty Girl. I turned off the ignition, leaned over the center console, and kissed her.

"Does that answer your question?" I asked. She smiled against my lips.

From the outside, the facility looked run-down. The inside wasn't much better. The waiting room furniture reminded me of something you'd find at a garage sale. It was mismatched and old. I could tell by Olivia's expression that she wasn't thrilled about the looks of the place, either.

After signing in, a woman in a nurse's uniform appeared.

"If you two will come with me, I'll take you to your mother, now," she said. We followed her down a long, dingy hallway. "Here we are." She opened one of several doors and ushered us inside. Across the room, sitting in a chair by the window, was my mother.

"Will you look who's come to see you, Francine? It's your son, Chaz!" the nurse called out. Slowly, my mother lifted her eyes to mine.

"Charles," I corrected. "She calls me Charles."

"I'll just leave you three to your chat. If you need anything, just holler," the nurse told us.

"Go," Olivia urged me forward.

"Hi, Mom. It's me, Charles," I said, as I started across the room in her direction. She sat there, staring at me with a blank expression on her face. Her dark hair had turned gray and her eyes were lifeless. "Do you mind if I sit with you for a minute?" Her eyes remained on me, but she didn't respond. As I circled her bed, I scanned the room. I couldn't help but notice the peeling paint and crappy carpets. Right then and there, I knew what I was going to do with Don's money. I was going to use it to get my mother into a better facility. Mom's eyes turned to me as I lowered myself down into the chair beside her. Olivia stood in the doorway with tears shimmering in her eyes. I held out my hand, and said, "Babe, come meet my mom."

Once Olivia was seated across from us on the side of my mother's bed, I introduced them. "Mom, this is Olivia Marshall. Olivia, this is my mother, Francine Dunn." With my eyes on Olivia, I leaned toward my mom, and loudly whispered, "I'm going to marry this girl." Olivia laughed, and I felt like I was on top of the world. For a guy who'd lived through hell, I'd finally found my slice of heaven.

"I had a boy named Charles," my mother quietly announced. Olivia sucked in a breath.

"You did? Why don't you tell us about him?" I urged.

"Well, he liked to make mud pies." She let out a brittle sounding laugh and shook her head. "My Charles...he was my shining star..."

# The End

# (BOOMSHAKALAKA)

Thank you for going on this journey with me!
While Meltdown is on a break, both Evan and Hank will be getting their own stand-alone stories.
Stay Tuned...

# Acknowledgments

~ Christian Brose – Thank you for talking me off the ledge and for not making me fire you again. I love you BIGLY!

~ Natalie Weston – My friend and PA. Thank you for believing in me, for sticking with me no matter what, and for putting up with my goofiness. Love your face, woman!

~ Joanne Thompson and Karen Hrdlicka – My amazing clean-up crew. As always, your feedback, notes, and words are invaluable. A million thanks to you both.

~ Betas: Danielle Brass, Lyndsey Hodson, Nicola Adams, Tara Slone, Jayne Wheatley, and Tara Champine - Thank you for the first read, and for LOVING Chaz and Olivia as much as I do!

~ Hilliard's Hellions – As always, you never disappoint. Thank you for sharing this wild ride with me and for your never ending support. I love you all to pieces!

~ My Fellow Authors – Your words are what it's all about, so keep writing!

~ Bloggers – Thank you for reading, reviewing, pimping, and believing in my stories.

# Other Books by RB Hilliard

His End Game
Not Letting Go
One More Time
Right Side Up
Keep It Simple
Utterly Forgettable
The Last Call
Fractured Beat
Broken Lyric

74081551R00172

Made in the USA
Middletown, DE
19 May 2018